# GCSE

# Information and Communication Technology

Liz Hankin

Endorsed by ICAA

GCSE

# Information and Communication Technology

Liz Hankin

Endorsed by ICAA

Heinemann Educational Publishers
Halley Court, Jordan Hill, Oxford OX2 8EJ
a division of Reed Educational & Professional Publishing Ltd

Heinemann is a registered trademark of Reed Educational & Professional Publishing Limited

OXFORD   MELBOURNE   AUCKLAND
JOHANNESBURG   BLANTYRE   GABORONE
IBADAN   PORTSMOUTH NH (USA)   CHICAGO

Copyright © Learning Solutions Partnership Limited 1998, 2001

First published 2001
2005  2004  2003  2002  2001
10  9  8  7  6  5  4  3  2  1

A catalogue record for this book is available from the British Library on request.

ISBN 0 435 44858 7

Designed and typeset by Artistix, Thame, Oxon
Original illustrations © Heinemann Educational Publishers 2001
Illustrations by Catherine Ward
Printed and bound in Spain by Edelvives

**Websites**
Examples of websites are suggested in this book. Although these were up to date at the time of writing we recommend that teachers preview these sites before using them with students to ensure that the URL is still accurate and that the content is suitable for your needs.

# Contents

# Preface

This new textbook and its accompanying Tutor Resource File are a further development of ICAA's strategy to improving standards of ICT. The book provides both stimulating and demanding work for students whilst the accompanying Tutor Resource File provides comprehensive guidance for teachers.

Whilst its major focus is the new ICT GCSE, it also provides a good foundation for the forthcoming VGCSE in ICT. Many teachers will also find it useful to support students following ICAA's ICT Competence Certificates. Some 200,000 students have participated in these schemes.

This book emphasises the importance of understanding how to use and develop ICT. The activities and tasks given represent suitable contexts for gaining and applying the competence and knowledge required for GCSE examinations in ICT.

Wherever possible, real contexts and typical systems problems have been provided.

Relevant levels of technical information have been included. Activities have been designed so that a user can work independently to achieve a high level of knowledge and understanding.

Teachers and writers directly involved with the ICAA ICT GCSE and Competence Certification programme have developed the activities through their own work in the classroom. Their constant enthusiasm has led to the development of the Case Studies in the format provided in the book. The use of the Case Studies provides the opportunity for the context to come to the user instead of the user having to seek out the context.

Liz Hankin, the author, is one of the leading ICT authorities in the UK and this textbook benefits from her extensive experience as a teacher, adviser and consultant. ICAA wishes to take this opportunity to express thanks to her for her excellent work.

Ben Kelsey
Chief Executive Officer
International Curriculum and Assessment
Agency (ICAA)

# Acknowledgements

The author and publishers would like to thank the following:

EdICTS, Jennie Clark, Peter Hammond, April Jones and Dave Dunn for their support and observations; Nottinghamshire Fire Service for the information about their communications; Rover Education Section for the data about the CAD/CAM methods used; Strand Lighting for the use of material from their 'Step into the Limelight' education pack; and Penni Bickle, picture researcher.

We are also grateful to the following for permission to reproduce photographs:

Alvey and Towers – page 207; BT Images – page 199; Trevor Clifford – p.53; Firepix – p.5, 184; MIRA – p.157; Yiorgos Nikiteas – p.11, 13, 25, 41, 81, 89, 151, 218, 220; Christine Osborne – p.93; Pictor Uniphoto – p.12; Shout – p.9, 62, 186; Stone – p.158; Stone/Chard Ehlers – p.15; Stone/Condina – p.192; Stone/Douet – p.8 (top right); Stone/Simmons – p.130; Stone/Taylor – p.78 (bottom left); Stone/Trip – p.137; Trip/Kaplan – p.148; Trip/Rogers – p.43

Every effort has been made to contact copyright holders of material published in this book. We would be glad to hear from unacknowledged sources at the first opportunity.

# How to use this book

This book has been written to help you understand **GCSE Information and Communication Technology** and practise the skills needed.

Each chapter deals with different ICT applications and is split into four **Case Studies**, all of which need to be studied. In each chapter, **Case Studies 1–3** provide information about a specific ICT application

and **Case Study 4** revises what you have learnt.

Each case study is laid out as shown below:

At the end of each chapter, there is an **Information Bank** that provides you with the information needed to carry out the tasks in the chapter. The Information Bank can also be used as a revision guide for your examination.

**Introduction** – gives you background information about the case study

**Action Point** – tasks you need to carry out

**Learning Objectives** – tell you what you will do in each activity

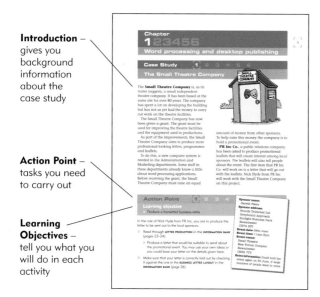

**Action Plus** – optional extra tasks

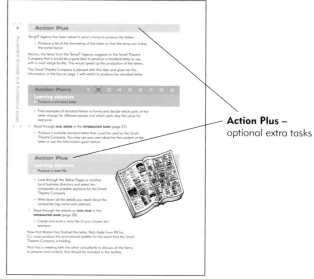

**Knowledge Points** – summarise what you should have learnt in the case study

**Skills Focus Point** – focuses on the practical skills you should use in the case study

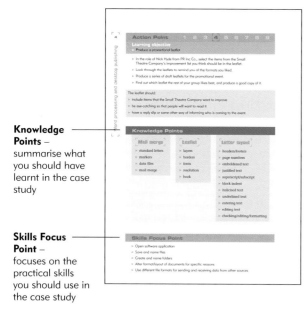

**Information Bank** – explanations to help you with tasks and revision

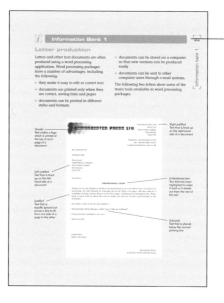

When all of the tasks have been completed you will be able to complete the **Review ICT** section. This section gives you the opportunity to make a record of the items you have covered in the tasks. The Learning Objectives table can be used to pick out any topics you think you need to revise or know more about. The Skills Objectives table can be used as a checklist to ensure you are confident about using your practical skills.

## Case study notes

The case studies describe four ICT-based companies, and show how they are used by different organisations.

In carrying out the tasks, you are asked to take on the role of a consultant from one of the companies.

### IS..IT Ltd

A company of ICT consultants who design and install new ICT systems

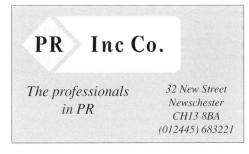

### PR Inc Co.

A company consisting of freelance public relations consultants who join together for large projects

### TempIT

A temp agency that provides temporary staff who have good ICT skills

### Control Systems Co.

A company of control technology consultants who help with development and installation of control systems

# Chapter 1 23456

## Word processing and desktop publishing

### Case Study 1 2 3 4 5 6

### The Small Theatre Company

The **Small Theatre Company** is, as its name suggests, a small independent theatre company. It has been based at the same site for over 80 years. The company has spent a lot on developing the building but has not as yet had the money to carry out work on the theatre facilities.

The Small Theatre Company has now been given a grant. The grant must be used for improving the theatre facilities and the equipment used in productions.

As part of the improvements, the Small Theatre Company aims to produce more professional-looking letters, programmes and leaflets.

To do this, a new computer system is needed in the Administration and Marketing departments. Some staff in these departments already know a little about word processing applications. Before receiving the grant, the Small Theatre Company must raise an equal amount of money from other sponsors. To help raise this money the company is to hold a promotional event.

**PR Inc Co.**, a public relations company, has been asked to produce promotional leaflets that will create interest among local sponsors. The leaflets will also tell people about the event. The first item that PR Inc Co. will work on is a letter that will go out with the leaflets. Nick Hyde from PR Inc will work with the Small Theatre Company on this project.

### Action Point 1 2 3 4

#### Learning objective

➤ Produce a formatted business letter

In the role of Nick Hyde from PR Inc, you are to produce the letter to be sent out to the local sponsors.

*i* Read through **LETTER PRODUCTION** in the **INFORMATION BANK** (pages 23–24)

➤ Produce a letter that would be suitable to send about the promotional event. You may use your own ideas or you could base your letter on the details given here.

*i* Make sure that your letter is correctly laid out by checking it against the one in the **BUSINESS LETTER LAYOUT** in the **INFORMATION BANK** (page 26).

**Sponsor name:**
Gareth Peers
**Sponsor address:**
Sounds Unlimited Ltd
Greyhound Approach
Sunlight Business Park
Newschester
CH74 8TT
**Event date:** 28th June
**Event time:** 11am–3pm
**Event venue:**
Small Theatre
New Forum Complex
Newschester
CH32 7TY
**Extra information:** Could hold the event again on 30 June, if large numbers of people want to come

## Action Plus

TemplT Agency has been asked to send a temp to produce the letters.

> Produce a list of the formatting of the letter so that the temp can follow the same layout.

Marion, the temp from the TemplT Agency, suggests to the Small Theatre Company that it would be a good idea to produce a standard letter to use with a mail merge facility. This would speed up the production of the letters.

The Small Theatre Company is pleased with this idea and gives her the information in the box on page 1 with which to produce her standard letter.

## Action Point     1   2   3   4   5   6   7   8   9

### Learning objective
> Produce a standard letter

> Find examples of standard letters or forms and decide which parts of the letter change for different people and which parts stay the same for everyone.

*i* Read through **MAIL MERGE** in the **INFORMATION BANK** (page 27).

> Produce a suitable standard letter that could be used by the Small Theatre Company. You may use your own ideas for the content of the letter or use the information given before.

## Action Plus

### Learning objective
> Produce a data file

> Look through the Yellow Pages or another local business directory and select ten companies as possible sponsors for the Small Theatre Company.

> Write down all the details you need about the companies (eg name and address).

*i* Read through the details on **DATA FILES** in the **INFORMATION BANK** (page 28).

> Create and store a data file of your chosen ten sponsors.

Now that Marion has finished the letter, Nick Hyde from PR Inc Co. must produce the promotional leaflets for the event that the Small Theatre Company is holding.

Nick has a meeting with the other consultants to discuss all the items, ie pictures and content, that should be included in the leaflets.

### Learning objective

➤ Copy a promotional leaflet

➤ Collect a range of different leaflets. Look through your leaflets and put them into order from the one you like the best to the one you like the least.

➤ Make notes about the two leaflets you like the best. Decide what it is that you like about them – is it the fonts, size of lettering, colours used, the way the leaflet folds or the layout.

*i*   Read through **LEAFLETS** in the **INFORMATION BANK** (pages 29–30).

➤ Produce a copy of one of the leaflets using a word processing package and a desktop publishing package. If you cannot create or copy the images, leave boxes of the correct size where they would be.

➤ Experiment with a range of fonts and layouts until you are pleased with the result.

➤ Ask other members of your group for their opinion of your leaflets, and alter them if necessary.

These are the areas that the Small Theatre Company wants to improve with the money from the grant:

➤ automate the use of special effects in the productions (eg use projected images)

➤ upgrade the sound system so that a range of sounds can be automated

➤ improve the design of stage sets

➤ install a control system for lighting and moving scenery

➤ introduce a sponsorship scheme

➤ produce a database containing details of the productions, and the characters and scenes within productions

➤ create the souvenir programmes in-house.

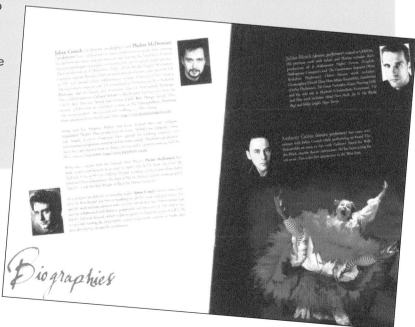

## Action Point 1 2 3 **4** 5 6 7 8 9

### Learning objective

➤ Produce a promotional leaflet

➤ In the role of Nick Hyde from PR Inc Co., select the items from the Small Theatre Company's improvement list you think should be in the leaflet.

➤ Look through the leaflets to remind you of the formats you liked.

➤ Produce a series of draft leaflets for the promotional event.

➤ Find out which leaflet the rest of your group likes best, and produce a good copy of it.

The leaflet should:

➤ include items that the Small Theatre Company want to improve

➤ be eye-catching so that people will want to read it

➤ have a reply slip or some other way of informing who is coming to the event.

## Knowledge Points

### Mail merge

➤ standard letters
➤ markers
➤ data files
➤ mail merge

### Leaflet

➤ layers
➤ borders
➤ fonts
➤ resolution
➤ book

### Letter layout

➤ headers/footers
➤ page numbers
➤ emboldened text
➤ justified text
➤ superscript/subscript
➤ block indent
➤ italicised text
➤ underlined text
➤ entering text
➤ editing text
➤ checking/editing/formatting

## Skills Focus Point

➤ Open software application
➤ Save and name files
➤ Create and name folders
➤ Alter format/layout of documents for specific reasons
➤ Use different file formats for sending and receiving data from other sources

**Newschester Fire Service** has decided that it needs to work with local schools to promote fire safety. The service often holds competitions for children and, although these are helpful, the fire officers would like the chance to hold a large event that many more people could attend.

The Senior Officer, Steve Thomas, decides that it would be a good idea to have an exhibition about the way fire officers work and how they use ICT.

He knows, from talking to children, that some of the new systems and equipment used by the fire service would be interesting for the children. Displays could be set up for children to find out about the systems.

The main areas he would like to include in the exhibition are:

> the work the fire officers do

> the way they use ICT in their work

> fire safety information

> fire prevention

> rescue services.

Steve Thomas does not know where to start with preparations for the exhibition. He is told about the ICT consultancy called **IS..IT Ltd** that helps people with ICT systems.

When he contacts the company, Frederick Muzungu, one of the consultants, suggests that the fire service needs an analysis report on its use of ICT systems. This report would help to identify which of the ICT systems are the most important ones, which would give a focus for the exhibition.

## Action Point   1 2 3 4 5 6 7 8 9

> Read through the following report called Fire Service Information to find out where and how ICT systems are used in the fire service.

# Fire Service Information

Newschester County Fire Brigade has been responsible for providing fire protection to the town of Newschester since 1948. The brigade serves the town's population as part of a county network of 40 fire stations, structured into three divisions.

Fire Brigade Headquarters, situated at Newschester in the centre of the county, contains the offices of the Chief Fire Officer and his senior management team. It also houses a computer-aided command, control and communications centre, which the brigade uses to handle the large number of incidents arising from, on average, the 55,900 calls for assistance it receives annually.

The county of Newscheshire is one of the largest in the UK, with a population of over 1.4 million and covering an area of 307,770 hectares. The county has 142 km of motorway out of a national total of 3,110 km. In addition to boasting the busiest seaside town in the country, Whitepond, there are major shopping complexes, leisure developments, business parks and rail links. All these factors combine to make exceptional demands on the brigade.

The brigade's mobilisation had been organised by a BT/Ferranti system since 1985. However, due to advances in technology, it was decided to establish a project team in July 1992 to provide the brigade with an integrated digital network and to replace the station end equipment. The new equipment was supplied and installed by BT and Fortek Computers Ltd. The tender for installation was awarded to GEC-Marconi.

The prime function of the command and control centre is to receive emergency calls and to mobilise fire appliances to attend emergency incidents. This is a complex task and consists of procedures for:

- receiving emergency calls
- entering incident details
- identifying the location of the incident
- determining which fire appliances should attend
- passing turnout instructions and other messages to the communications system for onward transmission to brigade appliances
- monitoring of the progress of the incident and providing additional resources when required.

The GEC-Marconi Integrated Command and Control System (ICCS) selected by the brigade receives emergency calls, and mobilises, controls and manages the brigade's operational resources.

The equipment that makes up the control installation comprises:

- a mobilisation system, supplied by GEC-Marconi, which presents real-time information for use by control staff
- an integrated communications control system (call handling) supplied by Advance Data Systems Ltd, which manages the various communications links and provides the interface between emergency callers and the mobilising system
- a geographic information system, supplied by PAFEC, which provides resource availability and status information, displayed as an overlay on screen
- recording equipment, which consists of instant replay recorders and Racal Rapidax equipment, supplied by Racal, which enables all telephone and radio communications to be stored
- a management information system, supplied by GEC-Marconi, which processes and presents data for assessment and analysis by management

● Chemdata information (information about chemicals) which can be transmitted to appliances, stations or designated printers by fax or remote printer via the mobilising system. Software is supplied by GEC-Marconi.

A fallback system is held on the mobilising terminal, supplied by GEC-Marconi, which is used in case of failure of the main mobilising system. The secondary control is equipped with the necessary software and hardware, ISDN lines, power and ancillary services to permit it to be used as a mobilisation centre if the headquarters building has to be evacuated.

Three separate and independent external communication routes provide a fail-safe means of conveying mobilising and administrative messages between the control room and each fire station.

## Mobilisation system

The control room at brigade headquarters has seven mobilising positions, including supervisors' positions, which are connected via a local area network (LAN) to the mobilising computers. The computers using mobilising software and action commands assist the Fire Control Operators in determining which resources to mobilise in response to a reported incident, and in despatching instructions to the appropriate fire stations. The Fire Control Operators receive information about incidents from various sources and enter it into the system. The system then suggests what action can be taken. The operators can accept, modify or ignore the suggestion.

## Integrated communications control system (call handling)

The call handling equipment permits supervisors and operators to connect with the radio and telephone services used by the brigade. Each position is equipped with a console from which all voice communications can be accessed. All functions are software controlled, allowing the system to provide flexibility of design and operation. The associated management information system provides a call-logging facility for statistical purposes.

## Geographic information system (GIS)

The GIS terminals permit monitoring of incidents by providing a graphical display of incidents and resources overlaid on maps of various scales. The operator can determine at a glance the distribution and commitments of the brigade's resources. The GIS monitors display information as an overlay on an electronic map of Newschester; this is then projected on two 52-inch monitors.

## Racal Rapidax recording equipment

The recording system is a rapid-access, 20-channel voice recorder. It is capable of recording communications over land lines and radio, providing instantaneous message recall, and is managed by a central system controller. A desktop console is situated at each terminal and can record, store and play back radio or telephone speech traffic from the operator's position. It is possible to continue recording whilst playing back a message.

## Management information system (MIS)

The management information system assists the brigade by producing high-quality operational and management information. This information covers both local managerial purposes and Home Office requirements for incident report and analysis. Statistical data is automatically transferred to the management information system from the mobilising system.

### Learning objectives

➤ Use and compare a word processing package and a DTP package for the production of a diagram

➤ Carry out a simple analysis of a system

One way of showing information is in a spider diagram. A spider diagram can be used to identify separate items of important information.

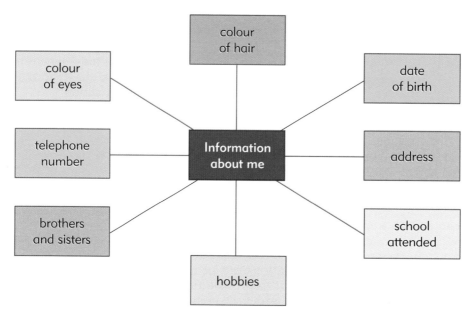

➤ Produce a spider diagram that shows the important items of information about the fire service's use of ICT.

➤ Produce a good copy of your diagram using both a word processing application and a DTP application.

➤ Make notes about which application was the easier one to use for the diagram.

The information from the analysis of ICT usage (your spider diagram) is to be used in a report for the fire service. Frederick could use either a word processing or a DTP application to produce the report.

### Learning objective

➤ Produce an analysis report

ℹ Read through **WP OR DTP?** in the **INFORMATION BANK** (page 31).

➤ Make a copy of the table overleaf and complete it to identify which application would be best for producing the items on the left. Give reasons for your choice.

| | Item ✓ | WP ✓ | DTP Reasons |
|---|---|---|---|
| Letters | | | |
| Newspapers | | | |
| Leaflets | | | |
| Diagrams | | | |
| User guide | | | |

> In the role of the IS..IT Ltd consultant, you are to produce the report about the use of ICT in the fire service.

> Choose either a word processing or a DTP package to produce the report. Your choice of application should be based upon your knowledge of their features and uses.

*i* Read through **DOCUMENT FORMAT** in the **INFORMATION BANK** (pages 32–33) to help you to plan the format of your report.

Frederick thinks that the fire service would benefit from using pre-printed documents. He suggests the use of templates for:

**Business letters**

| | |
|---|---|
| Page attributes: | Portrait |
| Page layout: | A4 |
| Font: | Courier |
| Header/footer: | Logo |
| Justification: | On |
| Line spacing: | Single |
| Margins: | 15 |
| Page numbering: | Off |

**Internal memos**

| | |
|---|---|
| Page attributes: | Portrait |
| Page layout: | A4 |
| Font: | Arial |
| Header/footer: | Memo |
| Justification: | Off |
| Line spacing: | Double |
| Margins: | 25 |
| Page numbering: | Off |

**Newsletters**

| | |
|---|---|
| Page attributes: | Landscape |
| Page layout: | A4 with columns and text wrap |
| Font: | Times New Roman |
| Header/footer: | Logo |
| Justification: | On |
| Line spacing: | 1.5 |
| Margins: | 10, 10, 10, 10 |
| Page numbering: | No |

## Action Point    1  2  3  **4**  5  6  7  8  9

### Learning objective

➤ Produce reusable template files

*i* Read through **TEMPLATES** in the **INFORMATION BANK** (pages 34–35).

➤ Produce the three templates that would be suitable for the fire service.

➤ Find or create a clip art image suitable for use as a logo, and import it into your template.

## Action Plus

➤ The templates need to be customised for the different sections in the fire station. Create a series of Paste/Links to enable the logo or section heading to be changed as necessary.

## Knowledge Points

### Document format

➤ page attributes

➤ portrait/landscape

➤ page layout

➤ bullet points

### Templates

➤ templates/wizards

➤ indents

➤ alignments

➤ line spacing

➤ margins

➤ tabulation

➤ imported images

## Skills Focus Point

➤ Obtain suitable hard copy by altering print quality and orientation

➤ Set up template files for pre-printed items, eg documents with letterheads, data entry into forms

➤ Make use of embedded objects/files in preference to linking objects/files

### Sezer's Savastores

The Sezer family own a number of corner shops and convenience stores. The stores are run by managers and family members. The Sezers want to increase the number of stores and are thinking about expanding into small supermarkets. To be able to compete on this scale, the Sezers know they will have to acquire new ICT systems and equipment.

They are already using computerised systems in each of their shops, but know they are not the best systems for the type of work they do now or need to do in the future.

Their existing system is a 286 machine running under DOS with 2 MB of RAM, a 20 MB hard drive, and a floppy drive. It has a word processing package installed and is connected to a dot matrix printer.

Before acquiring new systems for all the shops, the Sezer family would like to upgrade the central system they use so that they can produce information leaflets and 'special offer' posters.

A member of staff from **IS..IT Ltd**, John Peters, knows the Sezer family and suggests that the family should talk to one of the company's consultants about upgrading the system.

### Action Point    **1**   2   3   4   5   6   7   8   9

#### Learning objective

➤ Carry out an analysis of a graphics system

*i*   Read through **GRAPHICS SYSTEMS** in the **INFORMATION BANK** (pages 36–38).

➤ In the role of John Peters, draw up your ideas for an upgraded system. Remember that the Sezers are not computer experts, so select only the items they will need to use.

➤ Record your ideas in an analysis table like the one shown below, using either a word processing or a DTP package. Add any extra lines to your table as you need them.

| Item | Existing system | New system | Reason |
|------|-----------------|------------|--------|
| **Hardware** | e.g. 486 processor | | |
| **Software** | e.g. word processor | | |

The full specification for the hardware and software of the upgraded system has been prepared, and needs to be presented to the Sezer family.

**Action Point**    1   **2**   3   4   5   6   7   8   9

**Learning objectives**

➤ Prepare a specification

➤ Prepare a presentation

*i*   Read through **SYSTEM SPECIFICATION** in the **INFORMATION BANK** (page 39).

➤ Using the information from your analysis table, prepare a presentation for the Sezers about the upgraded system. For your presentation you should think about:

➤ the audience of the presentation

➤ whether information should be provided on paper

➤ how long the presentation should be

➤ technical terms that need to be explained

➤ providing full coverage of the system's specification.

The Sezer family are keen to go ahead with the upgraded system. John Peters suggests they should have training to help them use the new system. He puts them in touch with PR Inc Co., a company that offers small businesses courses in training staff to use computer systems.

The Sezers ask for training on the set-up of their system (technical information); the use of their system (a user guide); and the documents they can produce.

### Learning objectives

➤ Produce documentation to support a system

➤ Prepare a system for others to use

*i* Read through **SYSTEM SUPPORT** in the **INFORMATION BANK** (page 40).

➤ In the role of the PR Inc Co. trainer, you are to run a demonstration and training session on how to use either a word processing or a DTP application.

➤ To run the demonstration produce the documentation that the Sezers would need.

## Action Plus

➤ Produce 'help guides' as help files on the system that you are going to use to demonstrate the application.

➤ Ask another member of your group to try out your help guides. Refine and change the files as necessary.

The Sezers have started to produce their 'special offer' posters for a range of products, using the new system. They would like to be able to add images of the products in the posters.

John Peters has arranged to show the Sezers ways that images can be put into documents.

The consultant brings:

➤ a CD-ROM with clip art images

➤ a scanner and software

➤ a digital camera and photo editing software.

### Learning objective

➤ Capture/create images for use on a computer system

*i* Read through **IMAGES** in the **INFORMATION BANK** (pages 40–41) to find out more about how images can be used in computer systems.

➤ Make notes about the methods that can be used, and select a method suitable for the system you are using.

➤ Choose a product that you can buy from a supermarket and create or capture an image of the product to use on a computer.

## Action Plus

### Learning objective

➤ Alter resolution and dpi settings to affect the final outcome

➤ Describe how you captured your image and placed it into the document.

➤ Changing the resolution or dpi of the image will affect the final result. Explain what happens when they are altered.

## Knowledge Points

### Graphics systems

➤ computer processors
➤ monitors
➤ input devices
➤ output devices
➤ storage devices

### Images

➤ scanners and software
➤ CD-ROMs
➤ clip art
➤ digital cameras
➤ resolution
➤ dpi

### System support

➤ system documentation
➤ user documentation
➤ technical documentation
➤ on-line help
➤ technical support links

### System specification

➤ hardware specification
➤ software specification

## Skills Focus Point

➤ Incorporate two or more different formats of data into a single document

➤ Establish the size of a file, eg through 'Properties or Get Info'

➤ Customise toolbars for specific documents

➤ Compress files to maximise storage on a system

**Bayrich Motors** is a manufacturer of family and executive cars.

The company is based at Landlow, close to Newschester, where it was founded in 1924. The factory employs 3000 people including designers, production workers and administration staff.

The factory has changed little since it was last refitted in 1966. The directors are now planning to invest in new technology systems. They will start with the Administration section.

The Administration department is large. It includes a team of financial managers and accountants, marketing and sales teams and general administration staff. At present, all promotional materials are produced by a company called Promat from Taurchester.

## Action Point  **1** 2 3 4 5 6 7 8 9

### Learning objective
> Review analysis of systems

Catherine Hewitt, as a consultant from IS..IT Ltd, is asked to find out where WP and DTP applications could be used to help the administration staff.

> Use the information shown in the spider diagram below to carry out an analysis of existing work that could be done by WP and DTP applications.

> Record your findings in a table or chart.

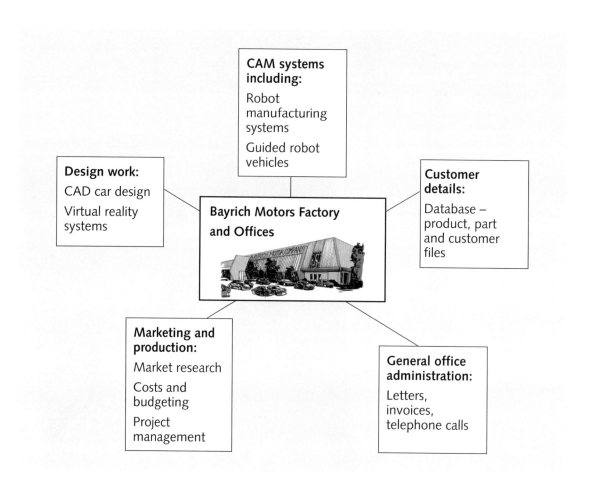

**CAM systems including:**

Robot manufacturing systems

Guided robot vehicles

**Design work:**

CAD car design

Virtual reality systems

**Bayrich Motors Factory and Offices**

**Customer details:**

Database – product, part and customer files

**Marketing and production:**

Market research

Costs and budgeting

Project management

**General office administration:**

Letters, invoices, telephone calls

## Action Plus

### Learning objective

➤ Identify the implications of using new technology in the workplace

You will be advising Bayrich Motors about where the introduction of WP/DTP applications will improve working methods.

➤ Consider the advantages and disadvantages of introducing the new system for the staff and the management.

➤ Draw up an advisory report for the directors identifying the implications of introducing new systems and working methods.

Bayrich Motors would like all the documents produced by the company to have a consistent look.

Catherine Hewitt asks a colleague from PR Inc Co. to provide a 'house style' for the company's documents. They will produce template files for letterheads, compliment slips, business cards, memos, fax covers, invoices, newsletters and address labels.

### Learning objective

➤ Review production and use of template files

➤ Select three items from the list of documents on page 16.

➤ Collect a range of samples of these documents as used by different organisations.

➤ Try out different fonts, sizes and layouts for these documents until you are satisfied that the documents are **clear**, **attractive** and **easy to use**.

➤ Produce template files for the items you have chosen, using either a DTP or a WP package. Do not use existing templates.

## Action Plus

➤ Make use of your template files to produce several documents from each of your templates, identifying what has to be added to personalise each item.

The staff in the Administration department of Bayrich Motors will need to feel confident when they use the new computer system.

To help both the permanent and temporary staff who will use the systems, PR Inc Co. is to produce documentation to support the type of work the staff will be doing.

## Action Point    1 2 `3` 4 5 6 7 8 9

### Learning objectives

➤ Review use of template files

➤ Review production of documentation

➤ Produce user support materials so that staff will be able to send out information as a letter from a template file. Use your own data or the sample given here.

> **From** Financial Manager, Bayrich Motors
> **To** Mr H Jones, Grimweld Ltd, Stocklington SK58 2JP
> **Text** Harry, Thank you for your telephone call last Thursday. I am sorry I was out of the office when you rang. The meeting will take place on Monday 23 March in the Conference Centre, Room III. I would be grateful if you would let Sarah Kiney know if you are able to attend.
>
> Phil.

## Action Plus

### Learning objective

➤ Review production and use of standard letters

This letter could also be produced as a standard letter to send out to a number of people.

➤ Change this letter into a standard letter that would be suitable for use by Bayrich Motors.

Catherine Hewitt has finished her work for the Bayrich Motors Administration department.

She is to meet all staff from the section in order to introduce the new system to them. She intends to show them how the new system will help them in their work.

## Action Point    1  2  3  4  5  6  7  8  9

### Learning objective

➤ Review production of leaflets

➤ Design an invitation to the launch meeting and a news-sheet about the new system.

You are invited to a

**CHAMPAGNE RECEPTION**

*celebrating the launch
of our exciting new model
at*
HILLVIEW MOTORS
Barkside, Newchester
*on*
*Friday 25 March 2002 at 6 pm*

**HILLVIEW MOTORS**

## Action Plus

### Learning objective

➤ Identify social and moral implications in the use of new technology

You should anticipate that some staff will not be happy about the introduction of the new system.

➤ List possible conflicts that could arise at the meeting.

➤ Prepare your own answers to these problems.

Throughout the case studies in this chapter, you have had the opportunity to explore a number of areas of knowledge. Make a copy of the following table and complete your table to show where you have used the Knowledge Points.

| Knowledge Points | Where Used |
|---|---|
| **Letter layout** | |
| ➤ headers/footers | |
| ➤ page numbers | |
| ➤ emboldened text | |
| ➤ justified text | |
| ➤ superscript/subscript | |
| ➤ block indent | |
| ➤ italicised text | |
| ➤ underlined text | |
| ➤ entering text | |
| ➤ editing text | |
| ➤ checking/editing/formatting | |
| **Mail merge** | |
| ➤ standard letters | |
| ➤ markers | |
| ➤ data files | |
| ➤ mail merge | |
| **Leaflets** | |
| ➤ layers | |
| ➤ borders | |
| ➤ fonts | |
| ➤ resolution | |
| ➤ book | |
| **Document format** | |
| ➤ page attributes | |
| ➤ portrait/landscape | |
| ➤ page layout | |
| ➤ bullet points | |

# Review ICT (continued)

| Knowledge Points | Where Used |
|---|---|

## Templates
- templates/wizards
- indents
- alignments
- line spacing
- margins
- tabulation
- imported images

## Graphics systems
- computer processors
- monitors
- input devices
- output devices
- storage devices

## System specification
- hardware specification
- software specification

## Images
- scanners and software
- CD-ROMs
- clip art
- digital cameras
- resolution
- dpi

## System support
- system documentation
- user documentation
- technical documentation
- on-line help
- technical support links

The following Learning Objectives have been covered in Chapter 1.

Decide whether you have sufficient knowledge about each item to be able to use or write about them in the future. Leave blank the 'tick' column for any objective that you need to know more about.

| Learning Objectives | ✓ |
| --- | --- |
| Produce a formatted business letter | |
| Produce a standard letter | |
| Produce a data file | |
| Copy a promotional leaflet | |
| Produce a promotional leaflet | |
| Use and compare a word processing package and a DTP package | |
| Carry out a simple anaylsis of a system | |
| Produce an analysis report | |
| Produce reusuable template files | |
| Carry out an analysis of a graphics system | |
| Prepare a specification | |
| Prepare a presentation | |
| Produce documentation to support a system | |
| Prepare a system for others to use | |
| Capture/create images for use on a computer system | |
| Alter resolution and dpi setting to affect the final outcome | |
| Identify the implications of using new technology in the workplace | |
| Identify social and moral implications in the use of new technology | |

## Skills Objectives

You should have used the practical skills listed below in following the case studies in this chapter. Copy this table for your records.

Decide whether you feel confident about using the skill again or are able to write about it. Leave blank the 'tick' column for any objective that you need to practise.

Record the filenames for any working drafts, showing how you developed at least two documents and print-outs. Keep records of how you saved information.

| Skills Objectives | ✓ |
|---|---|
| ➤ Open software application | |
| ➤ Save and name files | |
| ➤ Create and name folders | |
| ➤ Alter format/layout of documents for specific reasons | |
| ➤ Use different tile formats for sending and receiving data from other sources | |
| ➤ Obtain suitable hard copy by altering print quality and orientation | |
| ➤ Set up template files for pre-printed items, eg documents with letterheads, data entry into forms | |
| ➤ Make use of embedded objects/files in preference to linking objects/files | |
| ➤ Incorporate two or more different formats of data into a single document | |
| ➤ Establish the size of a file, eg through 'Properties or Get Info' | |
| ➤ Customise toolbars for specific documents | |
| ➤ Compress files to maximise storage on a system | |

## Letter production

Letters and other text documents are often produced using a word processing application. Word processing packages have a number of advantages, including the following:

➤ they make it easy to edit or correct text

➤ documents are printed only when they are correct, saving time and paper

➤ documents can be printed in different styles and formats

➤ documents can be stored on a computer so that new versions can be produced easily

➤ documents can be sent to other computer users through e-mail systems.

The following two letters show some of the main tools available in word processing packages.

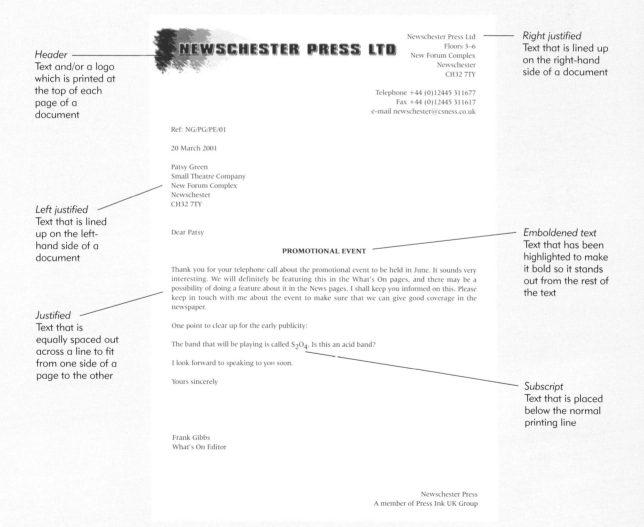

**Header**
Text and/or a logo which is printed at the top of each page of a document

**Left justified**
Text that is lined up on the left-hand side of a document

**Justified**
Text that is equally spaced out across a line to fit from one side of a page to the other

**Right justified**
Text that is lined up on the right-hand side of a document

**Emboldened text**
Text that has been highlighted to make it bold so it stands out from the rest of the text

**Subscript**
Text that is placed below the normal printing line

---

NEWSCHESTER PRESS LTD

Newschester Press Ltd
Floors 3–6
New Forum Complex
Newschester
CH32 7TY

Telephone +44 (0)12445 311677
Fax +44 (0)12445 311617
e-mail newschester@csness.co.uk

Ref: NG/PG/PE/01

20 March 2001

Patsy Green
Small Theatre Company
New Forum Complex
Newschester
CH32 7TY

Dear Patsy

**PROMOTIONAL EVENT**

Thank you for your telephone call about the promotional event to be held in June. It sounds very interesting. We will definitely be featuring this in the What's On pages, and there may be a possibility of doing a feature about it in the News pages. I shall keep you informed on this. Please keep in touch with me about the event to make sure that we can give good coverage in the newspaper.

One point to clear up for the early publicity:

The band that will be playing is called $S_2O_4$. Is this an acid band?

I look forward to speaking to you soon.

Yours sincerely

Frank Gibbs
What's On Editor

Newschester Press
A member of Press Ink UK Group

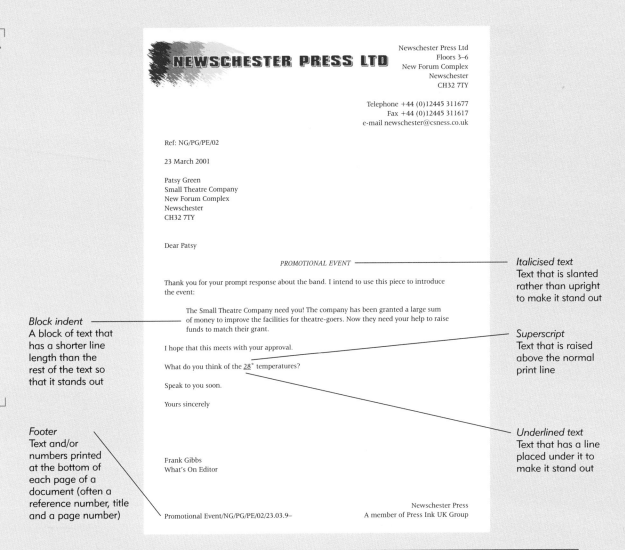

**NEWSCHESTER PRESS LTD**

Newschester Press Ltd
Floors 3–6
New Forum Complex
Newschester
CH32 7TY

Telephone +44 (0)12445 311677
Fax +44 (0)12445 311617
e-mail newschester@csness.co.uk

Ref: NG/PG/PE/02

23 March 2001

Patsy Green
Small Theatre Company
New Forum Complex
Newschester
CH32 7TY

Dear Patsy

*PROMOTIONAL EVENT* —————————————————— *Italicised text*
Text that is slanted
rather than upright
to make it stand out

Thank you for your prompt response about the band. I intend to use this piece to introduce
the event:

> The Small Theatre Company need you! The company has been granted a large sum
> of money to improve the facilities for theatre-goers. Now they need your help to raise
> funds to match their grant.

*Block indent*
A block of text that
has a shorter line
length than the
rest of the text so
that it stands out

I hope that this meets with your approval.

*Superscript*
Text that is raised
above the normal
print line

What do you think of the 28° temperatures?

Speak to you soon.

Yours sincerely

*Underlined text*
Text that has a line
placed under it to
make it stand out

*Footer*
Text and/or
numbers printed
at the bottom of
each page of a
document (often a
reference number, title
and a page number)

Frank Gibbs
What's On Editor

Promotional Event/NG/PG/PE/02/23.03.9–

Newschester Press
A member of Press Ink UK Group

---

You need to know how to use a word
processor for the following operations.

## Open/create a new document

You need to open an existing document or
create a new one after opening the word
processing application. Follow the on-
screen instructions to **open** a document,
when you are working on a document that
you have already created and saved. You
will use the **new** document routine when
creating a new piece of work.

## Save and re-save

It is a good idea to save your work often.
To be really safe, save your **new** document
as a file as soon as you start to work, and
then re-save every five minutes or so.

Some applications allow you to set up an
**auto save** routine. The software will then
save the file automatically at regular
intervals.

## Enter text

Entering text means keying in text using a
keyboard – as you key, the text will appear
on screen.

## Edit text

It is often necessary to alter the wording of
a document, or to correct errors. This
usually involves placing the cursor where
the change is to be made and re-typing
the text or back spacing in order to delete
an existing word.

## Style/format

Style facilities are used to enhance the look of the text. The main style features used in business letters are shown in the preceding letters.

The format of a document controls the way that the text will be placed on the page. The width of the margins, the justification of the text, and the page width are some of the ways that the document is formatted. Some of these features have been shown in the letters above.

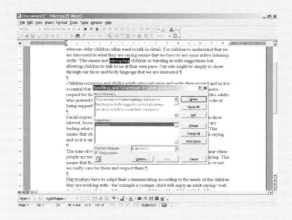

## Spell check

A spell-check facility is a useful tool in word processing. When text has been entered and before it is printed, a spell check can be used to make sure that all words are spelt correctly. Remember, however, that the spell check will not find words that are spelt correctly but used wrongly, such as using 'there' for 'their', or 'two' for 'too'.

## Print

If a printer is connected to the computer, hard copy can be made by using the print command. Some software has a 'print preview' facility, so that you can check how the document looks before you print it. Screen displays are not always what you get on paper!

A hard copy can be printed out from the computer

# Business letter layout

Most business letters follow the same layout. A sample of a letter showing the usual format is shown below.

**Letterhead**
Most business letters are printed on headed paper, or use a letterhead on the word processor

**Date**
The date should always appear at the top of the letter

**Address**
The name and address of the person to whom you are sending the letter should appear on the left-hand side

**Salutation**
This should include only the person's title (Mr, Mrs, Ms etc) and surname

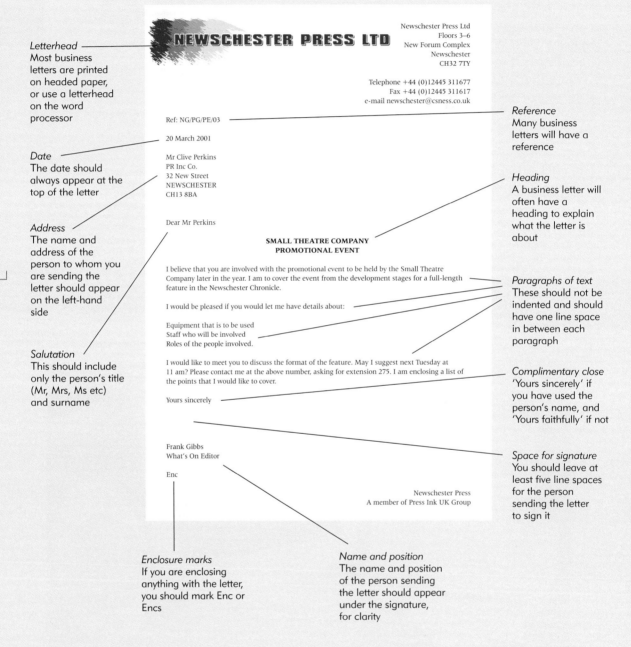

NEWSCHESTER PRESS LTD

Newschester Press Ltd
Floors 3–6
New Forum Complex
Newschester
CH32 7TY

Telephone +44 (0)12445 311677
Fax +44 (0)12445 311617
e-mail newschester@csness.co.uk

Ref: NG/PG/PE/03

20 March 2001

Mr Clive Perkins
PR Inc Co.
32 New Street
NEWSCHESTER
CH13 8BA

Dear Mr Perkins

**SMALL THEATRE COMPANY
PROMOTIONAL EVENT**

I believe that you are involved with the promotional event to be held by the Small Theatre Company later in the year. I am to cover the event from the development stages for a full-length feature in the Newschester Chronicle.

I would be pleased if you would let me have details about:

Equipment that is to be used
Staff who will be involved
Roles of the people involved.

I would like to meet you to discuss the format of the feature. May I suggest next Tuesday at 11 am? Please contact me at the above number, asking for extension 275. I am enclosing a list of the points that I would like to cover.

Yours sincerely

Frank Gibbs
What's On Editor

Enc

Newschester Press
A member of Press Ink UK Group

**Reference**
Many business letters will have a reference

**Heading**
A business letter will often have a heading to explain what the letter is about

**Paragraphs of text**
These should not be indented and should have one line space in between each paragraph

**Complimentary close**
'Yours sincerely' if you have used the person's name, and 'Yours faithfully' if not

**Space for signature**
You should leave at least five line spaces for the person sending the letter to sign it

**Enclosure marks**
If you are enclosing anything with the letter, you should mark Enc or Encs

**Name and position**
The name and position of the person sending the letter should appear under the signature, for clarity

# Mail merge

Companies often need to send standard letters to customers in which the contents of the letter is the same, and only the name, address and perhaps one or two other items need to be changed.

Once the standard parts of the letter are written, markers are put in to show where data from a data file will be put into the letter.

Newschester Press Ltd
Floors 3–6
New Forum Complex
Newschester
CH32 7TY

Telephone +44 (0)12445 311677
Fax +44 (0)12445 311617
e-mail newschester@csness.co.uk

<<Date>>

<<Title>><<First Name>><<Surname>>
<<Address 1>>
<<Address 2>>
<<Address 3>>
<<Postcode>>

Dear <<Title>><<Surname>>

I believe that you are involved with the promotional event to be held by the Small Theatre Company later in the year. I am to cover the event from the development stages for a full-length feature in the Newschester Chronicle.

I would be pleased if you would let me have details about:

Equipment that is to be used
Staff who will be involved
Roles of the people involved.

I would like to meet you to discuss the format of the feature. May I suggest next <<Day>> at <<Time>>? Please contact me at the above number, asking for ext. 275. I am enclosing a list of points that I would like to cover.

Yours sincerely

Frank Gibbs
What's On Editor

Enc

Newschester Press

*Markers*
Data items taken from a data file. These would change with each letter

*Standard letter*
The main text that does not change at all in the different letters

# Data files

A data file is made up of items of data that have been collected for some particular purpose. The data file is usually stored in a database application.

When using a mail merge facility, you can put the field names from a data file in place in the standard letter as markers. Each word processing and database application has its own coding for these markers.

Before the letters are printed, the word processing application reads the data from the data file and places it in the coded space in the standard letter.

The standard letter shown on page 27 has the field names in place ready to be taken from the data file. The field names used for this mail merge are:

| | |
|---|---|
| Date | This can be set automatically by the software |
| Title | Mr, Mrs, Miss, Ms, Dr, other |
| First name | Name or initial |
| Surname | Last name/family name |
| Address 1 | First line of an address |
| Address 2 | Second line of an address |
| Address 3 | Third line of an address |
| Postcode | Postcode/county/international zip code |
| Day | This can be set automatically by the computer or entered as a data item |
| Time | This can be set automatically by the computer or entered as a data item |

In future letters, the field names can be altered, added to or deleted.

# Leaflets

Leaflets can be produced using either a word processing or a desktop publishing (DTP) application.

DTP packages allow easier methods of moving and altering text and graphics.

To help with the layout of pages, DTP applications allow 'layers' to be used, so that items can be placed over each other.

| | | |
|---|---|---|
| **Small Theatre Company**<br><br><br>**A theatre for today!** | | **Small Theatre Company**<br><br><br>**A theatre for today!** |
| Layer 1 | Layer 2 | Combined layers |

Boxes and borders can be added to make the layers stand out.

Fonts can be changed. This is an important factor in the look of any document.

$$\textbf{a,}\; \alpha, \; \mathbb{A}, \; \textbf{a,} \; a, \; \mathfrak{a}, \; a, \; \textbf{a,} \; a$$
$$a, \; A, \; a, \; a, \; \textbf{a,} \; A, \; a, \; a, \; a, \; A$$

DTP applications can be used to sort the order of the pages so that they can be printed as a 'book'. The numbering of the pages is calculated automatically so that back-to-back printing will be correct.

## Layout points

➤ Leaflets can be produced by folding
paper in different ways. Pieces can also
be cut out or added.

**Folding methods**

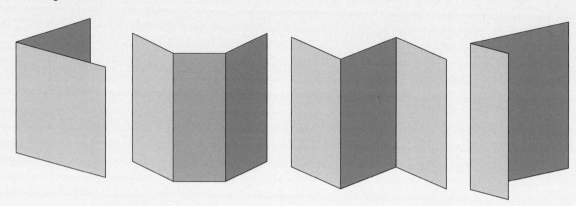

**Cut-away sections**

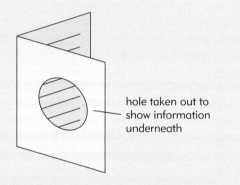

hole taken out to
show information
underneath

cuts used to
create effects

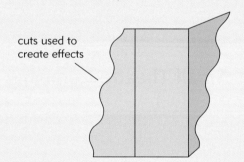

➤ Too many fonts on one leaflet can look
confusing. Decide how many different
fonts are really useful, and choose ones
that match the 'feel' of the leaflet.

➤ Pictures help to make leaflets attractive
and easy to understand. Decide whether
they should be photographs or clip art.

➤ The use of colour can improve or ruin
the look of a leaflet. Good use of colour
can emphasise the leaflet's message,
while clashing colours can make it
difficult to read.

# WP or DTP?

Deciding whether to use a word processing or a desktop publishing package has become more difficult. New word processing applications allow the user to carry out many of the same functions that can be done with DTP.

## What are the main differences?

### Word processing

The following are aspects of true word processing applications:

➤ *Text oriented.* Text can be handled efficiently and quickly. It also takes up less storage in a computer's memory.

➤ *Graphics and objects* can be imported, but are moved in connection with the text. Sometimes it is not possible to place graphics in the best place due to restrictions in the application.

➤ *Formatting* is given in terms of paragraphs, columns and page margins.

➤ *Line and page breaks* are inserted automatically by the application.

➤ *Text may flow* anywhere on the page.

➤ *Tables* can be created, which allows for the production of charts.

➤ *Linked objects*, such as a spreadsheets, can be embedded into a word-processed document. Any changes in the object can be made automatically in the document.

### Desktop publishing

➤ *Design and layout oriented.*

➤ *Graphics* can be moved without affecting text.

➤ *Formatting* is given in terms of position and size of frames, boxes or windows.

➤ *Text can be manipulated.* Text inside frames or boxes can be rotated or stretched to alter the appearance of the characters.

➤ *Graphics and linked objects* can be embedded and changes to the objects will be updated automatically in any documents.

## Which to choose?

Any documents that are mainly text based should be produced using a word processing package.

Documents that need to have graphics and text working together, and where the positioning of text and graphics needs to be changed, should be produced using a DTP package.

Text produced in a word processing application, such as reports and letters, can be cut or copied and pasted into a DTP application for a different type of presentation. This speeds up the use of DTP.

People who are involved in the production of DTP documents often do not type in the text themselves, but receive it in a format they can work with in the DTP application.

# Document format

Documents whose purpose is to report information must be clearly laid out, so that their contents are easy to follow.

Before a report or similar document can be produced, an appropriate format has to be chosen. Facilities within word processing and DTP applications let you set up the format for a particular document.

The Page Attribute facility allows the document to be produced in portrait or landscape orientation.

**Portrait**

**Landscape**

When the orientation has been set, the paper size needs to be selected.

Today, most commercial documents are produced in one of the following standard sizes:

| | |
|---|---|
| A3 | 420 × 297 mm |
| A4 | 210 × 297 mm |
| A5 | 148 × 210 mm |
| C5 Commercial Envelope | 162 × 229 mm |

Page Layout Attributes allows you to choose the way that text and graphics will look.

Text can be entered into columns so that when the end of a set column is reached the text will automatically start off in the next column. Columns can be set to different widths to fit areas of a page. Newspapers and magazines use columns.

Text can be entered into columns so that when the end of a set column is reached the text will automatically start off in the next column. Columns can be set to different widths to fit areas of a page.

Documents that need to have graphics and text working together, and where the positioning of text and graphics needs to be changed, should be produced using a DTP package.

Text can be set to flow around a graphic, behind a graphic or across a graphic

Reports often need to identify separate items of information so that reference can be made to appropriate sections when the report is being discussed.

To help the reader, numbered points can be used. WP and DTP applications will often automate the use of numbering.

Numbering can be used in different styles. A style is chosen to suit the amount of information that is held in the report. For example, a short report might use the simple system 1, 2, 3, etc, while a long report might use 1.1, 1.2, 1.3, 2.1, 2.2, etc.

| | | | | |
|---|---|---|---|---|
| 1 | 2 | 3 | 4 | 5 |
| i | ii | iii | iv | v |
| 1i | 1ii | 1iii | 1iv | 1v |
| 1.1 | 1.2 | 1.3 | 1.4 | 1.5 |
| a | b | c | d | e |

Text can be set into columns of different widths. Gaps between columns can also be altered to improve the layout of a document

Below is a section from an ICT GCSE syllabus, showing the use of numbered points.

**2**      Aims

**2.1**      The aims below are consistent with the National Curriculum requirements for ICT.

**2.2**      All candidates should:

i      solve problems through the use of information systems and associated principles and techniques;

ii      develop a broad and balanced view of the range of applications and information systems and an understanding of their capabilities;

iii      select from a range of ICT tools and information sources those that are appropriate for a variety of tasks.

# Templates

Using templates for documents saves time.

A template is a framework for a document, saved as a template file. Templates are used for a range of commercial documents such as business letters, business cards, memos, invoices and newsletters.

Some WP and DTP applications offer a range of templates. These are often known as 'wizards'.

When a business letter needs to be written, the appropriate template file is opened and the wording of the letter is typed into the template. All the formats are already set up in the template file, so all letters will look the same.

Companies may use letter-headed paper for their letters.

The pre-printed paper will have the company's logo, name and address in place at the top of the letter. Page Layout Attributes will be set so that any text starts under the space taken up by these items.

Letter-headed paper often has a logo printed in colour. The text would be added in black, and could be printed on an office printer, eg dot matrix, bubble jet or laser.

Instead of using a pre-printed letterhead, some companies will set their logo into the letter template file. This is a slower method, as each time a letter is printed the logo has to be printed as well.

This method would also be very costly if the company wanted to use colour in the logo, as they would have to use a colour printer for each letter.

Pre-printed logo ——

**NEWSCHESTER PRESS LTD**

Newschester Press Ltd
Floors 3–6
New Forum Complex
Newschester
CH32 7TY

Telephone +44 (0)12445 311677
Fax +44 (0)12445 311617
e-mail newschester@csness.co.uk

Newschester Press
A member of Press Ink UK Group

The range of formats stored in the template files can vary in different applications, but different types of indents are usually available.

Indents in text are used to emphasise or separate text, making it easier to read.

First-line indents look similar to a hand-written style.

Hanging indents are often used in numbered documents and reports.

This text has been written with a first line indent.

This text has been written to show how a document looks with a hanging indent.

1.1  Hanging indents allow the numbering of a document to stand out.

Other formats that can be set up in templates include the following.

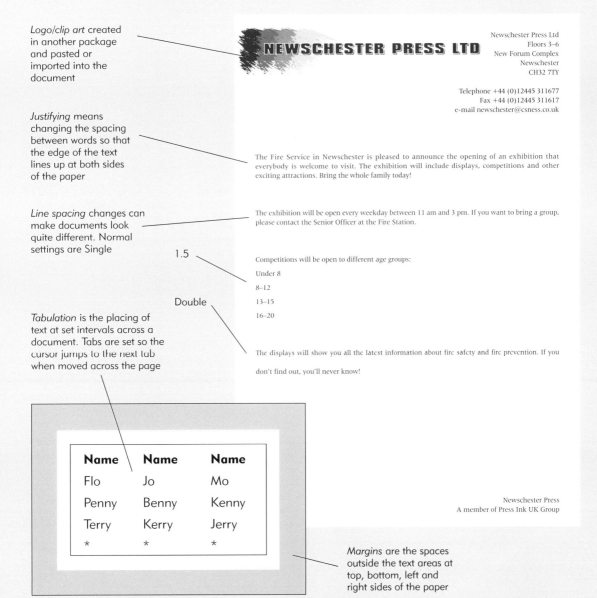

*Logo/clip art* created in another package and pasted or imported into the document

*Justifying* means changing the spacing between words so that the edge of the text lines up at both sides of the paper

*Line spacing* changes can make documents look quite different. Normal settings are Single

1.5

Double

*Tabulation* is the placing of text at set intervals across a document. Tabs are set so the cursor jumps to the next tab when moved across the page

*Margins* are the spaces outside the text areas at top, bottom, left and right sides of the paper

**NEWSCHESTER PRESS LTD**

Newschester Press Ltd
Floors 3–6
New Forum Complex
Newschester
CH32 7TY

Telephone +44 (0)12445 311677
Fax +44 (0)12445 311617
e-mail newschester@csness.co.uk

The Fire Service in Newschester is pleased to announce the opening of an exhibition that everybody is welcome to visit. The exhibition will include displays, competitions and other exciting attractions. Bring the whole family today!

The exhibition will be open every weekday between 11 am and 3 pm. If you want to bring a group, please contact the Senior Officer at the Fire Station.

Competitions will be open to different age groups:

Under 8

8–12

13–15

16–20

The displays will show you all the latest information about fire safety and fire prevention. If you don't find out, you'll never know!

Newschester Press
A member of Press Ink UK Group

| **Name** | **Name** | **Name** |
|----------|----------|----------|
| Flo | Jo | Mo |
| Penny | Benny | Kenny |
| Terry | Kerry | Jerry |
| * | * | * |

# Graphics systems

Today in the professional graphic design world, computers that are used for desktop publishing are also used for graphic design and multimedia projects.

The computers used in this kind of work have the same component parts as other systems, but the specification for the system is different. The main sections of a computer can be divided into input, processing and output components.

## Input

Data may be input in a range of ways. The most common devices used to input data or images into a computer include the keyboard, mouse, scanner, graphics tablet and digital camera.

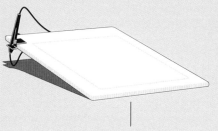

**Keyboard**
The keyboard is the most common input device for all computer systems. Data is keyed in using either full keyboards as shown in the illustration, or specialist overlay keyboards that have special functions programmed into the software

**Graphics tablet**
A graphics tablet is used along with an electronic pen or wand. Under the drawing area of the tablet is a fine grid of sensor wires which send and receive electric signals. The operation of the tablet appears to be continuous, because the system switches from 'send' to 'receive' mode approximately every 20 microseconds. In 'send' mode it supplies power to the pen, which is why the pen may be cordless.
In 'receive' mode, as pressure is applied to the nib, the distance between the electrode plates alters and so does the capacitance of the switch circuitry. The variable signal is communicated to the graphics software, and the software interprets the difference in pressure as the command for different quality marks.
Graphics tablets are used for freehand drawing, rendering and animation sequences. They are also used for manipulating images and adding special effects to images

**Mouse**
A mouse is a device used to select items from software menus, to draw images, and to complete editing procedures. A mouse may have one, two or more buttons. When a button is pressed, a signal is sent to the computer to carry out a process of some sort

**Scanners**
Flatbed scanners have a clear glass plate, under which is a light source and the recording unit on a moving arm. The recording unit is made up of an array of light-sensitive devices (CCD array). The number of these devices depends upon the type of scanner.
The scanning arm moves along under the glass plate, and the bright light allows the CCD array to pick up colours on a line-by-line basis from the image that is being scanned. The resolution of a scanner, expressed as dpi or dots per inch, is the number of pixels that can be picked up by the arrays across the width of its arm. This is why the resolution of some scanners is different horizontally as compared to vertically, eg 300 dpi X 600 dpi.

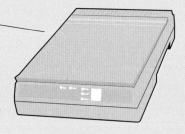

Scanners can also be hand-held or drum scanners, but the resolution obtained from these is not as good

**Digital camera**
Digital cameras are used in exactly the same way as an ordinary camera. The difference is in how the pictures are stored.
Images are stored in digital form, the same way as data is stored in a computer. The image is kept on a removable storage medium, eg a card or mini disk.
The data is then transferred into the computer either by attaching a link cable from the camera to the computer, or by downloading the image from the disk

# Processing

Each computer is set up differently, but the main components that perform the processing work of the computer are the motherboard, central processing unit (CPU), input/output ports, expansion cards, expansion slots, RAM, hard disk drive, CD-ROM drive, floppy drive, and removable hard drive.

**Motherboard**
The motherboard holds most of the electronic units. These are connected on metallic strips, known as the bus, and printed on to the motherboard

**Expansion cards**
An expansion card is equipped with a range of electronic components including chips. The card is used to add extra functions to a computer, eg a sound card allows the use of audio features

**RAM (random access memory)**
The RAM is the temporary storage medium for the data. The RAM is used when programs are running on the computer. Data stored in the RAM is lost when the system is turned off. The computer's performance is controlled by the speed of the processor and the amount of RAM it has

**ROM (read only memory)**
These are the chips built into a machine where data is stored permanently. Data can be read from the chips but cannot be written to them or altered. Programs built into a machine on ROM chips are called firmware as opposed to software, which is disk-based

**CD-ROM drive**
The CD-ROM drive allows the computer to take information from a CD

**I/O ports**
The input/output ports at the back of a computer enable data to be transferred. Keyboards, modems and printers are all I/O devices. I/O ports are also found on the back of expansion cards

**Hard disk drive**
Hard disks are used for the permanent storage of programs and data. Their storage capacity is measured in megabytes

**Expansion slots**
Expansion slots are used to hold expansion cards

**Floppy drive**
The floppy drive is used for floppy disks, which store data separately. The data is transferred from the system to the disk, which can be used as a backup of the data on the system

**Removable hard drive**
A removable hard drive is similar to an ordinary hard disk drive except that the metallic disk for storing the data is housed in a removable cartridge. This has two advantages: large amounts of data can be given directly to other users who have similar drives, and having several hard disk drives effectively increases the capacity of the system

**Central processing unit (CPU)**
The CPU acts as the brain of the computer; it is the part that does most of the actual computing.
The CPU acts upon programmed instructions, carrying out calculations and controlling the transfer of data.
To handle the amount of data involved in playing multimedia programs, the processor has to be fast and powerful. The processor can be upgraded by replacing it with a more powerful chip

# Output

Each computer system will be set up differently according to the type of output needed for the tasks carried out. The main output devices used with systems are monitors, printers, modems and speakers.

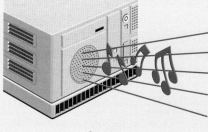

## Monitors

The type of monitor connected to a system can make all the difference for the user.

Monitors are available in two main types: an FST (flatter, squarer tube like a traditional TV shape); and a trinitron screen.

The FST screen is slightly curved in both the horizontal and vertical planes. This can make it difficult to avoid reflections on the screen.

The trinitron screen type has a mesh of wires instead of a solid grille, so that more light can pass through without reflection.

Software now allows for monitors to manage the colour display so that the colours viewed will also be the colours that are scanned or printed.

Screen dimensions are measured diagonally, and the standard sizes range from about 34 cm to 53 cm. Extra-large screens are available for displays or presentations, and these can be as big as 107 cm. The resolution of a monitor can affect how clearly images are displayed. Resolution is usually in the range of 1600 × 1200

## Speakers

Speakers will either be built into the computer or external speakers, plugged into the I/O port

## Modems

Modems are internal or external devices, used to send and receive data from external systems. Modems are used in communication technology. They are really an input, process and output device.

The name means Mo(dulator), Dem(odulator). This refers to the way that signals are received from a telephone line, and changed into a form that the computer can handle; or when sent, changed into a format from the computer into one that telephone systems can handle

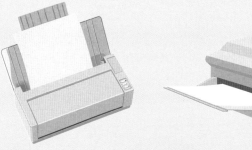

## Printers

A range of printer types are used with systems. The most common printers used are inkjet and laser. Some dot matrix printers are used for long print runs, such as for address labels and cheques.

*Inkjet printers* are cheap to buy and are capable of printing high-resolution images. The drawback is that they are slow, and images have to be printed on to special paper.

*Laser printers* are cheap for standard mono prints, but are expensive to buy for colour work. For general work the most important thing to consider is what type of documents are to be printed. Inkjet printing is never as sharp as laser printing. Because the ink is liquid when it reaches the paper, it tends to soak in, making the dots blur a little. However, on specialist paper this effect is practically removed.

It is also important to think about how fast you need the documents to be printed. Some printers can take minutes to print a single page. If the printer is being used by a single user, then a print rate of about 4ppm (pages per minute) is adequate.

The resolution of the print is important. Most standard printers now fall into the range of 300 dpi–720 dpi. Higher-resolution printers are often used for camera-ready images for professional printers.

With colour printing, the finished quality is important. Inkjet printers are far cheaper both to purchase and to run without losing too much quality. If colour work is large in size, it is quickest to use a modern bubble jet system

# System specification

When producing a specification for a
system, the following points have to be
carefully considered.

---

**People**

> Who will use the new system?

> The effects the new system will have on the way people work

> Who needs to be consulted as the design and implementation stages of
> the new system progress?

---

**Equipment**

> The hardware requirements for the new system

> The setup and configuration of the hardware

> The software requirements for the new system

---

**Data**

> The type of data items needed

> The methods of data capture that will be used

---

**Documentation**

> The type of documentation needed

> Who needs it and why?

# System support

The main types of support that should accompany a system are the following.

## System documentation

Any project manager needs an accurate record of the complete system covering all stages in the analysis, design, implementation and testing.

It should also provide details about file structures for input and output. Finally, it should include lists of the files generated by the system and describe the processes used in carrying them out.

## User documentation

All the people who are going to be direct users of the system need detailed instructions as to how to operate it.

Manuals should fully describe the use of the system, from how it is set up right through to achieving final output.

## Technical documentation

Programmers, software engineers, and all people who have to deal with problems in a system once it is up and running, need technical documentation.

This should provide details about all the hardware and software used in the system.

The program listings and 'dry run' tests performed when the system was tested should be included, to show what the system should do.

Lists of any directories, data files and their structures will be needed to help solve any problems with the system, and these should include any data links.

## Help

New users often need a lot of support. Documentation should describe how they can access any on-line help facilities. It is also important to provide details about the nature of the technical support that is available.

---

# Images

## Activities and tasks

A design studio carries out tasks such as the production of hard copy for advertisements, leaflets and other documents. Images are created so that they can be used in documents or further developed by

customers. Slide shows and presentations with timed and phased changes between screen images are also prepared.

Most systems used for multimedia work will have the facility to run video clips.

## Colour work

A graphic system will manage colour imaging (perhaps using ColourSync) and allow documents to be created in the simple RGB (red, green, blue) mode or in the more professional CMYK (cyan, magenta, yellow and black) mode. This produces files that can be printed out in different ways. They use the Pantone colour system as a reference so that clients can choose the colours to be used in documents.

## Processor speed

The processor used has to be fast to manage the manipulation of screen images and the processing of data. As the speed and nature of processors change continually, it is important to 'future proof' a system by buying one at the top of the range.

## RAM

A system used for images would need a high level of RAM to deal with the complicated and memory-hungry processing of graphic images.

## CD-ROM

The CD-ROM capability should also be high speed, to cope with the transfer of data and images as the software demands.

## Scanning image production

A flatbed scanner capable of capturing images in sizes up to A3, in millions of colours, would be needed. To enable someone to draw freehand into the system, a graphics tablet and pen should be included. A normal keyboard and mouse will also be needed for the production of text and for system operation.

Scanning into the computer

A digital camera could also be used to capture images of buildings, objects, scenes or people that need to be included in documents.

## Transfer of files/communications

If an internal fax modem is included, the designer can send the files direct to a print studio at a different location.

## Printing/dpi

A laser printer should be used for mono camera-ready images, although colour images for single users could be produced on a colour bubble jet printer. The laser printer should support at least 600 dpi and the colour printer at least be a 300 × 600 dpi machine.

## Clip art

To help create images a bank of clip art items could be used. A designer can then import and position prepared images, instead of having to create them. The images can be in simple line form, be coloured or fully photographic images. They can either be used under licence or purchased outright to be used whenever wanted.

## Backup and security routines

Finally, to secure the work, an external hard drive could be used to back up any files and also to prepare files for printing.

# Chapter 1 2 3 4 5 6
## Databases

## Case Study  1 2 3 4 5 6
### The Small Theatre Company

The **Small Theatre Company** is pleased with the response to the leaflets sent out about the promotional event. There will be many new contacts for future use. At the moment the staff use a paper-based system to store all the data about their customers, suppliers, administration and production personnel, and the actors and actresses.

The Small Theatre Company has a stand-alone computer that is used for word processing and some desktop publishing. The **IS..IT Ltd** consultant, Frederick Muzungu, advises the company that they could use a database to keep a record of all of the different groups of people they contact. The consultant feels that they should start off with a small database that holds data about some of the staff belonging to the company. He thinks that this would show how a database could help in day-to-day work.

The paper-based system holds data about the following groups of people:

- the Small Theatre Administration department staff
- suppliers
- cast members
- production teams
- sponsors.

Frederick knows that a lot of work is involved in setting up a database and wants to make sure that any database created would really help the staff.

## Action Point  1 2 3 4 5 6 7 8 9

### Learning objective
> Identify and report on various types of database systems

Read through **DATABASE SYSTEMS** in the **INFORMATION BANK** (page 72) to find out why a computerised database system would be an improvement on the existing system.

> Make notes about why the database would improve day-to-day work for the Small Theatre Company staff.

Frederick thinks that the best type of database for the company will be a relational database.

*i.* Read through **FLAT FILE/RELATIONAL/DISTRIBUTED DATABASES** in the **INFORMATION BANK** on pages 73–74 to find out why Frederick might think a relational database is the best type for the company.

➤ Make notes about the types of database systems, and state whether you would support Frederick in his choice of database for the Small Theatre Company.

The Administration staff from the Small Theatre Company do not know how to prepare the data for entry into a computer database.

The TempIT Agency has been asked to provide someone who could help the staff to prepare the data for the database. Shirin Amir has worked with a lot of different companies on their database systems and is recommended for the job.

Shirin needs to spend some time finding out about the types of data that the staff need and use. She has her own checklist of what she needs to know about the data to be stored in the database.

Here is her checklist.

1 In what format is the data stored at the moment?

2 How is the data collected?

3 Has any form of coding been used on the data?

4 What checks are carried out to make sure that the data is accurate?

5 Are there legal implications under the Data Protection Act?

## Action Point   1 **2** 3 4 5 6 7 8 9

### Learning objective

➤ Identify the data types and requirements

*i.* Read through **DATA REQUIREMENTS** in the **INFORMATION BANK** on pages 74–76 to find out why Shirin might need this type of information.

➤ Make notes about the data types that could be used in the system.

Here are Shirin's notes about the paper-based system that is used at the moment. She made the notes based upon her own checklist items.

In what format is the data stored at the moment?

All paper-based, stored in filing cabinets in alphabetical order. No separate files or sections for different groups of people.

How is the data collected?

Data is on a lot of different types of sheets, some are hand-written, there are memos, invoice and delivery notes as well as formal letters from sponsors.

Has any form of coding been used on the data?

No formal coding has been used by the staff. Different staff have used some different forms, eg 'Mr', 'Mrs', 'Miss', 'Ms' would be used as a title and would also be used to note the gender of the person.

What checks are carried out to make sure that the data is accurate?

Visual checks are carried out on the data. When contacting someone, the letters or replies are checked for spelling and punctuation.

Are there legal implications under the Data Protection Act?

On some of the data yes. Not much security in place to protect the data.

To help the staff at the Small Theatre Company, Shirin knows that she needs to create a data capture form. To make sure that she is clear about all of the data that is needed, she carries out an analysis of the system used at the moment.

## Action Point    1  2  **3**  4  5  6  7  8  9

### Learning objective

➤ Carry out a simple analysis of an existing system in a logical way

ℹ️ Look through **ANALYSIS** in the **INFORMATION BANK** on page 77 to identify the issues that Shirin will need to think about in her analysis of the paper-based system.

➤ Produce a chart like the one below for the issues you have identified in the analysis. Add as many boxes as you need to carry out your analysis.

| | | |
|---|---|---|
| **Issue No. 1**<br><br>Look where paper-based system is used ... | **Issue No. 2**<br><br>Make note about ... | **Issue No. 3**<br><br>Find out what data ... |
| **Issue No. 4**<br><br>Make notes about where the data ... | **Issue No. 5** | **Issue No. 6** |

### Learning objective

➤ Discuss the implications of the storage of personal information on computer systems

➤ Make a list of the items of information that you know your school keeps about you. Work out and write down:

- where and how the information is stored

- who has access to the information

- who should and who should not be allowed to see the data

- what the information can be used for.

## Action Plus

### Learning objective

➤ Identify the main issues relating to personal data and the Data Protection Act

ℹ Read through **DATA PROTECTION ACT** in the **INFORMATION BANK** on page 77.

➤ Make notes about how the Act might affect the school and yourself, regarding the personal information you have identified as being stored in school.

Having carried out an analysis of the paper-based system, Shirin has begun to work out how a data capture system could be used by the staff of the Small Theatre Company. The system must be simple to use, because the staff are not used to computerised systems.

She knows that the following methods will be the best ones to use.

| | |
|---|---|
| **Data entry** | Via the keyboard, with data entry staff typing the data items into a prepared database |
| **Data types** | Where possible, single key entry, with coding used on the data capture form to cut down the amount of data to be entered |
| **Checks** | Carried out by the software and by visual checks made by data entry staff |
| **Data capture forms** | Filed and stored for a maximum of six months. |

## Action Point      1  2  3  4  5  6  7  8  9

### Learning objective

➤ Reflect critically over the methods of data capture used within a specified system

Read through **DATA CAPTURE** in the **INFORMATION BANK** on pages 78–79 to identify why Shirin might have chosen the methods listed above.

➤ State whether you agree with her choice, or give reasons why she should choose different methods.

## Action Plus

Shirin has to talk through her ideas with the consultant from IS..IT Ltd and the Office Manager from the Small Theatre Company. She needs a discussion document that pulls together all the ideas for the data capture system.

➤ In the role of Shirin, present a discussion document to two members of your group in the roles of the IS..IT Ltd consultant and the Office Manager.

➤ Your presentation should convince them that you have chosen the right methods. Evaluate your results.

Having looked closely at the data that is kept on different groups of people, Shirin finds that one data collection form covering all the groups would be too difficult to fill in. She decides to produce different forms for different groups of people.

The first data collection form she works on is for the cast members. Below is a copy of her first ideas about the form.

| | |
|---|---|
| **Production** | Coded entry/alphanumeric × 8 |
| **Character played** | Text × 40 |
| **Acts appear** | Numeric × 5 |
| **Scenes appear** | Numeric × 10 |
| **Cast member surname** | Text × 20 |
| **first name(s)** | Text × 20 |
| **title** | Coded entry/text × 4 |
| **Gender** | Coded entry/text × 1 |
| **Address** | Will need 5 lines alphanumeric × 40 per line |
| **Telephone** | Numeric × 15 |
| **Agent's surname** | Text × 20 |
| **first name(s)** | Text × 20 |
| **title** | Coded entry/text × 4 |
| **Gender** | Coded entry/text × 1 |
| **Address** | Will need 5 lines alphanumeric × 40 per line |
| **Telephone** | Numeric × 15 |

## Action Point   1   2   3   4   5   6   7   8   9

### Learning objective

➤ Produce a data collection form

You are to create a data collection form using Shirin's data items as fields and her ideas of field lengths.

➤ Look back through your notes on data requirements, data analysis and data capture to help you with the data collection form.

➤ Collect a sample of data collection forms, eg application forms, reply slips, order forms and questionnaires, to compare different types of layout.

ℹ Read through **DATA COLLECTION** in the **INFORMATION BANK** on page 80 to help you with your ideas for layouts.

## Action Plus

### Learning objective

➤ Produce data tables for a relational database

Shirin has decided that the following information would be needed for the other groups of people. She knows it is necessary to include some of the data from the cast member data capture form.

| | |
|---|---|
| **Suppliers:** | Company name/contact name<br>Goods supplied |
| **Admin. staff:** | Job/role/title<br>Full/part time<br>Employee no<br>Section |
| **Production staff:** | Job/role/title<br>Full/part time<br>Employee no<br>Specialism, eg lighting, sound, scenery, etc |
| **Sponsors:** | Company name/contact name<br>Type of sponsor, eg money, goods, loan of equipment, etc<br>Offered in return, eg advertisement, free seats. |

➤ Create data tables that could be used within a relational database to hold data about all of the groups, including the cast members.

ℹ Read through **DATA TABLES** in the **INFORMATION BANK** on page 81 for more help with tables.

To try out her data capture form, Shirin uses data about the main cast members of the recent production of *Cinderella*.

The data she used can be found on the next page.

Databases

| Cast member | Character | Acts | Scenes | Agent |
|---|---|---|---|---|
| Miss Susan Rhodes<br>Old Hall Mews<br>Bishops Strand<br>Newschester<br>Newscheshire<br>012445 3678890 | Fairy Godmother | 1<br>2 | 1,4,5,7,8<br>2,6,7 | Mr Peter Franks<br>New Block<br>Feldshow<br>Newschester<br>Newscheshire<br>012445 6788903 |
| Mrs Dollie Henry<br>25 Smith Street<br>Upton<br>Milnbury<br>Newscheshire<br>012445 3554421 | Cinderella | 1<br>2 | 2,4,7,8<br>1,2,3,5,7 | Mr Peter Franks<br>New Block<br>Feldshow<br>Newschester<br>Newscheshire<br>012445 6788903 |
| Mr Abdul Nazir<br>Old Hall Mews<br>Bishops Strand<br>Newschester<br>Newscheshire<br>012445 3678890 | Baron Hardup | 1<br>2 | 2,4,6,8<br>1,4,5,7 | Mr Cyril Mathews<br>Smart Suite 2<br>Office Rd<br>Newschester<br>Newscheshire<br>012445 2225810 |
| Mr Brian Thomas<br>7 James Road<br>Dovedale<br>Hoyton<br>Newscheshire<br>012445 2546344 | Ugly Sister 1 | 1<br>2 | 4,6,8<br>1,4,5,7 | Mr Peter Franks<br>New Block<br>Feldshow<br>Newschester<br>Newscheshire<br>012445 6788903 |
| Mr Hugh Peters<br>28 Garlic Hill Close<br>Ferndale<br>Hoyton<br>Newscheshire<br>012445 6573988 | Ugly Sister 2 | 1<br>2 | 4,6,8<br>1,4,5,7 | Mr Peter Franks<br>New Block<br>Feldshow<br>Newschester<br>Newscheshire<br>012445 6788903 |
| Mr Dave O'Sullivan<br>17 Nova Brow<br>Bishops Strand<br>Newschester<br>Newscheshire<br>012445 3678472 | Buttons | 1<br>2 | 2,4,5,6,8<br>1,4,5,7 | Mr Peter Franks<br>New Block<br>Feldshow<br>Newschester<br>Newscheshire<br>012445 6788903 |
| Miss Jessica Tsang<br>Flat 2, Grove House<br>Ferndale<br>Hoyton<br>Newscheshire<br>012445 6534441 | Dandini | 1<br>2 | 3,5,6<br>1,2,3,5,6,7 | Mr Cyril Mathews<br>Smart Suite 2<br>Office Rd<br>Newschester<br>Newscheshire<br>012445 2225810 |
| Miss Catherine Peers<br>11 Airlie Close<br>Dovedale<br>Hoyton<br>Newscheshire<br>012445 2341189 | Prince Charming | 1<br>2 | 3,5,6<br>1,2,3,5,6,7 | Mr Cyril Mathews<br>Smart Suite 2<br>Office Rd<br>Newschester<br>Newscheshire<br>012445 2225810 |

## Action Point · 1 2 3 4 5 6 **7** 8 9

### Learning objective

➤ Record data on a data capture form ready for input into a database

➤ Use your data collection form to record the cast members' data.

➤ Change the layout of your form if needed. If you do make any changes to the form, state why you have changed it.

Shirin's form is working well and the staff are quite happy to transfer the data from the paper-based system on to the new data capture forms.

When all of the information has been collected, Shirin prepares the computer database application so that the data can be entered. She will have to think about how she will check the accuracy of the data as it is entered.

## Action Point · 1 2 3 4 5 6 7 **8** 9

### Learning objectives

➤ Create a database to hold a number of records

➤ Identify validation and verification procedures

ℹ Read through **DATA ENTRY** in the **INFORMATION BANK** on page 82.

ℹ Read through **VALIDATION** and **VERIFICATION** in the **INFORMATION BANK** on page 82.

➤ Use a database application to create the database of the cast members.

➤ Set in place your own validation checks.

➤ Enter the data directly from your data capture forms.

## Action Plus

### Learning objective

➤ Refine and improve the database system in the light of evaluation

➤ Carry out 'dry run' tests on your system.

➤ Produce some test data for someone else to enter into your database system. Make sure that you include some invalid data items that the system should reject.

➤ Produce an evaluation form like the one shown below. Ask the user to fill in the form to show you how well they think your system performed. Add lines to the table for any other parts of the system that you would like to be evaluated.

| Database | Comment | Good ✓ | Poor ✓ |
|---|---|---|---|
| Screen layout | | | |
| Ease of entering data | | | |
| Error messages | | | |

➤ Make any alterations to your database systems that are necessary in the light of the comments made.

➤ Make notes about any alterations that you have made.

Now that the cast members' database is up and running, Shirin has to show the staff how the database system can help them in their work. The best way to do this would be by performing one of the tasks that can take the staff a long time to do with the paper-based system.

She carries out some searches and sorts on the database, to show the staff how easy it is to use.

## Action Point          1  2  3  4  5  6  7  8  9

### Learning objective
➤ Produce a series of database reports showing the results of searches and sorts

ℹ Read through **DATABASE REPORTS** in the **INFORMATION BANK** on page 83.

➤ Produce a report showing the results of a search carried out on your database for all of the cast members that appear in Act 2, Scene 4.

➤ Produce a report that shows the result of the database being sorted so that the characters appear in alphabetical order.

## Action Plus

### Learning objective
➤ Investigate and use a method of securing data from unauthorised use

You need to make sure that the personal data on the system is protected against improper use.

ℹ Read through **DATA SECURITY** in the **INFORMATION BANK** on page 83 to find some methods that can be used to protect data against unauthorised users.

➤ Select one of these methods, or an alternative of your own, and set it in place in your system.

➤ Ask someone to try to retrieve data from the protected areas, to check that your method works.

## Database systems

- flat file
- relational
- distributed

## Data requirements

- character data
- numeric data
- keys:
  simple
  compound/
  composite
  primary
  secondary
  foreign
- coding data

## Analysis of a system

- Data Protection Act (DPA)
- data collection
- data tables
- data entry
- validation and verification
- database reports

## Data capture

- bar codes
- keyboard
- document readers:
  optical mark readers (OMR)
  optical character recognition (OCR)
  magnetic ink character recognition (MICR)

## Data security

- passwords
- encryption
- restricted access (privileges)
- firewall

## Skills Focus Point

- Open software application
- Save and name files
- Create and name folders
- Alter format/layout of documents for specific reasons
- Enter data
- Move files and folders
- Find location of files stored on a system
- Enable security procedures on a system

### Sezer's Savastores

The Sezer family are pleased with their upgraded computer system. They would like to offer the same type of systems and facilities to all the other Savastores.

As all the Savastores are in different types of location (eg corner shops, in busy main streets, or inside shopping precincts), they would like the staff in each of the stores to be able to produce posters and leaflets that are appropriate for their area.

Mr and Mrs Sezer often spend hours on the telephone talking to staff in other stores about promotional or administrative issues.

An **IS..IT Ltd** consultant, Peter Jones, is called in to talk about development ideas for the Savastore group.

Peter explains to the Sezers that there are a few ways in which they could develop their ICT systems:

- set up *stand-alone systems*, like their newly upgraded one, in each store;
- set up *local area network systems* (LANs) in each store – they could have terminals in the stores, offices and private areas that are linked together and make use of the same data;
- look into setting up a *wide area network system* (WAN) so that information can be transferred around all the stores.

## Action Point     1  2  3  4  5  6  7  8  9

### Learning objective
➤ Identify a range of network systems

ℹ️ Read through **NETWORKS** in the **INFORMATION BANK** (pages 84–86) to find out about the different stand-alone, LAN and WAN systems that are available.

  ➤ Produce a chart like the one opposite to show the advantages and disadvantages of each of the types of systems.

  ➤ In the role of Peter Jones, write a short report for the Sezers advising them of the best system to develop. Remember to state why you have chosen a particular system.

| | | Advantages | Comments |
|---|---|---|---|
| Stand-alone systems | | Advantages | |
| | | Disadvantages | |
| Local area networks | Ring | Advantages | |
| | | Disadvantages | |
| | Star | Advantages | |
| | | Disadvantages | |
| | Ethernet | Advantages | |
| | | Disadvantages | |
| Wide area networks | | Advantages | |
| | | Disadvantages | |

## Action Plus

### Learning objective

➤ Find out about OS and GUI systems

Peter Jones knows that a number of items could need changing if the Sezers go ahead and develop a network system. One important item that will need to be checked is the operating system that is in use.

*i* Read through **OPERATING SYSTEM** in the **INFORMATION BANK** on page 87 to find out what an OS does.

Peter also feels that the staff in the Savastores would find a graphical user interface (GUI) system easy to use.

Read through **GRAPHICAL USER INTERFACE** in the **INFORMATION BANK** on page 88 to see if you agree with him.

> Make a bullet-point list of all of the features you find out about for OS and GUI systems.

The Sezers like the idea of networking their stores and will budget for a full WAN network sometime in the future.

At present, each Savastore is responsible for its own stock control. Some of the stores use a simple EPOS system and their re-ordering is done directly from the supplier.

The planned expansion of the Savastore group will mean that tighter control is needed over stock and administration. It is hoped that a centralised store and distribution system will save money as less stock will need to be kept and larger discounts can be obtained through larger bulk purchases from suppliers. Delivery could be from the depot on a daily basis.

The stores that use EPOS systems all have PCs in their offices, on which the stock control program is linked to the EPOS terminals at the tills. The program records the sales made that day and gives a financial breakdown that is used by the staff at the main Savastore office to prepare the group accounts. Data is printed out in the Savastores and is taken to the main office at the end of each week.

Sales are recorded by the store system, and as the level of stock becomes lower new stock is ordered manually from the main supplier.

Customers at each shop can pay by cheque or cash, but the Sezers wish to extend this service to include debit card and credit card payments, just like larger chains. It is hoped that this will attract more customers, as many prefer this type of payment.

## Learning objectives

➤ Identify and report upon EPOS and EFTPOS systems

➤ Identify advantages of EFTPOS systems for a range of users

➤ Describe what is meant by smart cards and BACS, and how they could be useful for the Sezers

Read through **ELECTRONIC POINT OF SALE AND ELECTRONIC FUNDS TRANSFER AT POINT OF SALE** in the **INFORMATION BANK** on pages 89–90.

➤ In the role of Mr or Mrs Sezer, talk through with a member of your group the advantages of introducing EPOS systems into all of the Savastores.

➤ Discuss the additional features the EFTPOS system would provide.

## Action Plus

➤ Identify the implications for the introduction of an EFTPOS system for customers, staff and management.

When Mrs Sezer was at a Small Business Group meeting, some people were talking about the Health and Safety at Work Act. She already knew about the Act as she has to make sure that all the Savastore managers follow the regulations in all of the stores.

SAVASTORE

# FIRE PROCEDURES
## INSTRUCTIONS TO ALL STAFF

Your assembly point is **DUKE STREET CAR PARK**

What you <u>must</u> do in the case of a fire or other emergency

**When the fire alarm sounds**

● Leave the building immediately by the nearest exit and report to the person in charge of the assembly point at the place indicated above. A roll call will then be taken.

● The senior person or authorised deputy on each floor of the building will take charge of any evacuation and ensure that no one is left in the area.

**Remember**

● use the **nearest** available exit

● do **not** use the lift

● do **not** stop to collect personal belongings

● do **not** re-enter the buildings for any reason until the safety officer or his or her representative gives you permission.

A special meeting of the Small Business Group was set up to look at any aspects of the Act that apply particularly to computers and computer operators.

## Action Point   1  2  **3**  4  5  6  7  8  9

### Learning objective

➤ Identify the main issues related to the use of computers within the Health and Safety at Work Act

Read through **HEALTH AND SAFETY** in the **INFORMATION BANK** on page 91.

➤ Produce a leaflet or poster for Savastore staff that highlights the main issues they should know about.

## Knowledge Points

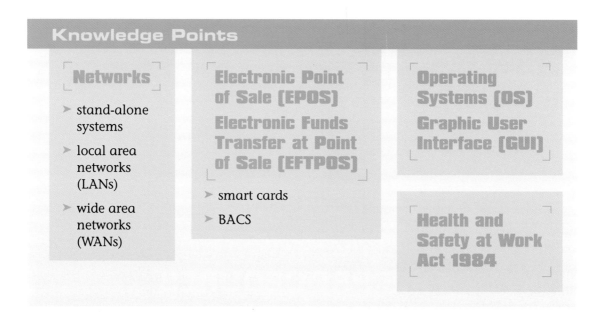

### Networks

➤ stand-alone systems

➤ local area networks (LANs)

➤ wide area networks (WANs)

### Electronic Point of Sale (EPOS)

### Electronic Funds Transfer at Point of Sale (EFTPOS)

➤ smart cards

➤ BACS

### Operating Systems (OS)

### Graphic User Interface (GUI)

### Health and Safety at Work Act 1984

## Skills Focus Point

➤ Obtain suitable hard copy by altering print quality and orientation

➤ Create and make use of sub-directories

➤ Demonstrate the ability to set the system settings for a specified user

## Bayrich Motor Company

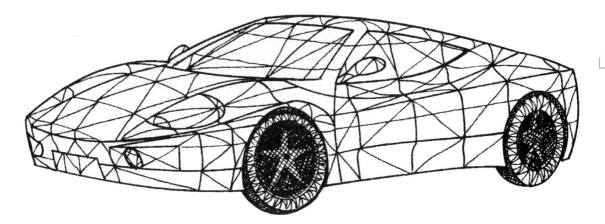

The **Bayrich Motor Company** is developing a new model of car. The first stages of the development have been finished by the design team. The team have presented their ideas to the development group.

The development group are interested in the design, but find it very different from the models that Bayrich usually makes. Before they will allow the development to go any further, they want to carry out some consumer research to find out what the average car buyer will think of the new model.

Bayrich Motors often makes use of **PR Inc Co**. to carry out market research. Two PR Inc Co. consultants are asked to attend a development group meeting to work out some ideas for the research.

Although the consultants, Anand and Suzy, are quite used to holding briefing meetings before carrying out research, they want to make sure that they are well prepared for this development group meeting.

## Action Point  1  2  3  4  5  6  7  8  9

### Learning objective
➤ Identify the main issues in market research

*i* Read through **MARKET RESEARCH** in the **INFORMATION BANK** on page 92 to gain ideas about how market research could be conducted.

Anand and Suzy intend to use a database system to record their findings. They will also use the system to analyse car buyers' response to the new design.

They hold a planning meeting to make sure that they are thinking the same way about the research. Here are the notes that Anand made at their planning meeting.

**Suzy**

Car buyers are very clear about what they want in a car. They make clear decisions based on hard facts. At the same time, they say things like 'I don't like that curved bit on the bonnet', or 'That yellow is horrible'.

**Anand**

Before a car goes into production, the development team need to invite members of the public to come to the factory and look at different car designs, including the new one, and to answer different questions. A sample of about 20 people of different ages, who do different types of work, would be good.

**Suzy**

We need to ask them what they think is important in a car. We could ask 'Is comfort more important than fuel economy?' or 'Would you buy a car that did not have airbags for safety?' We could also show them pictures of cars provided by the development group, and ask them what they like or dislike.

**Anand**

Before they arrive, we can produce a questionnaire on a word processor. We could use the Pentium 4 machine in the PR Inc Co. main office. It has 128MB RAM and 20GB hard disk drive.

**Suzy**

We need a word processing package, like Microsoft® Word, and a database, like Microsoft® Access.

**Anand**

It is important to make sure that the questionnaire we give the public is designed well. It must enable the interviewee to give very specific answers. A question like 'What do you like about this car?' is a poor question, because it will get a vague answer. It is better to ask, 'Do you like the shape?' If they say no, you ask them what specifically they don't like.

**Suzy**

Yes, only if we have detailed answers can we use the database to process the data. We can use the database to search for things like what is considered the best feature of the car, or we can see how many people liked the design of the bumpers.

**Anand**

It is really important that the questions on the questionnaire match the fields that we create in the database. It is pointless asking a question and not being able to put the response into the database. When we have all the data in the database, we can export it into a spreadsheet to produce graphs of the results.

Case study 3

### Learning objective

➤ Identify how ICT can be used in market research

➤ Read through the planning meeting notes carefully. Identify how ICT systems could be used to record the consumer research.

➤ Write a report for the Bayrich development group stating how you, in the role of a PR Inc Co. consultant, will carry out the consumer research.

➤ Discuss your report with members of your class taking the role of the PR Inc Co. consultant and members of the Bayrich development group.

Suzy is to carry out the research. Her first task is to produce a questionnaire that will be given to car buyers when they visit Bayrich Motors.

The development group have selected the car buyers for the research, and issue her with the list opposite.

Before issuing her questionnaires to the car buyers, Suzy creates a database to store the data.

**Data sheet**

| Name | Gender | Occupation |
|---|---|---|
| Belmont | M | Dentist |
| Browning | F | Bank worker |
| Deal | M | Solicitor |
| Edwards | M | Planner |
| Farooq | M | Engineer |
| Foster | F | Music teacher |
| Gallino | M | Buyer |
| Hamilton | M | Shop worker |
| Jones | F | Designer |
| Lane | M | Steel worker |
| Miliwood | M | Sales person |
| Neale | F | Care assistant |
| Rafeeq | M | Chemist |
| Sanderson | M | Hotelier |
| Taylor | F | Solicitor |
| Tyler | M | Teacher |
| Underwood | M | Lorry driver |
| White | F | Teacher |
| Yeates | F | Engineer |
| Zaffar | M | Finance officer |

## Action Point    1   2   **3**

### Learning objectives

➤ Construct a questionnaire using appropriate types of closed and open questions

➤ Create a database to hold specified data

➤ Produce a sample questionnaire that is also to be a data collection form for a database.

➤ Check the questionnaire for accuracy. Your questionnaire should examine car buyers' needs and wants. Consider carefully the questions you need to ask.

➤ Give out your questionnaire to 20 people who are likely to buy a car. It is not advisable to issue them to other class members, as they are not yet car buyers! If you cannot give the questionnaire to enough people, you could use the list of names that was issued to Suzy and fill in various answers yourself.

➤ Produce a database that can be used to store the data from the questionnaires. The database should hold all the personal details about the car buyers (as on the data sheet issued to Suzy) as well as their responses to the questions.

## Action Plus

➤ Construct a personalised questionnaire by using a mail merge facility. Refer back to the **INFORMATION BANK** material on setting up a mail merge if you are not sure (see page 27).

When the questionnaires have all been completed, Suzy has to draw the information together and enter it into her database. She will have to analyse the data and report directly to the development group and design team at Bayrich Motors.

Suzy thinks that the best way to give the information to the groups will be through a presentation.

## Action Point  1  2  3  4  5  6  7  8  9

### Learning objectives

➤ Enter data into a database and analyse the results

➤ Deliver a presentation to a selected audience

➤ Collect your completed questionnaires and enter the data into your database.

➤ Focus upon a few of the questions in your questionnaire. Conduct a series of searches and sorts on the responses to those questions, and identify any trends in car buyers' responses.

➤ Prepare and deliver a presentation to a selected audience (which will represent the Bayrich Motors development and design teams).

## Action Plus

### Learning objective

➤ Export or embed data directly from a database into a graphing application

➤ Export the relevant data from the database into a spreadsheet or charting program to produce a graphical representation of the data. If you haven't yet learnt about charts or spreadsheets, make a note to return to this task when you have the knowledge.

The development group at Bayrich are pleased with the results of the consumer research. They would like to know more about how PR Inc Co. produced the results.

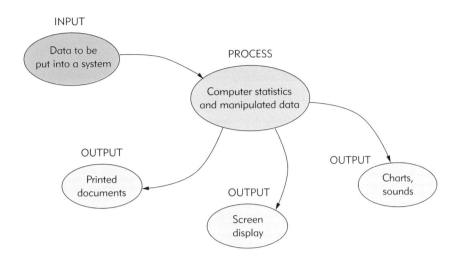

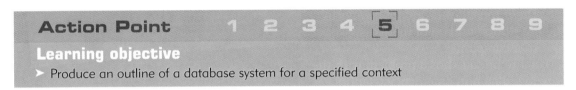

## Learning objective
➤ Produce an outline of a database system for a specified context

*i* Using the database you have created, produce an outline of the system. State where and how the data was obtained, how it was processed (this will include details of the data types) and the range of outputs available.

## Knowledge Points

### Market research

➤ interview technique

➤ questionnaires:
closed questions
open questions

## Skills Focus Point

➤ Set up template files for pre-printed items

➤ Use linking facility to link objects/files

➤ Incorporate two or more different formats of data into a single document

➤ Transfer files to external devices, eg writable CD, zip cartridges, for use on other systems

## Case Study    1   2   3   **4**   5   6

## Newschester Fire Service

Within the **Newschester Fire Brigade** headquarters there are several different sections. There is a general administration section, the emergency room (where all incoming emergency calls are dealt with), a public relations section, and an inspection section. Some of the staff in these sections are consultants and are employed as temporary staff by the fire service only when they are needed for a job. These consultants are not always in the fire station and all of them also work for other companies.

The fire brigade has a problem with the way in which non-emergency telephone calls are dealt with at the fire station. The secretarial staff are finding it very difficult to pass on appropriate messages from clients and the public to the consultants in the fire station.

Secretarial staff often do not know if the call is personal or involves the fire service. Therefore it has been decided to create a suitable method for the capture and recording of data, so that when a call comes in the secretarial staff have ready access to information. Sam, one of the temporary consultants in the public relations section, also works for **PR Inc Co**. He has been asked to develop the system for the secretarial staff.

Sam needs to find out what type of data is required by the secretarial staff. At present ten consultants work in the different sections of the fire station. As far as the secretaries know, each consultant has approximately ten clients with whom he or she regularly works. Members of the public call frequently, and do not have a particular contact at the fire station but need to be put in touch with a consultant.

The secretarial staff say that the minimum information they need is:

- Name of caller
- Name of fire station consultant
- Name of the company calling
- Address of the company calling
- Telephone no/fax no
- Contact within the company
- Type of business
- Private or fire station business.

## Action Point    **1**   2   3   4   5   6   7   8   9

### Learning objectives

➤ Review the analysis of a system

➤ Review the production of a data collection form

➤ Review data entry

➤ Look at the information the secretarial staff asked for. Add any other fields you think are of use to the fire brigade or individual consultants.

*i* Look back through the **INFORMATION BANK** sections on **DATA REQUIREMENTS** and **ANALYSIS** on pages 74–77 if you need help.

➤ Produce a suitable data collection form and issue it to five of the fire station staff. Ask them to fill in the data (you may wish to work as a group to do this). The form should enable them to record all the data about all their clients.

*i* Look back through the **INFORMATION BANK** section on **DATA COLLECTION** on page 80 if you need help.

## Action Plus

➤ Design a suitable data capture form for use on a computer system. The form should be available to be opened up whenever a telephone call is made.

*i* Look back through the **INFORMATION BANK** section on **DATA CAPTURE** on pages 78–80 if you need help.

Before a lot of data is collected, Sam needs to create the database to store the data. He has to make sure that it is easy to enter data and that the system is user-friendly. As the secretarial staff are always very busy, he will set in place a range of validation checks on the data.

## Action Point    1 **2** 3 4 5 6 7 8 9

### Learning objective
➤ Review the creation of a database

➤ Create the database, making sure you consider issues such as ease of entry and validation checks when you design the structure of the database.

➤ Collect the completed data collection forms and enter the data into your database.

Some of the staff are not happy with the idea of personal information about them being kept on a computer system. They want to know how unauthorised people will be prevented from taking the data and using it.

Sam has already decided that the information would need to be protected under the terms of the DPA. He has decided to issue each of the secretarial staff with an ID number and also to password-protect the database. He feels confident that with these security procedures in place, he can convince the staff that their data is safe.

## Action Point    1 2 **3** 4 5 6 7 8 9

### Learning objectives
➤ Review data security procedures
➤ Review DPA

➤ Create data security procedures on your database to prevent unauthorised people from gaining access to the data.

To make sure that the data entered into the database is accurate, Sam advises the Fire Station Manager that all clients should be contacted to verify their data. He suggests that a standard letter should be produced and sent to new clients as their data is entered. For this purpose he shows the secretarial staff how to carry out a mail merge.

## Action Point  1  2  3  **4**  5  6  7  8  9

### Learning objectives

➤ Review the production of a standard letter

➤ Review the use of the mail merge facility on a computer system

➤ Devise a standard letter that could be sent to clients of one member of the fire station staff, asking them to check data for accuracy.

➤ Run a mail merge using this data.

The Fire Station Manager is glad to see that the secretarial staff are now using the new system and that it is keeping track of telephone calls in a much more efficient way. To find out exactly how well the staff are managing the system, and if it needs any improvement, he issues an evaluation questionnaire.

## Action Point  1  2  3  4  **5**  6  7  8  9

### Learning objective

➤ Review the production of questionnaires using appropriate methods of questioning

➤ Write a list of questions that would need to be included in the questionnaire.

*i* If you need help, look back through the **INFORMATION BANK** section on **MARKET RESEARCH** on page 92.

➤ Produce a questionnaire that could be used to gain information about the new system.

➤ Ask several different people to use your database, by giving them all the same test data to enter, and then ask them to complete a questionnaire about your system.

## Action Plus

### Learning objective

➤ Identify appropriate error trapping and evaluation procedures

Sam would like to use the new system to carry out an evaluation while the staff are actually using it. He decides to set up a tracking system that counts the number of times the secretarial staff hit the 'help' button, and the number of times data is rejected.

➤ Create a routine within your database that is capable of keeping track of errors.

The Management Committee of the Newschester Fire Brigade wants to know:

- the breakdown of the number of fire station clients and private clients each member of the staff has
- what type of business these clients are in
- the proportion of private to fire station business that each member of staff is engaged in.

## Action Point    1  2  3  4  5  6  7  8  9

### Learning objectives

➤ Review methods of searching and sorting data on a database system

➤ Review the production of database reports

➤ Search the database and provide the committee with the information required.

➤ Take print-outs of any searches made, or graphics produced, and make notes on these to show how each search was carried out and how it helped to find the data needed.

The telephone recording system is at present working on the stand-alone computers that the secretarial staff have in their section. The data they record would be very useful in some other sections. In order to share this data, the computers would have to be networked.

The Management Committee is willing to provide the money needed for installing a suitable network.

## Action Point    1  2  3  4  5  6  7  8  9

### Learning objectives

➤ Review the types of networks available

➤ Review the advantages of network systems

➤ Explain which type of network would be most suitable for the fire station. Think about the safety and security issues that could be involved. It would be important to keep the emergency room completely separate, for example.

➤ Produce a report for the committee that describes the installation of a suitable network.

➤ Include details about the setup, and possible alterations or upgrades to existing machines that could be necessary.

## Action Plus

Some of the staff at the fire station are not convinced that their jobs will be safe if a network is installed. They have asked for a meeting to discuss the implications for their futures if a network is installed.

➤ Brainstorm with four of your class members to draw up a list of objections staff might raise. Then, on your own, prepare a presentation for this group of staff that supports the idea of installing a computer network. Plan answers to the points they might raise.

➤ Working with other members of your class representing the staff, hold a discussion that allows you to put forward your case as to why they should welcome the installation of a network.

The Management Committee would like to be able to send information to and maintain a close and effective contact with all the fire stations in other areas of Newscheshire.

The County Fire Service often holds special promotional events, on topics such as fire safety in the home. Leaflets, T-shirts and other items that are given away at these events are stored at the Newschester headquarters. The fire stations around the county buy these items from headquarters whenever they are planning to run an event. The Management Committee would like the area stations to be able to order directly using a network link.

## Action Point    1  2  3  4  5  6  7  8  9

### Learning objective
➤ Review the use of network systems

➤ Describe what type of network system could be installed to allow appropriate contact with all the other Newscheshire fire stations.

If you are unsure, look through the **INFORMATION BANK** section on **NETWORKS** on pages 84–86 for help.

➤ Read through the items that are available for order, and describe how a stock ordering system could be set up on the network so that the fire stations could all order items as they need them.

**Promotional items available on order**

| **Leaflets** | Fire safety in the home 1 | | | |
|---|---|---|---|---|
| | Fire safety in the home 2 | | | |
| | Fire safety in the home 3 | | | |
| | Storing chemicals safely in the home and garage | | | |
| | List of dangerous chemicals | | | |
| | Smoke alarms | | | |
| | Is your company safe? | | | |
| | Fire regulations for small and medium-size businesses | | | |
| **T-shirts** | **Sizes** | Small | Medium | Large | X-Large |
| | **Colours** | Blue | White | Black | Red |
| **Key rings** | Large | Small | | |
| **Tea towels** | **Designs** | Kitchen Care | Put it Out! | |
| **Mugs** | **Colours** | Blue | White | Red |
| **Pens** | **Colours** | Blue | Black | |
| **Pencils** | Single | Packs of 10 | Packs of 20 | |

## Action Plus

### Learning objective

➤ Review the use of EPOS and EFTPOS systems

➤ Work out a suitable coding system for the items that can be ordered.

➤ Describe how coding the data in this way could make the system more efficient.

➤ The fire stations would all like to pay as they order. Describe the type of order system that would allow this to happen.

## Review ICT

Throughout the case studies in this chapter, you have had the opportunity to explore a number of areas of knowledge. Make a copy of the following table and complete your table to show where you have used the Knowledge Points.

| Knowledge Points | Where Used |
|---|---|
| **Database systems** | |
| ➤ flat file | |
| ➤ relational | |
| ➤ distributed | |
| **Analysis of a system** | |
| ➤ Data Protection Act (DPA) | |
| ➤ data collection | |
| ➤ data tables | |
| ➤ data entry | |
| ➤ validation and verification | |
| ➤ database reports | |
| **Data requirements** | |
| ➤ character data | |
| ➤ numeric data | |
| ➤ keys:<br>simple<br>compound<br>primary<br>secondary<br>foreign | |
| ➤ coding data | |
| **Data capture** | |
| ➤ bar codes | |
| ➤ keyboards | |
| ➤ document readers:<br>optical mark readers (OMR)<br>optical character recognition (OCR)<br>magnetic ink character recognition (MICR) | |

| Knowledge Points | Where Used |
| --- | --- |

**Data security**

> passwords
> encryption
> restricted access (privileges)
> firewall

**Networks**

> stand-alone systems
> local area networks (LANs)
> wide area networks (WANs)

**Electronic Point of Sale (EPOS)**

**Electronic Funds Transfer at Point of Sale (EFTPOS)**

> smart cards
> BACS

**Operating Systems (OS)**

**Graphical User Interface (GUI)**

**Health and Safety at Work Act 1984**

**Market research**

> interview technique
> questionnaires
> closed questions
> open questions

## Learning Objectives

The following Learning Objectives have been covered in Chapter 2.

Decide whether you have sufficient knowledge about each item to be able to use or write about them in the future. Leave blank the 'tick' column for any objective that you need to know more about.

| Learning Objectives | ✓ |
|---|---|
| Identify and report on different types of database systems | |
| Identify the data types and requirements for a database system | |
| Carry out a simple analysis of an existing system in a logical way | |
| Discuss the implications for the storage of personal information on computer systems | |
| Identify the main issues relating to the Data Protection Act | |
| Reflect critically over the methods of data capture used within a specified system | |
| Produce a data collection form | |
| Produce data tables for a relational database | |
| Record data on a data capture form ready for input into a database | |
| Create a database to hold a number of records | |
| Identify validation and verification procedures | |
| Refine and improve the database system in the light of evaluation | |
| Produce a series of database reports showing the results of searches and sorts | |
| Investigate and use a method of securing data from unauthorised use | |
| Identify a range of network systems | |
| Find out about OS and GUI systems | |
| Identify and report upon EPOS and EFTPOS systems | |
| Identify advantages of EFTPOS systems for a range of users | |
| Describe what is meant by smart cards and BACS, and how they could be useful | |
| Identify the main issues related to the use of computers within the Health and Safety at Work Act | |
| Identify the main issues relating to market research | |
| Identify how ICT can be used in market research | |
| Construct a questionnaire using appropriate types of open and closed questions | |
| Create a database to hold specified data | |

## Learning Objectives ✓

Enter data into a database and analyse the results

Deliver a presentation to a selected audience

Export or embed data directly from a database into a graphing application

Produce an outline of a database system for a specified context

## Skills Objectives

You should have used the following practical skills in following the case studies in this chapter. Copy this table for your records.

Decide whether you feel confident about using the skill again or be able to write about it. Leave blank the 'tick' column for any objective that you need to practise.

Record the filenames for any working drafts, showing how you developed the database and print-outs or prints of a static or dynamic screen display of your final work, including examples of text, images and numbers. Also keep records of how you saved information.

## Skills Objectives ✓

➤ Open software application

➤ Save and name files

➤ Create and name folders

➤ Alter format/layout of documents for specific reasons

➤ Enter data

➤ Move files and folders

➤ Find location of files stored on a system

➤ Obtain suitable hard copy by altering print quality and orientation

➤ Create and make use of sub-directories

➤ Demonstrate the ability to set the system settings for a specified user

➤ Set up template files for pre-printed items

➤ Use linking facility to link objects/files

➤ Incorporate two or more different formats of data into a single document

➤ Transfer files to external devices, eg writable CD, zip cartridges, for use on other systems

Databases

## Database systems

A database is an organised collection of structured data. So that large amounts of data can be managed within a computerised database, the data is arranged into fields, records and files.

A field is an item of data kept in a record. Fields can hold different types of data, eg numeric (1,2,3) or character (a,b,c,2a,2b).

A record is a collection of related fields holding all the data about one person or object, eg a person's name, address, telephone number, date of birth, and club membership details.

A file contains all the records under one category, eg a membership file containing details on all members.

The membership file would contain a record for each member

The records would contain personal information about the members

| **File:** | Membership |
| **Record 1:** | Membership ID |
| | Title |
| | Surname |
| | First name(s) |
| | Date of birth |
| | Address |
| | Telephone no |
| | Membership type |
| | Clubs |
| **Record 2:** | Membership ID |
| | Title |
| | Surname |
| | First name(s) |
| | Date of birth |
| | Address |
| | Telephone no |
| | Membership type |
| | Clubs |

The fields would be all of the items of personal data needed by the organisation

## Advantages of computerised database systems

Databases are very useful when items of data need to be found quickly from large amounts of stored information.

Databases can be searched to produce reports on selected items. This work could be done manually, but would take a long time.

The accuracy of data can be checked automatically by features in software programs, leaving less scope for error when the data is used.

Distributed databases can be accessed through modem telephone links (see page 74). Users from all around the world can gain access to systems in other parts of the world, eg by using the Internet.

Data can be entered into a database using different methods, some of which have little or no manual input.

# Flat file/relational/ distributed databases

Databases are used to carry out many different tasks. Different types of database perform some tasks more efficiently than others.

## Flat file databases

Flat file databases are the simplest type to create and use. A flat file database deals with one data file at a time. Each record contains the same field headings. The data held can be 'interrogated' by carrying out searches and sorts and producing reports.

Because each record contains all the information about a person or object, this process can be very slow. The files can also take up a lot of valuable computer memory.

**Record 1:**

Membership ID
Name
Address
Telephone no
Membership type

**Record 2:**

Membership ID
Name
Address
Telephone no
Membership type

**Record 3:**

Membership ID
Name
Address
Telephone no
Membership type

## Relational databases

Relational databases are more difficult to set up, but much quicker to use. The different files in a relational database can be handled at the same time. Related items of data can be stored in separate files so that the data is accessed only when

needed. This cuts down on the number of separate data items stored in the computer memory. It also makes it quicker to interrogate the database for items of related information.

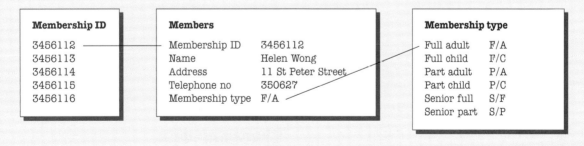

**Membership ID**

3456112
3456113
3456114
3456115
3456116

**Members**

Membership ID    3456112
Name             Helen Wong
Address          11 St Peter Street
Telephone no     350627
Membership type  F/A

**Membership type**

Full adult    F/A
Full child    F/C
Part adult    P/A
Part child    P/C
Senior full   S/F
Senior part   S/P

# Distributed databases

Large organisations such as banks and travel booking agencies make use of distributed databases. A distributed database is a large-scale relational database with an 'on-line' (active) feature for users to contact the system.

A user has direct access to the database from his or her computer terminal. The database contacted could be miles away (even in a different country). The connection is through a modem telephone link (or in some specialist systems, via a satellite link).

Access to distributed database systems is strictly controlled, with users being allowed into specific parts of the system at any time. Security of the data is very carefully monitored.

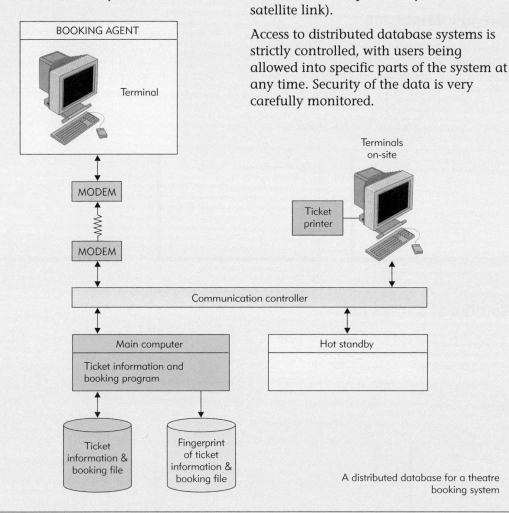

A distributed database for a theatre booking system

# Data requirements

The structure of a database has to be planned carefully. The data types have to be chosen before starting to create the database. The amount of storage space needed for each of the data items also has to be known before work can begin.

# Character data

Character data is stored in different formats:

➤ as text data (a, cat, CD),

➤ as alphanumeric data (2a, CH3 4NQ), or

➤ as any other data item that is not numeric (***@).

The character field is set at a maximum length, known as the character field length. The field length shows the maximum number of characters that can be stored in a field. For example, a field that is to hold someone's name may be set to a maximum of 30 characters.

| Membership | ID3456112 |
|---|---|
| Name | Helen Smith |
| Date of birth | 25/11/78 |
| Tel no | 350627 |

Showing a simple key field

## Numeric data

Numeric data can be stored in different formats:

➤ as whole numbers (integers) 1, –1, 1998, 42,

➤ as decimal numbers 1.001, –1.001, 42.5, or

➤ as special data types, eg as a date 25/11/98, 25 November 1998; as money 100.50, 5.50.

The number field length shows the maximum value of a number in a field. For example, if all items for sale cost under £1000 each, the maximum value that would have to be stored in the field would be £999.99.

Date fields are set up as the format chosen to show the date. The date format 25/11/98 is 8 characters long.

## Keys

Some items of data within a record or file are more important or useful than other items. These are known as 'key fields'. A key field holds a unique value that applies to only one record.

There are different types of keys and each one has a different use.

### Simple key

This a single field. It could be a reference number or a membership number, which can identify only one person. Care has to be taken in establishing a simple key field,

as some items of personal data are not unique (eg a date of birth).

### Compound/composite key

Where no single item can be guaranteed to be unique, a compound or composite key can be used. This key is made up by joining two or more fields together, so that the key is then unique.

Below is a sample of three records held in a database.

A compound or composite key could be made from Gender, Date of birth and Telephone number. From the records shown, this would give:

F251178350627    F291078344121
M251178350121

### Primary key

A primary key can be either a single or a compound/composite key, but it must have the following properties:

➤ it must uniquely identify a record

➤ it must have a value, so it cannot be 0

➤ it must be kept as short as possible to ensure uniqueness.

Examples include National Insurance numbers and product codes.

### Secondary key

A secondary key is a useful item of data within a record, which would often be used in searches, but is not always unique.

| **Name:** | Helen Smith | **Name:** | Susan Smith | **Name:** | Peter Smith |
|---|---|---|---|---|---|
| **Gender:** | (F)emale | **Gender:** | (F)emale | **Gender:** | (M)ale |
| **Date of birth:** | 25/11/78 | **Date of birth:** | 29/10/78 | **Date of birth:** | 25/11/78 |
| **Tel no:** | 350627 | **Tel no:** | 344121 | **Tel no:** | 350121 |

| Membership ID: | 3456112 | Membership ID: | 3456113 | Membership ID: | 3456114 |
|---|---|---|---|---|---|
| **Name:** | Helen Smith | **Name:** | Susan Smith | **Name:** | Peter Smith |
| **Gender:** | (F)emale | **Gender:** | (F)emale | **Gender:** | (M)ale |
| **Date of birth:** | 25/11/78 | **Date of birth:** | 29/10/78 | **Date of birth:** | 25/11/78 |
| **Tel no:** | 350627 | **Tel no:** | 344121 | **Tel no:** | 350121 |
| **Clubs attended:** | Jazz Dance | **Clubs attended:** | Jazz Dance | **Clubs attended:** | Football |
| | Swimming | | Football | | Swimming |

The field 'Clubs attended' would make a good secondary key. For example, the database could be interrogated using the secondary key 'Clubs attended' to find all the members who go to the football club.

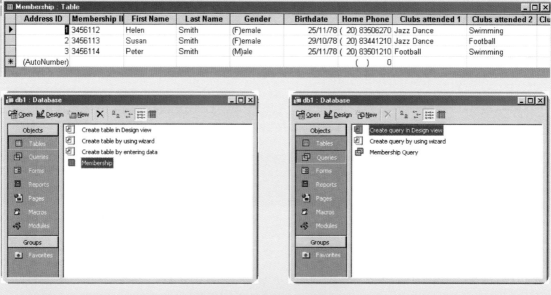

## Foreign key

A foreign key is a field in one record or file that is a primary key in another record or file, eg

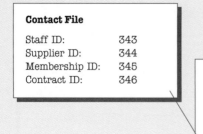

**Contact File**

| Staff ID: | 343 |
|---|---|
| Supplier ID: | 344 |
| Membership ID: | 345 |
| Contract ID: | 346 |

**Membership ID File 345**

*Membership ID 3456112*
| Name: | Helen Smith |
|---|---|
| Date of Birth: | 25/11/78 |
| Tel no: | 350627 |

## Coding data

To help ensure the accuracy of data, it is often entered using coding. We use coded data every day without thinking about it. Coding for gender is the most common, ie M=Male, F=Female, but we also code people's titles, eg Mr, Mrs, Ms, Dr, and people's addresses as postal codes, eg CH32 7NQ. Coded data takes less time to enter into a computer and takes up less storage space in the memory.

# Analysis

Carrying out an analysis of an existing system involves:

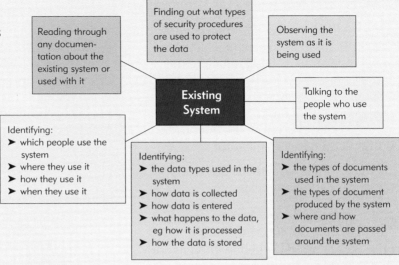

Reading through any documentation about the existing system or used with it

Finding out what types of security procedures are used to protect the data

Observing the system as it is being used

**Existing System**

Talking to the people who use the system

Identifying:
➤ which people use the system
➤ where they use it
➤ how they use it
➤ when they use it

Identifying:
➤ the data types used in the system
➤ how data is collected
➤ how data is entered
➤ what happens to the data, eg how it is processed
➤ how the data is stored

Identifying:
➤ the types of documents used in the system
➤ the types of document produced by the system
➤ where and how documents are passed around the system

# Data Protection Act (DPA) 1984

The Data Protection Act (DPA) 1984 was replaced with an updated version in 1998.

The increased use and storage of electronic data required changes to the earlier Act.

Details of the Act can be downloaded from:

http://www.legislation.hmso.gov.uk/acts/acts1998

The wording of the new Act is:

*'An Act to make new provision for the regulation of the processing of information relating to individuals, including the obtaining, holding, use or disclosure of such information.'*

The new Act has taken the protection of personal data further than the 1984. It also includes paper-based copies of data. An individual can expect to be informed of:

(i)   *the personal data of which that individual is the data subject,*
(ii)  *the purposes for which they are being or are to be processed, and*
(iii) *the recipients or classes of recipients to whom they are or may be disclosed.'*

They are protected in these ways:

➤ Any organisation holding personal data in a computer system must register with the Data Protection Registrar. In doing so it has to state what type of information it is going to store and exactly what it is going to use the data for.

➤ The data held must have been obtained legally and may be held and used only for the stated purpose.

➤ The data must be accurate and be kept up to date. No data other than the items stated may be stored, and it must be discarded when finished with.

➤ The data must be protected from any unauthorised access, and must not be passed on to any other organisation or person.

➤ In most cases, everyone can request that they see the data stored about them. They must apply in writing to the named data controller, who must then satisfy themselves that the request is coming from an individual who has the right to see the information. Appeals to look at the data (or restrict the use of the data) can be made by an individual or the data controller and where it is found that the use of incorrect data has caused personal damage, he or she has the right to compensation.

# Data capture

Many methods are used to compare the data for a database. The data collection forms or documents filled in before the data is transferred to a computer system are known as the source documents. Some source documents are pre-printed and do not have to be filled in as the data is actually printed on to the form.

The most common methods used for data capture are discussed below.

## Bar codes

A bar code is a pre-printed method of data capture.

The bar code is a set of black lines and white spaces of different thickness. These lines are used as a code that carries data about a product. The most commonly used bar code system is the EAN code (European Article Number).

The code is 13 digits long and is made up as follows:

| First 2 numbers | Country of origin |
| Next 5 numbers | Factory/company |
| Next 5 numbers | Item |
| Last number | Check digit |

A hand-held scanner reading a bar code

A bar code can be read by an infra-red beam that measures the reflected light from the bars and spaces. Different types of scanners can be used to read the codes. Some scanners are hand-held. They are placed over the bar code and moved across the code to read it. Others are vertical or flat-bed scanners. A flat-bed scanner reflects infra-red beams through mirrors so that the bar code can be read from different angles.

A flat-bed scanner reading a bar code

## Keyboard

Keyboards have long been used for entering data. Data is often collected on forms such as questionnaires, application forms, reply forms or order forms, and keyed into the computer system using a standard keyboard. The way that the information is prepared for entry is very important if accuracy is to be ensured. The screen image and the data collection form should look alike so that the data-entry clerk can key in the data without much chance of error. Where coded items are to be entered, the data collection form should show the codes.

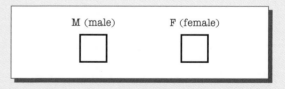

The keyboard method allows flexibility. A data collection form can quickly be altered in layout, whereas some other methods would be costly to alter.

# Document readers

Document readers are devices that can read data directly from a data collection document. The data-entry clerk does not have to enter data via a keyboard, but feeds the documents through a reader. Some common document readers are described below.

## Optical mark reader (OMR)

Data is transferred directly from a pre-printed form. The form is designed so that users mark with a pencil or pen on to set spaces on the form.

When the form is passed through the reader the marks are detected, or if there is not a mark where there could be one its absence is noted.

The software interprets the signals from the reader into a form that a computer can work with.

Examples of OMR forms in use every day include multiple-choice examination papers and market research questionnaires.

## Optical character recognition (OCR)

Characters (text) can be read by a device that detects light reflected from a page and its inked areas.

The readings are converted into signals for the software. The software has stored data about character sets (fonts). The signals are checked against the stored information to make a screen image of the document.

Organisations using OCR forms include gas and electric companies, which use them in their billing systems.

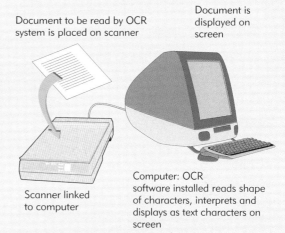

Document to be read by OCR system is placed on scanner

Document is displayed on screen

Scanner linked to computer

Computer: OCR software installed reads shape of characters, interprets and displays as text characters on screen

## Magnetic ink character recognition (MICR)

In this case, special ink containing iron oxide is used to print the source documents. When the document is passed through the reader, the ink is magnetised and the magnetised patterns can be identified as characters.

Bank cheques (see the next page) make use of magnetic ink character recognition.

| Marks | – For Examiners Use | | |
|-------|---------------------|--|--|
| O | | | |
| 5 | | | |
| A | | | |
| 20 | | | |
| 64 | | | |
| NS | | | |
| 100 | | | |
| 220 | | | |

Example of an OMR form

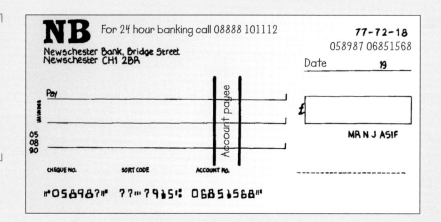

## Data collection

The methods commonly used by small companies to collect data in the correct format for entry into a database are paper-based. They may be forms giving results of a questionnaire, application forms, order forms or reply slips.

The layout of a data collection form is very important. The layout sheet below shows how the fields, their length, the data types and codes can be placed on to a form. These all have to be designed before the form can be created.

# Data tables

**Membership ID**

*345*
3456112
3456113
3456114
3456115
3456116

**Clubs**

| Jazz dance | JD |
| Swimming | S |
| Football | F |
| Hockey | H |
| Aerobics | A |
| Circuit | C |
| Diving | D |

**Members**

| *Membership ID* | 3456112 |
| Title | Ms |
| Surname | Smith |
| First name | Helen |
| Date of birth | 25/11/78 |
| Address | 11 St Peter Street |
| | Kingsham |
| | Lowton |
| Telephone no | 350627 |
| *Membership type* | F/A |
| *Clubs* | JD/S |
| | |
| *Membership ID* | 3456113 |
| Title | Miss |
| Surname | Smith |
| First name | Susan |
| Date of birth | 29/10/78 |
| Address | 23a Bloom Hill Rd |
| | Kingsham |
| | Lowton |
| Telephone no | 344121 |
| *Membership type* | P/A |
| *Clubs* | JD/F |

**Membership type**

| Full adult | F/A |
| Full child | F/C |
| Part adult | P/A |
| Part child | P/C |
| Senior full | S/F |
| Senior part | S/P |

Data tables allow data to be structured so that it takes up the minimum amount of computer memory. Tables also allow data to be changed easily. The four tables above show information about club members. It is easy to change data in any of the tables without affecting the data held in other tables.

If a new club, tennis, were to be started, it would be easy to add an extra field '**Tennis    T**' to the Clubs table.

There would be no need to go through all other tables to make this change. As members joined the new club, their records would be changed.

If Helen Smith decided to join the tennis club, her record would need to be changed. To change her record, the Membership ID table would be searched on her **Membership ID**, 3456112. This would bring up her record and the **Clubs** field would have 'T' added.

It would be quicker to search the Membership ID table to access her record than to search through all the members' records until hers is found.

Data tables must be carefully planned, taking into account how data will be used. Before decisions can be made about the number of tables needed for a database, the requirements for queries, reports and access must be worked out.

# Data entry

Another important factor in data accuracy is the screen layout for data entry. A screen form can be made to look like a paper-based data collection form, but will often have to be altered to fit it all on the screen.

Forms are designed using the **form design** feature of a software application. This allows for background and foreground colours to be set. Multiple-choice user controls can be set, allowing a user to select an option from a small list of possible items.

The default values (the ones in the computer memory, which are restored when the computer is switched off) can be set.

Validation checks (see below) can be put in place so that checks happen automatically when data items are entered.

Each entry form is a design based upon a record (or table) or a query that has been formed by linking records (or tables) together.

## Validation and verification

Two methods of checking accuracy of data are commonly used.

### Validation

Validation is a check to see that the data being used is realistic. Software applications will often contain validation checks.

Some of the most common checks are described below.

#### List check

This is a check to see that a data item comes from a given list of items that are acceptable.

#### Range check

A check can be made to see that the data item does not fall outside a given range, eg that a date entry does not exceed the 31st of the month.

#### Type check

A type check sees that a data item is in the correct format, eg in either a character or numeric format.

#### Check digit

An extra digit called a check digit can be added to a number so that the number can then be verified using a pre-set calculation. If any digit in the number has been entered wrongly, the calculation will be recognised as incorrect.

### Verification

Where data is entered by a data-entry clerk into a computer, there are plenty of chances to make mistakes. A verification check is carried out to make sure that data items have been entered into the database correctly. When the data has been entered, it is checked either by comparing the entries on screen with the original documents, or by re-entering it into the system and comparing the two versions. If the first and second entry versions are the same, then the data is most likely to be accurate.

---

**Microsoft Access**

 **The value you entered isn't valid for this field.**

For example, you may have entered text in a numeric field or a number that is larger than the FieldSize setting permits.

OK

## Database reports

Reports produced by a database may be simple lists, or based on queries that show data from several records or tables.

A report is printed as a hard copy. It may be many pages long, so a screen image would not be appropriate. A report is in either portrait or landscape format.

Reports usually have a header and footer (perhaps titles and dates); page headers and footers (perhaps page titles and page numbers); and the body of the report, which is the data taken from the database and clearly laid out.

### Names of materials

| | |
|---|---|
| **Name:** | Broadlands |
| **Code:** | D897C |
| **Width in m:** | 90 |
| **Description:** | Blue and cream stripes |
| **Stock level in m:** | 100 |
| **Suppliers:** | Oakland Materials |
| **Price per 120 m:** | £20.00 |
| | |
| **Name:** | Criss-cross |
| **Code:** | K734U |
| **Width in m:** | 150 |
| **Description:** | Blue criss-cross pattern on a green background |
| **Stock level in m:** | 456 |
| **Suppliers:** | Old Warehouse & Co. |
| **Price per 120 m:** | £6.00 |

## Data security

Security is part of database design, because data has to be protected. Data with personal information has to be protected under the Data Protection Act, and commercial data has to be safeguarded against theft. Data can be protected in a number of ways, eg:

➤ passwords
➤ restricted access (privileges)
➤ encryption
➤ firewalls.

### Passwords

A database application or the computer system may be protected by a password. A password has to be keyed in to gain access, and may be made up of characters, numbers or in an alphanumeric form. The password is issued only to those authorised to use the system and is changed regularly to keep the data secure.

### Restricted access (privileges)

Different data areas can be set up so that only authorised users can gain access to certain data. All users may be able to access the Clubs file in the database, but only certain staff may be allowed to access the Member file.

This can be managed through the use of additional passwords or by setting up the system so that only certain terminals can gain access to certain data.

### Encryption

Data can be stored in a format that is 'encrypted'. This means that a code is applied to the data in order to scramble it. If anyone did gain access to the data, they would find it in a format that could not be used. To unscramble the data, an encryption key is used.

### Firewall

A software application known as a firewall can be used to separate part of a hard disk and deny access to the data in that part of the disk. This is used over a network system.

## Stand-alone systems

Any computer system that is not linked to other systems is working as a stand-alone. These systems will often be connected to output devices such as a printer.

The software on a stand-alone system is usually bought for only one system, allowing one user. Stand-alone systems can be useful if expensive software is needed for certain purposes only. The software can be put on to a stand-alone system and used when necessary. Software for use on networks is bought with licences allowing set numbers of users, eg a five-, ten- or twenty-user licence. Licences can be expensive for small organisations and it is often economical to buy single-user versions.

If data is to be transferred from a stand-alone system without a network connection, it has to be transferred on to disk and manually moved from one system to the other. If there is a lot of data or a lot of computer users need the data, this can be very time-consuming and unreliable.

## Setup

Computers can be linked together to form networks. Different types of networks can be set up, with the shape and structure of the network depending upon how the links are made and the distances that they are designed to cover.

Computers linked directly into a network need to have an additional item of hardware called a network card. The network will also need special software to operate, called network software.

Networks usually have a file server. This is a computer that organises the running of the network, eg sharing files between the different computers and allowing access to software. The software applications are stored on the file server's hard disk. When a computer is used, the software runs from the server, and the files created are stored in disk space reserved for that user.

A file server is sometimes used as a printer server. Otherwise, a separate computer on the network will act as the printer server. The printer server organises access to the printers attached to a network. There can be a number of printers, and these can be accessed by all computers on the network.

When a document is sent to print, the printer server could be dealing with many documents waiting to print at the same time from computers on the network, so the software organises a 'printer queue'. This allows a user to continue to work on the system as the document is stored on the network hard disk until printed.

## Local area networks

Local area networks (LANs) are used within a locality, eg a school campus or a factory unit (with several buildings). They are linked via cables. Several types of network can be considered. The layout of a network is called its topography. Machines connected to it are called nodes.

The most common types are described on the next page.

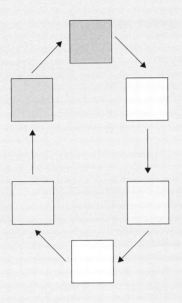

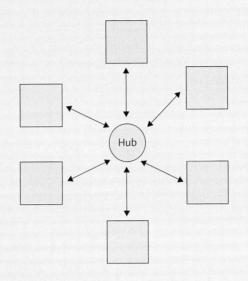

## Ring plan network

In this network all of the components are connected to a cable that runs from one machine to the next in a circle or ring. This includes computers and other items of hardware (eg printers).

This is often known as a token passing ring as all of the information passes in one direction. Therefore, a machine may have to pass information all the way round the network to contact its neighbour. Each component takes in the information and then transmits it to the next along the line.

If the link goes down, the whole network is useless.

## Star plan network

In a star network all the components are connected to a central hub, which receives and transmits data to the appropriate component.

This system can be very fast, and has the advantage that if one component goes down the links to the others are maintained and the whole system does not 'crash'.

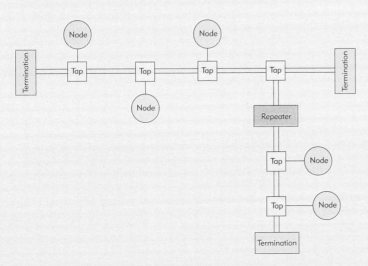

## Broadcast (ethernet) network

Ethernet is the most common type of LAN network and is becoming the standard. It is reasonably efficient, fast and cost effective for most installations. The nodes of the system are connected to a coaxial cable via taps which are spaced regularly along the network. Along the cable are repeaters which amplify and preserve the signals between cables.

When laying out such a network some physical restraints need to be observed. No cable segment can be longer than 500 m. The cables are marked out in 2.5 m lengths, and it is at these points that the taps can be placed. Larger networks can be created with special types of repeater which enable sizes up to 2500 m to be created, although the norm is a maximum of 1500 m. Communication is broadcast by the nodes on to the cable system, and it includes the destination address to ensure it goes to the correct receiver. Once on the cable it goes throughout the system (hence the name broadcast), including the termination where it is absorbed, and is taken in by the intended receiver.

Only one node can broadcast at any one time, so a facility called 'carrier sense multiple access with collision detect' is used to control the system, making other nodes wait until the current user is finished.

## Wide area network

A wide area network (WAN) does not have all its terminals permanently linked. A WAN will be spread over a wide geographical area, or could even be world wide. The Internet is a global WAN network.

Wide area networks require the use of a **modem** to connect to the telephone network, so that computers can communicate anywhere in the world. A modem translates the sound waves (analogue) signals that travel along telephone lines into digital ones that computers use, and vice versa. Modem stands for **mod**ulator/**dem**odulator.

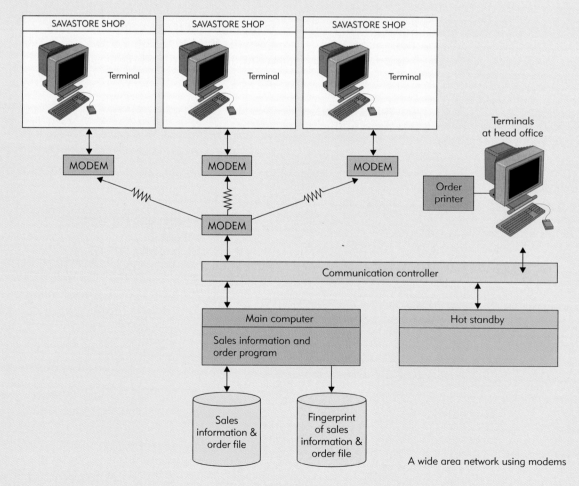

A wide area network using modems

# Operating system (OS)

An operating system performs a number of tasks in a computer system. Some of the most important are described below.

## Controlling hardware

The operating system software allows the OS user programs to communicate with the hardware of the system.

As users, we do not see the masses of electronic signals and the process of interpreting data. The computer's standard operating routines ensure that each time an action takes place, the same result occurs.

## Monitoring programs

As programs run, the OS monitors them to check that there are no problems. It will overcome any problems wherever possible, otherwise the system usually crashes.

## Data transfer

Where data has to be transferred from one system to another, the OS will ensure that the data is in the correct format. Where files are being transferred from one type of system to another, eg PC to Mac, or Mac to Acorn, the software and OS allow for file transfer in set formats.

## File management system

The OS provides utilities to ensure files are stored, deleted, re-named or copied correctly. OS systems keep catalogues of file locations, their length and the dates and times of their creation.

It is the OS system that checks, when a file is being saved, that the filename does not already exist. If it does, a warning message will show on screen before the existing file is overwritten with the new one.

## Prioritising the use of resources

When computers are running a number of programs at the same time (multitasking), the OS has to work out the order in which they should happen. If a document has been sent to print, and the user still wants to work on the system, the OS manages the data through the spooler.

The OS will also set priority so that certain users can have high priority. Different resources can be set at different priorities depending upon the work being done and the users who are doing it.

## Security checks

Where systems have been protected by access codes or user ID numbers, the OS stores the data and will carry out checks to see whether a user is authorised to gain access to a system.

# Graphical user interface (GUI)

GUI systems have been developed to make it easier to use a computer. For the maximum convenience of users, systems make use of windows, icons, menus and pointers (WIMPs). Today most computers are sold with a GUI system installed and ready to run as soon as the computer is switched on.

The separate parts of the systems are described below.

## Windows

Windows are areas on the screen that hold all the information about programs stored or running on the system. The size of the windows can be varied from tiny to filling up the whole of the screen area. When the system is multitasking, a series of windows can be opened at the same time allowing the user to move between different windows while working in different applications.

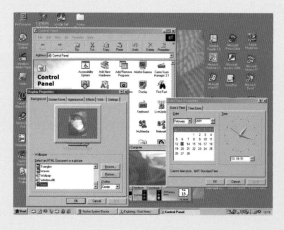

## Icons

Icons are symbols used in the WIMP system to represent different processes or items. For example, an hourglass may show when the computer is processing, and a wastebin icon may be used to put files in for deletion.

## Menus

Software and system programs can all have 'drop-down' or 'pull-down' menus. These contain options from which a user may select one appropriate to the task.

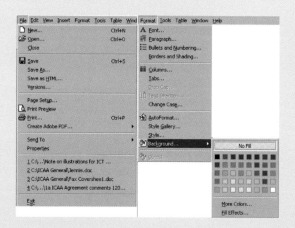

## Pointers

When a user moves the mouse over the mouse-mat or a flat work surface, a pointer on the screen moves. When an icon or menu item is touched with the pointer, the item may be selected using the mouse, by clicking a button. Different systems make use of different controls on the mouse. Some have one button, others have two and still others have three. The choice of button, the number of clicks and the combination of menu and pointer location allow a wide range of tasks to be carried out.

# Electronic Point of Sale (EPOS) and Electronic Funds Transfer at Point of Sale (EFTPOS)

Most shops, supermarkets and commercial outlets make use of either an EPOS or EFTPOS system.

Bar codes are used in both systems. Find out about bar codes on page 78.

## EPOS systems

Once a bar code is identified by the till reader, the information is converted into electrical pulses and communicated to the computer, which searches the stock file for the product EAN (European Article Number).

This information is sent back to the till and the item price and name are printed on the receipt for the customer.

Scales at the tills are also connected to the stock file, and as loose products such as fruit and vegetables are weighed, the code for the item is input by staff, the price is calculated automatically and it is added to the receipt. The total is also calculated and printed on to the receipt.

With each bar code scan, one item registers as sold on the stock records. Sophisticated systems will automatically generate an order when stock falls to a pre-set level. This can ensure an adequate supply of goods for customers.

For safety and security, most branches have two computers both storing this

information from the tills. This ensures that they have a check for verification purposes, and also a back-up in case of system failure. In larger stores these computers are linked to a central distribution system via modem for the purposes of collecting stock data. This data is analysed and compared to a forecast of sales (generated from data that has been collected earlier), taking into account the weather and time of year. The system will then automatically order the correct amount of stock for the store. The orders are transmitted to distribution centres to ensure stock arrives the next day.

Any information on price changes or special offers are also transmitted to the store and the stock files are updated accordingly in readiness. New price labels for the shelves are printed, and night staff in the supermarket put these on the shelves for the next day.

## Electronic Funds Transfer

Many supermarkets also offer the use of debit and credit cards for purchases.

The additional equipment needed is a card reader at each till and a modem link to the banking system. The customer's card is swiped through the reader and the amount spent is communicated to his or her bank. If authorised, the funds are automatically transferred from the customer's account into the supermarket's account. Because this cash is guaranteed, the supermarket can also offer a cash-drawing facility. The customer can pay for goods and also take away cash.

On the backs of the cards is a metallic strip which contains information about the customer's account number and the expiry date of the card. These cards are very useful to both shops and customers.

An EPOS system helps to keep the shelves filled

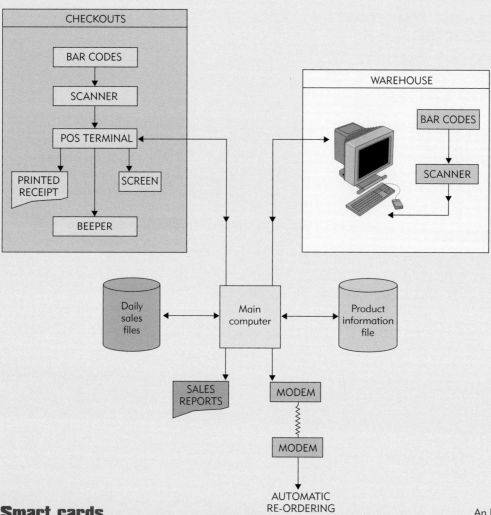

CHECKOUTS

BAR CODES

SCANNER

POS TERMINAL

PRINTED RECEIPT

SCREEN

BEEPER

WAREHOUSE

BAR CODES

SCANNER

Daily sales files

Main computer

Product information file

SALES REPORTS

MODEM

MODEM

AUTOMATIC RE-ORDERING

An EPOS system

## Smart cards

An innovation currently in development is the smart card. These cards are similar to phone cards in that they record an amount of money that is deducted from the card itself.

Customers decide how much money to have on the card. They can add or subtract it by contacting their bank via a modem and a special machine which transmits the data on to the smart card's memory circuits.

One advantage of these cards is that any amount of money can be deducted, no matter how small, so the customer no longer needs to carry cash, even for the purchase of a newspaper.

If the card is stolen only the amount on the card is lost – once the amount of money stored on the card is spent there is

no access to any more from the account. This benefits both bank and customer, as fraudulent losses on cards cost millions of pounds each year.

## Bankers' Automated Clearance System (BACS)

A further development of the electronic funds transfer systems is BACS. This is the banking service that allows direct payment of wages into employee or client accounts, and the clearance of other electronic transactions.

The risk of theft is much reduced, as there is no large transfer of money from banks to the wages departments in companies and back again via employees making visits to their own banks with their wages.

# Health and Safety

Computer operators, like other workers, are covered by the Health and Safety at Work Act 1984, and a number of European Union directives.

## Health and Safety at Work Act

To comply with the Act, employers are required to make sure that their place of work is a safe environment.

All electrical equipment has to be regularly checked to make sure it is safe to use.

Employees are responsible for undertaking safe working practices, and are required to:

➤ deal with any hazards (relating to computers this could include trailing computer leads, loose wiring, etc)

➤ avoid lifting heavy equipment unless trained to do so

➤ take breaks at regular intervals

➤ maintain good posture when sitting at terminals (see below).

Other issues include eyestrain, repetitive strain injury (RSI), and radiation hazards.

### Eyestrain

The constant use of monitors can affect a user's eyes. Regulations have been laid down to help prevent serious eye damage.

➤ Staff have the right to free eye tests before they start to work on VDU screens. They can also ask for tests if they are already working on systems.

➤ Screens should be free from flickering.

➤ Screens should not be placed where they reflect light and systems should be matt so that they do not create glare.

➤ The user should be able to change the angle of the screen (VDU).

➤ Lighting should be bright so that there is not too great a contrast between the screen and the background light.

➤ Users should be able to adjust the screen brightness and contrast.

### Posture

Sitting at a terminal for lengthy periods of time can lead to back, neck and arm injuries. To help to prevent such injuries:

➤ chairs should be designed to swivel and move (best if they have castors) and should also be adjustable for the individual user in the angle of the chair-back and the height of the seat

➤ operators should not work for long periods without taking a break. The break allows for a change in posture.

### Repetitive strain injury (RSI)

Over the past few years, some operators have experienced pains in their fingers, hands, wrists and arms caused by making repeated small movements. In some cases, operators have been permanently injured. Operators need to set up their systems to prevent injury. The keyboards should:

➤ have concave-shaped keys

➤ lie flat or be at an angle of about 10°

➤ be separate from the VDU so that operators can adjust them for their own height and angle.

### Radiation

Special shields are available for VDU screens to protect users from radiation. Although it has not been proved that screens emit dangerous amounts of radiation, it has been suggested that some women operators might have miscarried their babies due to radiation from VDUs.

## Techniques

Before any decisions are made about the manufacture of new products or the provision of new services, market research is carried out.

Possible users of the products or services are contacted to find out what they think about the ideas for the new items.

Two of the most common ways that contact is made with the potential customers are:

> by questionnaire, either sent in the post, included in magazines or sent as e-mail communications;

> by interview, over the telephone, at special meetings or in the street.

Whichever method is used, the most important consideration is the questions to be asked. The decision about the type of questions used will affect the type of data that comes back.

If companies want to know exactly what the potential customer wants, they should ask closed questions.

Closed questions allow only for Yes or No responses, or answers chosen from a list.

Here is an example of a closed question:

Do you like the new colour? **YES** [ ]   **NO** [ ]

If companies need more detailed information, they can follow on with other carefully set questions.

If you answered **NO** to the last question, please state if you thought the colour was:

Too bright [ ]

Too pale [ ]

The wrong colour completely [ ]

Other reason [ ]
(please state)

_____

This allows for databases to be set up showing the results, and these can then be searched to help with decision making.

## Methods of carrying out market research

### Questionnaires

The **advantages** of questionnaires are that they:

> can be sent to a large number of people, providing a large sample of results to get an accurate picture of public opinion

> can target a particular audience for specialist information. This could be achieved by placing a questionnaire in a specialist journal or magazine.

The **disadvantages** of questionnaires are that they:

> cannot guarantee that anyone will complete and return them

> are expensive because of postage, distribution and printing costs.

### Interviews

The **advantages** of interviews are that they:

> can be done at the customer's convenience, so they are popular

> can guarantee a response to questions

> can ask a wider variety of questions and use interviewers' observations about the responses, eg the customer smiled, or frowned and hated the ideas.

The **disadvantages** of interviews are that they:

> can be time-consuming

> need trained staff to produce good results.

# Chapter 123456

## Spreadsheets

## Case Study [1] 2 3 4 5 6

## Newschester Fire Service

Briony Phillips is one of the freelance agents working with **PR Inc Co**. and the fire brigade at Newschester. She is responsible for helping with the organisation of the exhibition that the fire brigade is organising.

The Senior Fire Officer, Steve Thomas, wants to know how much Briony's time is going to cost. Briony has been asked to produce a breakdown of her costs for her organisation work.

Briony has been thinking about using computer technology to enable her to budget efficiently this year. She has asked another colleague at PR Inc Co. to help her to set up a computer model, a spreadsheet, of her annual expenditure.

Briony will then be able to use the model to help her to work out her costs for the fire station work.

## Action Point [1] 2 3 4 5 6 7 8 9

### Learning objective
➤ Identify the uses for computer models

*i* Read through **COMPUTER MODELS** in the **INFORMATION BANK** on page 119 to find out why a computer model might be useful.

The first thing Briony has to work out are all the different areas on which she spends money at work. This does not include personal spending. From her diary and records she can put together the following information about payments to PR Inc Co. and the fire station.

| | |
|---|---|
| **Rent** | Pays a flat fee each year to PR Inc Co. for office space. This covers the use of all of the resources in the office. The fire brigade do not charge her. |
| **Stationery** | Fees are charged for any paper, card, reprographics and printing needed. |
| **Telephone** | The cost of calls and faxes is charged, but the line rental is covered in the rent fee. |
| **Petty cash** | She spends a certain amount of money entertaining clients, for coffees and lunches. |

Briony's records show that she has paid out the following amounts of money over the past twelve months.

| Month | Rent | Stationery | Telephone | Petty Cash |
|---|---|---|---|---|
| January | 200 | 160 | 60 | 56 |
| February | 200 | 157 | 75 | 45 |
| March | 200 | 190 | 98 | 70 |
| April | 200 | 200 | 12 | 10 |
| May | 200 | 179 | 130 | 40 |
| June | 200 | 200 | 69 | 13 |
| July | 200 | 150 | 133 | 59 |
| August | 200 | 250 | 49 | 34 |
| September | 200 | 120 | 88 | 10 |
| October | 200 | 136 | 78 | 60 |
| November | 200 | 258 | 97 | 30 |
| December | 200 | 250 | 110 | 12 |

## Action Point   1  **2**  3  4  5  6  7  8  9

### Learning objectives

➤ Create a financial spreadsheet model

➤ Use the model to carry out basic calculations on data

*i.* Read through **SPREADSHEET LAYOUT** and **SPREADSHEET FEATURES** in the **INFORMATION BANK** on pages 119–120 to find out how to construct a spreadsheet.

➤ Use the data that Briony worked out about her expenditure over the past twelve months to construct a financial model to calculate her total outgoings for last year. The model should also display the monthly totals for each item and the overall total.

➤ To help her with the budgeting, Briony would like to know what percentage of her outgoings is spent on each of the items. Use your spreadsheet to find out and report on the percentages.

*i.* Read through **CELL CONTENT** in the **INFORMATION BANK** on pages 121–122 to help you to set up the correct way of calculating these percentages.

## Action Plus

Briony has also heard that the PR Inc Co. management group are proposing a rise in the rent. This could be either 3% or 5%.

➤ Use your model to calculate the increase in her monthly and annual bills in either case.

➤ Alternatively, they may increase the contribution to the stationery by the same amount. Using your model, calculate both increases and work out which one would be the most costly to her.

Briony is ready to work out her fees for the fire station. She will be working a set number of days for both PR Inc Co. and the fire station.

She outlines her model for the colleague who is helping her with the spreadsheet.

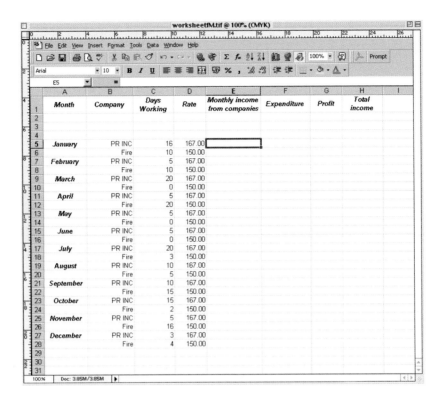

| | A | B | C | D | E | F | G | H | I |
|---|---|---|---|---|---|---|---|---|---|
| 1 | Month | Company | Days Working | Rate | Monthly income from companies | Expenditure | Profit | Total income | |
| 2 | | | | | | | | | |
| 3 | | | | | | | | | |
| 4 | | | | | | | | | |
| 5 | January | PR INC | 16 | 167.00 | | | | | |
| 6 | | Fire | 10 | 150.00 | | | | | |
| 7 | February | PR INC | 5 | 167.00 | | | | | |
| 8 | | Fire | 10 | 150.00 | | | | | |
| 9 | March | PR INC | 20 | 167.00 | | | | | |
| 10 | | Fire | 0 | 150.00 | | | | | |
| 11 | April | PR INC | 5 | 167.00 | | | | | |
| 12 | | Fire | 20 | 150.00 | | | | | |
| 13 | May | PR INC | 5 | 167.00 | | | | | |
| 14 | | Fire | 0 | 150.00 | | | | | |
| 15 | June | PR INC | 5 | 167.00 | | | | | |
| 16 | | Fire | 0 | 150.00 | | | | | |
| 17 | July | PR INC | 20 | 167.00 | | | | | |
| 18 | | Fire | 3 | 150.00 | | | | | |
| 19 | August | PR INC | 10 | 167.00 | | | | | |
| 20 | | Fire | 5 | 150.00 | | | | | |
| 21 | September | PR INC | 10 | 167.00 | | | | | |
| 22 | | Fire | 15 | 150.00 | | | | | |
| 23 | October | PR INC | 15 | 167.00 | | | | | |
| 24 | | Fire | 2 | 150.00 | | | | | |
| 25 | November | PR INC | 5 | 167.00 | | | | | |
| 26 | | Fire | 16 | 150.00 | | | | | |
| 27 | December | PR INC | 3 | 167.00 | | | | | |
| 28 | | Fire | 4 | 150.00 | | | | | |
| 29 | | | | | | | | | |
| 30 | | | | | | | | | |
| 31 | | | | | | | | | |

Briony has listed the number of days that she knows she is going to work for the two organisations in column C. She charges them different daily rates for her work, as is shown in column D.

She will use the monthly expenditure that she worked out before, and split it between the two organisations equally.

## Action Point       1   2   **3**   4   5   6   7   8   9

### Learning objectives
➤ Create a spreadsheet to set criteria
➤ Use formulae to carry out calculations

➤ Create a spreadsheet model of this plan.

➤ Use formulae to work out the figures that should go into the empty cells.

➤ Print a copy of your spreadsheet with the formulae and explain what each of them is doing.

➤ Briony will be doing the exhibition work for the fire station in April and May. Use your spreadsheet to find out how much she will have to charge the fire station for this work on the exhibition.

➤ Produce a report for the Senior Fire Officer stating how much the costs will be.

Now that Steve Thomas, the Senior Fire Officer, knows how much he is going to have to pay Briony Phillips, he can go ahead and plan the exhibition.

There is a fixed budget for the exhibition. The whole budget is £53 000, although £2500 of this total is reserved for emergencies. Some of the staff thought that this sounded a lot of money to spend on an exhibition.

Some fixed costs have to be met. All of the staff time, including that of Briony Phillips, must be counted as well as the cost of merchandise used as free gifts, and publicity that might be needed at the exhibition.

Steve asks Briony if she could produce a spreadsheet to work out the cost of the exhibition. Briony agrees to set one up, but says that the administration staff at the fire station should enter the data and produce any reports that Steve needs. Before starting on the spreadsheet, she has to agree a proposal with Steve for what the system should do.

| Action Point | 1 2 3 **4** 5 6 7 8 9 |
| --- | --- |

### Learning objective

➤ Develop a design and development plan for a system

Read through **SYSTEM DESIGN** in the **INFORMATION BANK** on page 123.

> ➤ Produce a design and development report on the proposed spreadsheet system for the exhibition under these headings:
> *Purpose*
> *Data*
> *Methods*
> *Support*

The issues that must be considered for the spreadsheet are as follows.

● The exhibition will be open and need staffing for five days. There will also be a set-up day and a take-down day.

● Briony Phillips' fee is extra to the staffing listed below.

---

**Known fixed costs**

| | |
| --- | --- |
| Hire of the hall for the exhibition | 30 m² @ £238 per m² |
| Cost of the design and publicity work | £25 000 |
| Newspaper publicity & delivery of leaflets | £12 500 |
| Electricity for the exhibition | £45.00 per day |
| Hire of transport van | 2-day hire @ £75.00 per day (+VAT at 17.5%) |
| Fuel for van | £60.00 max. |

---

**Staffing for the exhibition**

Six extra staff are to be brought in for the exhibition. They have agreed to work at the overtime rate of £12.50 per hour.

They are needed for five days. The exhibition is open from 10.00am to 6.00pm. The staff are needed shortly before the opening and a short time after closing. They will work half-day sessions, ie from 9.00am to 2.00pm or 1.30pm to 6.30pm, in teams of three at one time.

### Free gifts for visitors

A local promotional company has offered to produce a range of gifts that could be given out at the exhibition. The costs are given below.

| | | |
|---|---|---|
| Key rings | £50 per 100 | Minimum order £100 |
| Pens | £25 per 60 | Minimum order £50 |
| Pencils | £10 per 100 | Minimum order £10 |
| Cloth hats | £25 per 10 | Minimum order £100 |
| Card hats | £10 per 100 | Minimum order £30 |
| Balloons | £20 per 50 | Minimum order £40 |
| Plastic carrier bags | £15 per 1000 | Minimum order £75 |

All items are exclusive of VAT at 17.5%.

## Action Point    1  2  3  4  5  6  7  8  9

### Learning objectives

➤ Create a spreadsheet to set criteria

➤ Produce a meaningful graphical representation of the spreadsheet data

➤ Develop a spreadsheet model of the costs of the exhibition

ℹ Read through **GRAPHS** in the **INFORMATION BANK** on page 123.

➤ Produce a graphical representation of all the expense items for the exhibition, showing the relative expenditure on each item.

## Action Plus

➤ There is a difference of opinion amongst the staff about which free gifts should be selected. Select those that you think would be appropriate from the list.

➤ Use your spreadsheet to work out the maximum number of gifts of the kinds you have selected, which could be afforded in the budget, when everything else is taken into account.

## Knowledge Points

### Computer models

- spreadsheets
- simulations

### Cell contents

- numbers
- characters
- formulae
- functions
- absolute and relative values

### System design

- purpose of system
- data
- methods
- support

### Spreadsheet layout

- row, columns and cells
- cell format
  number
  alignment
  font
  border
  patterns
  protection
- cell width and height

### Data capture

- axes
- legends

### Spreadsheet layout

- moving, cutting and pasting
- sorting
- printing

## Skills Focus Point

- Discuss how to install software on a system
- Open software application
- Save and name files
- Create and name folders
- Enter data
- Delete files
- Find location of files stored on a system
- Customise toolbars for specific documents

The **Bayrich Motor Company** is moving ahead with its development of a new car. The design team has changed the design of the car quite considerably. The team has had to work on some new parts for the car, as the existing ones would not fit into the new shape.

The engineers are pleased to see all of the ICT systems being upgraded, and have worked out some simple computer models of the existing cars in production. The computer models that they have developed so far hold information on:

- car parts
- dimensions
- weights
- forces and structures

They need to experiment with their new parts to see how these can affect the car design.

The engineers call out a consultant from **IS..IT Ltd**, Frederick Muzungu, to help them use their spreadsheet model correctly. They are sure that they can speed up the process of selecting the best parts by working through a modelling exercise.

### Learning objective

➤ Analyse and report upon the effectiveness of a simple computer model

➤ After reading through the following section about the Bayrich Motor Company's computer modelling, make notes about the way the model has been constructed, and suggest any improvements that you think could be made.

### Action Plus

➤ The engineers would like to be able to use the data that they already have entered into other files. Describe the most effective way that the data could be transferred from one file to another.

Spreadsheets

# Bayrich Motors computer modelling

Bayrich Motors staff are investigating the way in which the weights of different car parts will affect the total weight of the car. Some standard parts (Type 1) are currently in use, and a series of new parts (Type 2) are under consideration.

The car must not weigh more than 880 kg in total.

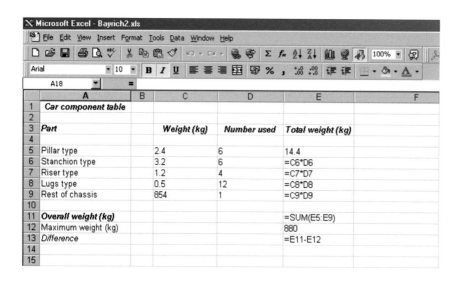

| | A | B | C | D | E | F |
|---|---|---|---|---|---|---|
| 1 | Car component table | | | | | |
| 2 | | | | | | |
| 3 | Part | | Weight (kg) | Number used | Total weight (kg) | |
| 4 | | | | | | |
| 5 | Pillar type | | 2.4 | 6.0 | 14.4 | |
| 6 | Stanchion type | | 3.2 | 6.0 | 19.2 | |
| 7 | Riser type | | 1.2 | 4.0 | 4.8 | |
| 8 | Lugs type | | 0.5 | 12.0 | 6.0 | |
| 9 | Rest of chassis | | 854.0 | 1.0 | 854.0 | |
| 10 | | | | | | |
| 11 | Overall weight (kg) | | | | 898.4 | |
| 12 | Maximum weight (kg) | | | | 880.0 | |
| 13 | Difference | | | | 18.4 | |
| 14 | | | | | | |
| 15 | | | | | | |

(Microsoft Excel - Bayrich1.xls)

| | A | B | C | D | E | F |
|---|---|---|---|---|---|---|
| 1 | Car component table | | | | | |
| 2 | | | | | | |
| 3 | Part | | Weight (kg) | Number used | Total weight (kg) | |
| 5 | Pillar type | | 2.4 | 6 | 14.4 | |
| 6 | Stanchion type | | 3.2 | 6 | =C6*D6 | |
| 7 | Riser type | | 1.2 | 4 | =C7*D7 | |
| 8 | Lugs type | | 0.5 | 12 | =C8*D8 | |
| 9 | Rest of chassis | | 854 | 1 | =C9*D9 | |
| 10 | | | | | | |
| 11 | Overall weight (kg) | | | | =SUM(E5:E9) | |
| 12 | Maximum weight (kg) | | | | 880 | |
| 13 | Difference | | | | =E11-E12 | |
| 14 | | | | | | |
| 15 | | | | | | |

(Microsoft Excel - Bayrich2.xls)

- The weights of the parts are multiplied by the number of parts used (C5*D5) to give a total weight as shown in E5.

- The totals are added together, including the weight of the chassis (=sumE5:E9), to give the overall car weight, which is shown in E11.

- The total weight allowed (880 kg) is in cell 12. To find out if the car would be less than this weight, the overall total in cell E11 is subtracted from E12. The difference in weights is then recorded in cell E13.

In this second model, the new parts that have just been developed are put into the model, replacing the older ones.

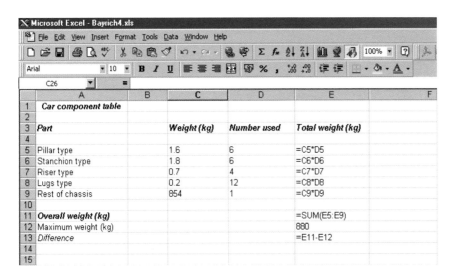

The weight for the new parts has decreased. Look at the total weight for the Type 2 parts compared to the Type 1 parts shown in column E.

## Summary

Using the spreadsheet model the engineers could input information on different parts, mixing Type 1 and Type 2 parts, to see what effect this would have on the overall weight of the car. Because of the use of formulae, the figures would change according to the rules decided upon.

The computer models have proved very useful, but the management group has identified a problem with the development. The Type 2 parts might be lighter in weight, but they are not the cheapest. The Type 2 parts are more expensive at the moment as they are made from more expensive materials, and the production process also takes longer.

The management group gives the engineers the following costings (on page 102) for both types of parts.

| Part | Cost £ |
|---|---|
| **Type 1** | |
| Pillar | 9.65 |
| Stanchion | 4.80 |
| Riser | 3.10 |
| Lugs | 2.96 |
| Rest of the chassis | 3127.00 |
| **Type 2** | |
| Pillar | 23.10 |
| Stanchion | 16.98 |
| Riser | 12.86 |
| Lugs | 8.00 |
| Rest of the chassis | 3127.00 |

## Action Point    1 2 3 4 5 6 7 8 9

### Learning objective

> Create a computer spreadsheet model for given data

The spreadsheet can calculate the costs of using the two types of car parts.

> Use the costs above to create a costs spreadsheet based on the car part spreadsheet.

## Action Plus

### Learning objective

> Use a computer spreadsheet model to answer a 'What if?' question

> Use a computer spreadsheet feature of goal setting

Read through **'WHAT IF?' ANALYSIS** and **GOAL SETTING** in the **INFORMATION BANK** on page 124.

> Use the spreadsheet models for the car parts and costs to find out which combination of parts would give the cheapest and lightest design.

Before the new car can go into production, the financial directors want a breakdown of the full production costs. Examine the figures given below.

> Each model in the new car range costs £40.15 per hour in labour.

> The overhead cost for each car is £1765.

> From the cost of each car, Bayrich Motors can deduct £513, known as an 'offset'.

> The basic model of the new car, the 1.1L, takes 20 hours to build and costs £2145 in materials.

> The mid-range model, the 1.3L Sprite, takes 22 hours to build and costs £2564.70 in materials.

> The top-of-the range model, the 2.4LX G, takes 30 hours to build and costs £3017.50 in materials.

## Learning objectives

➤ Produce a spreadsheet for given data

➤ Use a range of formulae and functions within the computer model

➤ Produce a spreadsheet which will show:
*the total cost of each car model,* and
*the average materials cost of the 3 models together.*

➤ Show the formulae you have used in your spreadsheet.

➤ Explain what each of the formulae is doing.

➤ State why it is useful to have a spreadsheet for this task.

## Action Plus

### Learning objective

➤ Use appropriate import techniques to produce a report

*i* Read through **IMPORT/EXPORT** in the **INFORMATION BANK** on pages 125–126.

➤ The financial directors require a report indicating the costs. Decide which method of importing the spreadsheet files would be best for your report.

➤ Produce the report, including the production costs spreadsheets.

The financial managers plan to launch the new range of cars at a big motor show held in November.

To make sure that their new range will be priced competitively with similar models, they ask for a computer model to be set up to analyse the price range they can offer to dealers.

They produce an outline for the spreadsheet as follows:

| A | B | C | D | E | F |
|---|---|---|---|---|---|
| Model/range | Cost | % profit | Total cost | Market price | Difference |
| Landau 1.3L | 4200 | 50 | | 6200 | |
| Landau 1.3LS | 4800 | 50 | | 6600 | |
| Landau 1.3 Coupe | 5000 | 50 | | 7000 | |
| *New model* | | | | | |
| Cryon 1.1 | 4200 | 50 | | 6100 | |
| Cryon 1.3L Sprite | 4600 | 50 | | 6400 | |
| Cryon 2.4LX G | 6500 | 50 | | 9000 | |
| Lacourt 1.8L | 6700 | 50 | | 9100 | |
| Lacourt 2.0L | 7400 | 50 | | 9900 | |
| Lacourt 2.0LX | 7600 | 50 | | 10000 | |
| Lacourt 2.4Gfi | 8000 | 50 | | 11300 | |

Their suggestion is that:

Column A          Shows the range and model

Column B          Shows the cost of producing the car

Column C          Gives the amount of profit the financial directors would like to make on each car

Column D          Shows the cost so far if the percentage in Column C is added on

Column E          Gives the maximum price that the Marketing department thinks should be charged. The final selling price cannot be more.

Column F          Shows the difference between the total cost and the suggested market price.

## Action Point     1  2  3  4  5  6  7  8  9

### Learning objectives

➤ Create a spreadsheet model of a given situation

➤ Use a model to carry out simple calculations

➤ Create a spreadsheet based upon the financial directors' ideas.

➤ Set up formulae to calculate the cost price for Column D, and the difference for Column F.

➤ Produce a report for the financial directors stating the information that can be gained from the spreadsheet about each model of car.

➤ Decide whether to include the spreadsheet in your report. If you do, look through **IMPORT/EXPORT** in the **INFORMATION BANK** (pages 125–126) to help you decide how to do it.

## Action Plus

### Learning objective

➤ Use comparative operators within formulae and functions

In some cases, the cost price of a car is greater than the suggested market price. The financial directors agree to adjust the profit percentage to make the cost price meet the market price.

*i*  Re-read the information on comparative operators under **CELL CONTENT** in the **INFORMATION BANK** on pages 121–122 to help you work through the task.

➤ Use your spreadsheet to adjust '% profit' to bring the 'Cost price' to no more than £100 greater than the 'Market price'.

**Import/export procedures**

**'What if' questions**

**Cell contents**

➤ comparative operators

➤ formulae and functions

**Goal setting**

**Skills Focus Point**

➤ Obtain suitable hard copy by altering print quality and orientation

➤ Discuss how to connect peripheral devices to a computer

➤ Create and make use of sub-directories

➤ Demonstrate the ability to set the system settings for a specified user

➤ Add labels, axes, legends and titles to charts

## Case Study  1 2 **3** 4 5 6

### Sezer's Savastores

Now that the Sezers have introduced an upgraded system into each of their Savastores, they are keen to extend the services that they offer to customers. For years, each of the branches has run a Christmas Club savings plan for its customers. Now the Sezers would like to have one scheme throughout all the stores.

Under the existing schemes, customers pay a regular amount into their club plan each week or month. Customers are given a quarterly bonus of 1% on their balance. The schemes run from 1 January to 30 November each year.

At the end of the period customers can cash in their savings. To get them to spend the money in its own stores, the company has added an incentive bonus of a further 2% if the money is spent there.

The managers of six stores decide to try a joint scheme for one year, and if successful will extend it to all other Savastores.

The table below gives the monthly income of the savings plan in each of the shops for the previous year. This is the income from all customers, with each shop keeping details of the individual customers on a spreadsheet in the shop.

At the moment a bonus of 1% is awarded on the total income in the account on 31 March, 30 June, 30 September and 30 November.

| Store | Jan | Feb | Mar | Apr | May | Jun | Jul | Aug | Sep | Oct | Nov |
|-------|-----|-----|-----|-----|-----|-----|-----|-----|-----|-----|-----|
| Shop 1 | 500 | 500 | 300 | 600 | 400 | 600 | 600 | 800 | 800 | 800 | 700 |
| Shop 2 | 700 | 600 | 600 | 500 | 700 | 700 | 500 | 400 | 900 | 900 | 500 |
| Shop 3 | 300 | 500 | 700 | 400 | 600 | 900 | 800 | 200 | 400 | 700 | 600 |
| Shop 4 | 700 | 700 | 900 | 800 | 900 | 700 | 500 | 900 | 500 | 800 | 400 |
| Shop 5 | 200 | 400 | 700 | 600 | 600 | 200 | 400 | 500 | 600 | 400 | 600 |
| Shop 6 | 800 | 800 | 500 | 700 | 800 | 600 | 900 | 400 | 400 | 500 | 800 |

## Action Point  **1** 2 3 4 5 6 7 8 9

### Learning objective

➤ Create a spreadsheet model using appropriate formulae and functions

➤ Use the information in the table to create a spreadsheet to calculate the total bonus cost for:
*each quarter; the total income from the scheme; the final cost to the company when it pays the bonuses.*

The company invests the income from the scheme into a long-term investment account in order to generate interest. This usually nets 5% interest over the period.

> ➤ Calculate the profit the company will make on this deal with the customer details given.

The additional bonus of 2%, if customers qualify, is calculated on the final total on 30 November, and the money is given to the customers in the form of vouchers they can use in the store.

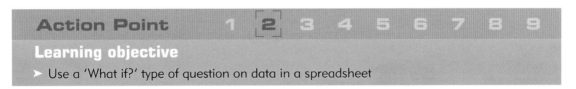

## Action Point    1 **2** 3 4 5 6 7 8 9

### Learning objective
> ➤ Use a 'What if?' type of question on data in a spreadsheet

> ➤ Calculate the extra cost of the 2% bonus for the company if all customers qualify for it, and the new level of profit.

The staff who keep the records find it very time-consuming to go through all the processes of opening up the file, adding in the amount of money a customer would like to deposit, and calculating the new balance. The staff also find it time-consuming when they have to alter the records to credit the 1% interest every quarter.

Mr Sezer wants the scheme to succeed, so he mentions the staff's problems to the IS..IT Ltd consultant, Frederick Muzungu, who has been working with them. Frederick tells him about macros, and how they can be written to perform some tasks automatically.

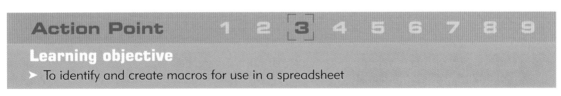

## Action Point    1 2 **3** 4 5 6 7 8 9

### Learning objective
> ➤ To identify and create macros for use in a spreadsheet

*i*   Read through **MACROS** in the **INFORMATION BANK** on page 127.

> ➤ Choose a task involving the spreadsheet you have set up for the Savastore saving scheme and replace it with a macro.

## Action Plus

The use of macros can ensure that all data is processed in the same way.

> ➤ Analyse the use of the spreadsheet system you have created, from the time that the computer is turned on, to identify where macros could be used to ensure consistency in each of the Savastores.

> ➤ Develop a series of macros to make the running of the spreadsheet as simple as possible for the user.

The Savastores all find that competition for customers is growing. It has been decided to improve the existing bonus scheme to give an added incentive to savers. The managers think that an improved scheme running in the smaller shops will attract customers from other local shops and bring in new ones as the number of Savastores increases.

## Action Point   1  2  3  **4**  5  6  7  8  9

### Learning objectives

➤ Carry out a 'What if?' exercise

➤ Represent data in graphs or charts

➤ Use your spreadsheet to model different levels of bonus, eg 1.5%, 2%, 2.5%, to find out the maximum bonus level that can be given before a loss is made. You may need to look at either the quarterly or the annual bonus, or both.

➤ Present your results using a suitable graph or chart.

➤ Write a report to summarise your findings for the board. This should show the present situation and how profit decreases with each increased level of interest before you reach a loss situation.

➤ Recommend which bonus scheme to use.

A new Savastore has been opened. The Sezers decide that this store will run the scheme from the start, so this store must be added to the six that are currently running the scheme.

From customer profiles, the following forecast has been made about the income expected from the store.

| Store | Jan | Feb | Mar | Apr | May | Jun | Jul | Aug | Sep | Oct | Nov |
|-------|-----|-----|-----|-----|-----|-----|-----|-----|-----|-----|-----|
| Shop 7 | 300 | 600 | 400 | 500 | 700 | 400 | 500 | 700 | 600 | 500 | 600 |

The income from the other six shops is likely to remain the same over the next twelve-month period.

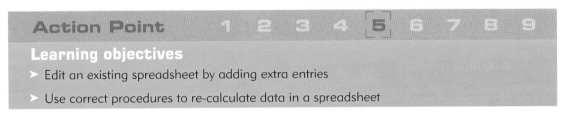

**Action Point**  1  2  3  4  **5**  6  7  8  9

**Learning objectives**

➤ Edit an existing spreadsheet by adding extra entries

➤ Use correct procedures to re-calculate data in a spreadsheet

If you are unsure how to add additional rows and columns, look again at **SPREADSHEET FEATURES** in the **INFORMATION BANK** (page 121).

➤ Add the new shop to the spreadsheet and work out the forecast income figures for the next twelve months.

➤ With the new figures in your spreadsheet, re-calculate the profit made under your proposed bonus award scheme.

Mr Sezer is pleased to see that the use of the system is increasing every day. A number of changes have been made, and features have been added. He is now concerned that errors could be creeping into the system.

Frederick Muzungu arranges to test the systems thoroughly. To do this he has to use the system in exactly the same way as the staff in the Savastores. Frederick asks for some test data to be prepared so that he can use it to test the system.

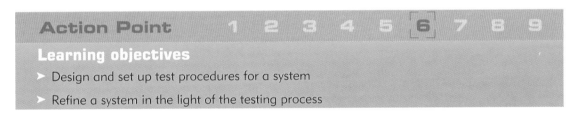

**Action Point**  1  2  3  4  5  **6**  7  8  9

**Learning objectives**

➤ Design and set up test procedures for a system

➤ Refine a system in the light of the testing process

Read through **TESTING SYSTEMS** and **DETECTING ERRORS** in the **INFORMATION BANK** on pages 127–128.

➤ Prepare some test data for your spreadsheet system. Ask a member of your class to enter the data into your spreadsheet and report any problems.

➤ Refine your system in the light of the testing carried out.

Spreadsheets

## Knowledge Points

### Macros

- uses of a macro
- recording a macro

### Test procedures

- test data
- dry run tests
- evaluation forms

### Detecting errors

## Skills Focus Point

- Use linking facility to link objects/files
- Incorporate two or more different formats of data into a single document
- Compress files to ensure maximum storage efficiency on a system
- Transfer files to external devices, eg writable CD, zip cartridges, for use on other systems

## The Small Theatre Company

The **Small Theatre Company** wants to develop a sponsorship scheme. After considering the types of people who visit the theatre, they decide that three different types of sponsorship should be available to them.

**Company sponsors**
Companies sponsor the theatre productions by donating set amounts of money. In return they receive advertising space in the souvenir programme and a set number of seats at reduced rates for staff and clients.

**Friends of the Theatre Company**
Some people regularly buy season tickets. Three types of season tickets are available: annual, single season and monthly. Purchasers could be designated as Friends of the Theatre Company.

**Group sponsors**
Social clubs and similar organisations often contribute an annual donation and receive reduced price seats for groups.

The finance group has drawn up the following proposals for the sponsorship scheme:

---

Tickets are available in the following price bands:

|  | A | B | C | D |
|---|---|---|---|---|
| Full price | £25.00 | £15.00 | £7.50 | £5.00 |
| Concessionary rate | £15.00 | £7.50 | £5.00 | £2.50 |

(*for children under 14 and senior citizens*)

---

The Small Theatre has:

50 seats at price A　　100 seats at price B　　150 seats at price C　　300 seats at price D

It runs seven productions over 38 weeks of the year.

---

The scheme for company sponsors is based upon the following levels of donation:

Annual donation of:
£5000 allows a 20% reduction on the price of 1000 seats
£10 000 allows a 15% reduction on the price of 2000 seats
£20 000 allows a 10% reduction on the price of 5000 seats

---

**Group sponsors**

| Groups of up to 10 | 20 groups of 5 people in band C |
|---|---|
|  | 50 groups of 8 people in band D |
| Groups of 11–20 | 5 groups of 20 people in band B |
|  | 20 groups of 15 people in band C |
|  | 80 groups of 12 people in band D |
| Groups of 21–50 | 16 groups of 25 people in band C |
|  | 18 groups of 30 people in band D |
| Groups of above 50 | One group of 120, given a 35% reduction on band C |

The Small Theatre Company's Accounts department will be responsible for the running of the scheme and know that they will need a specific spreadsheet on which to record the sponsor scheme data. They ask for the help of IS..IT Ltd to advise them how to create it.

## Action Point  1  2  3  4  5  6  7  8  9

### Learning objective
➤ Review system design and development

➤ In the role of Frederick Muzungu, identify the areas that must be considered when designing this system for the Small Theatre Company. If necessary, re-read the section on **SYSTEM DESIGN** in the **INFORMATION BANK**.

➤ Produce a system design and development report for the Accounts department to show them how the spreadsheet will be laid out and what it will do.

➤ Discuss the report with people from your class (in the roles of Accounts staff) to check that it is going to be a suitable system.

With the outline of the system agreed, Frederick is to develop his system.

## Action Point  1  2  3  4  5  6  7  8  9

### Learning objectives
➤ Review the creation of a spreadsheet for a specified context
➤ Review the use of formulae and functions appropriate to the spreadsheet

➤ Use the information provided to create a spreadsheet for the sponsor scheme.

➤ Make notes about the structure of the spreadsheet and of any formulae you use.

➤ Print a copy of the spreadsheet.

The system needs to be thoroughly tested before it can be used by the Accounts department. Frederick wants someone to try using the system to make sure that it does exactly what it should.

## Action Point  1  2  3  4  5  6  7  8  9

### Learning objective
➤ Review the testing procedures needed for a system

➤ Identify which members of staff would be the best ones to test the system. State the reasons for your choice.

➤ Prepare test data for the system and ask someone from your class to enter the data into your spreadsheet.

➤ Refine the spreadsheet in the light of this testing.

## Action Plus

### Learning objective

➤ Review the use of formulae and functions

The Accounts department staff at the Small Theatre Company want to know more about formulae and functions and what they do within the spreadsheet model.

➤ Draw up a glossary of the most commonly used formulae and functions in spreadsheets, which would be suitable for someone who knows little or nothing about them.

The spreadsheet has now been installed for the Accounts department to use. Their first task will be to find out what type of revenue they can expect for the first few years of the scheme.

The staff have also found that some of the routines they have to perform each time they use the system are complex, and that sometimes they make mistakes.

## Action Point          1   2   3   4   5   6   7   8   9

### Learning objectives

➤ Review the use of a spreadsheet to carry out simple calculations

➤ Review the development and use of macros

➤ Use your spreadsheet to calculate the projected revenue from the sponsorship scheme for next year.

➤ Add macros to the spreadsheet to speed up the way in which it can be used. If necessary, re-read the section on **MACROS** in the **INFORMATION BANK** on page 127.

The directors of the Small Theatre Company know that their expenses are increasing, so the total money received from ticket sales will have to increase by at least 3% overall next year. They want to increase each band of ticket prices by the minimum amount to result in this overall increase.

## Action Point   1 2 3 4 [5] 6 7 8 9

### Learning objectives

➤ Review the use of formulae and functions

➤ Review the use of import, cut and paste procedures

➤ Review the use of graphs

➤ Review the use of goal setting and 'What if?' questions

➤ Use your spreadsheet to show how a 3% increase in ticket prices would affect the income of the Small Theatre Company.

➤ Produce a report to illustrate how they could implement this increase, showing the amounts received from each of the ticket price bands. You should incorporate a copy of your spreadsheet into your report document.

➤ Add graphs or charts to illustrate your points where necessary.

## Action Plus

➤ Use your spreadsheet to work out the rates of increase that can be applied to different price bands, so that the effective increase in overall income is 3%. Try to minimise the alterations to the price bands where most sales occur, or alternatively, increase those the most and leave the rest unchanged.

➤ Incorporate these development ideas into the report, with suitable graphical representation of the data.

Throughout the case studies in this chapter, you have had the opportunity to cover a number of areas of knowledge. Make a copy of the following table and complete your table to show where you have used the Knowledge Points.

| Knowledge Points | Where Used |
|---|---|
| **Computer models** | |
| ➤ spreadsheets | |
| ➤ simulations | |
| **Spreadsheet layout** | |
| ➤ row, columns and cells | |
| ➤ cell format<br>number<br>alignment<br>font<br>border<br>patterns<br>protection | |
| ➤ cell width and height | |
| **Spreadsheet features** | |
| ➤ moving, cutting and pasting | |
| ➤ sorting | |
| ➤ printing | |
| **Cell contents** | |
| ➤ numbers | |
| ➤ characters | |
| ➤ formulae | |
| ➤ functions | |
| ➤ absolute and relative values | |
| **Graphs** | |
| ➤ axes | |
| ➤ legends | |

## Review ICT (continued)

| Knowledge Points | Where Used |
|---|---|
| **System design** | |
| ➤ purpose of the system | |
| ➤ data | |
| ➤ methods | |
| ➤ support | |
| **'What if' questions** | |
| **Goal setting** | |
| **Import/export procedures** | |
| **Cell contents** | |
| ➤ comparative operators | |
| ➤ formulae and functions | |
| **Macros** | |
| ➤ use of macros | |
| ➤ recording a macro | |
| **Test procedures** | |
| ➤ test data | |
| ➤ dry run test | |
| ➤ evaluation forms | |
| **Detecting errors** | |

The following Learning Objectives have been covered in Chapter 3.

Decide whether you have sufficient knowledge about each item to be able to use or write about them in the future. Leave blank the 'tick' column for any objective that you think you need to know more about.

| Learning Objectives | ✓ |
| --- | --- |
| Identify the uses for computer models | |
| Create a financial spreadsheet model | |
| Use the model to carry out basic calculations on data | |
| Create a spreadsheet to set criteria | |
| Use formulae to carry out calculations | |
| Develop a design and development plan for a system | |
| Produce a meaningful graphical representation of the spreadsheet data | |
| Analyse and report upon the effectiveness of a simple computer model | |
| Create a computer spreadsheet model for given data | |
| Use a computer spreadsheet model to answer a 'What if?' question | |
| Use a computer spreadsheet feature of goal setting | |
| Use a range of formulae and functions within the computer model | |
| Identify and create macros for use in a spreadsheet | |
| Edit an existing spreadsheet by adding extra entries | |
| Use correct procedures to re-calculate data in a spreadsheet | |
| Design and set up test procedures for a system | |
| Refine a system in the light of the testing process | |

## Skills Objectives

You should have used the practical skills listed below in following the case studies in this chapter.

Decide whether you feel confident about using the skill again or are able to write about it. Leave blank the 'tick' column for any objective that you need to practise.

Record the filenames of the spreadsheets you have created and copies of source materials. Make sure that there is at least one chart and one diagram within the files. Keep your own records of the information you obtained and the types of calculations you identified to get the results you needed.

Remember to record how you checked your findings and calculations.

| Skills Objectives | ✓ |
|---|---|
| ➤ Discuss how to install software on a system | |
| ➤ Open software application | |
| ➤ Save and name folders | |
| ➤ Enter data | |
| ➤ Delete files | |
| ➤ Find location of files stored on a system | |
| ➤ Customise toolbars for specific documents | |
| ➤ Obtain suitable hard copy by altering print quality and orientation | |
| ➤ Discuss how to connect peripheral devices to a computer | |
| ➤ Create and make use of sub-directories | |
| ➤ Demonstrate the ability to set the system settings for a specified user | |
| ➤ Add labels, axes, legends and titles to charts | |
| ➤ Use linking facility to link objects/files | |
| ➤ Incorporate two or more different formats of data into a single document | |
| ➤ Compress files to ensure maximum storage efficiency on a system | |
| ➤ Transfer files to external devices, eg writable CD, zip cartridges, for use on other systems | |

# Computer models: spreadsheets and simulations

Computer models are created to give a representation of a real-life situation on a computer. Computer models can be said to fall into two types:

➤ Models created through **spreadsheet applications**, which a user can set up for specific purposes. These models usually allow data to be presented in worksheets and as graphs or charts, making them very flexible. The most common uses for spreadsheets include:
  - *analysing finance and budget models*
  - *recording and calculating tax, loan and accounts*
  - *recording and analysing statistics.*

| | A | B | C | D | E | F | G | H | I | J |
|---|---|---|---|---|---|---|---|---|---|---|
| 1 | District | North | Foods £ | Papers £ | Extra £ | Total £ | | | | |
| 2 | Month | | Sales | Sales | Sales | Sales | | | | |
| 3 | January | | 150.78 | 344.00 | 60.00 | 554.78 | | | | |
| 4 | February | | 62.89 | 235.00 | 55.00 | 352.89 | | | | |
| 5 | March | | 123.00 | 123.75 | 35.45 | 282.20 | | | | |
| 6 | April | | 250.00 | 222.50 | 26.75 | 499.25 | | | | |
| 7 | May | | 165.75 | 136.80 | 45.30 | 347.85 | | | | |
| 8 | June | | 128.67 | 102.75 | 23.50 | 254.92 | | | | |
| 9 | | | | | | | | | | |
| 10 | | | | | Total | | | | | |
| 11 | | | | | | 2291.89 | | | | |
| 12 | | | | | | | | | | |

➤ Models that are created to **simulate** a real-life situation. Although these models cannot be altered, they can be controlled by the user. Simulation models can be used to develop ideas that would otherwise be costly or hazardous. It is important to remember that these simulations are only *representing* a real-life situation, and could never replace one. Some typical uses of simulations include:
  - *CAD (computer-aided design) of cars, boats, aeroplanes and buildings*
  - *weather forecasting*
  - *predicting events*
  - *computer games.*

Models in both of these formats are frequently used in commercial and industrial organisations. In today's world, accurate predictions about the future can make the difference between being a successful organisation and failing. Computer models are becoming an essential tool.

Organisations can gain a number of benefits from using a computer model to aid their work. These benefits include:
  - *shorter processing time for calculations*
  - *convenient to transfer information, and use in different locations*
  - *avoiding expensive mistakes in developing items or products*
  - *a safer environment for developing ideas for dangerous items*
  - *'What if?' and predictive questions can be asked.*

## Spreadsheet layout

A computer spreadsheet is displayed as a worksheet. The worksheet is made up of a series of columns and rows. Where the columns and rows join, a cell is created.

The cell reference is made up from the column (A, B, C, etc) and the row (1, 2, 3, etc) so the cell shown here is C12.

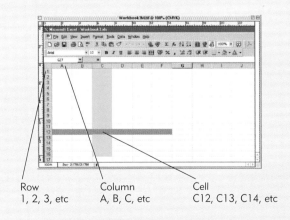

Row
1, 2, 3, etc

Column
A, B, C, etc

Cell
C12, C13, C14, etc

It is sometimes necessary for a number of cells to be active at the same time. This is done by highlighting the cells or using a cell range reference, eg C1:C16, or A12:F12 as shown on page 119. This form of cell reference is often used in a formula to calculate totals of rows or columns.

A cell can contain data as numbers, characters or formulae.

## Cell format

Cells can be formatted so that they are displayed differently. This screen displays the options available for formatting the cells in a typical spreadsheet. The options are:

*Number, Alignment, Font, Border, Patterns, Protection*

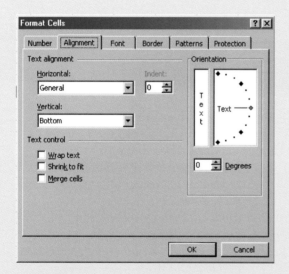

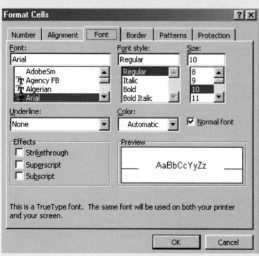

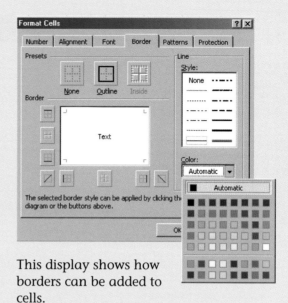

This display shows how borders can be added to cells.

This final formatting screen shows how the cells could be shaded, coloured or have a pattern added to the presentation of the worksheet.

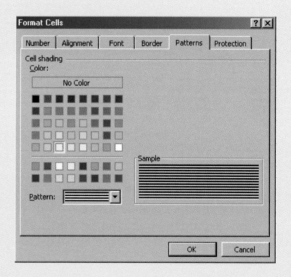

## Cell width and height

It is possible to change the width of cells to allow for long data items or titles.

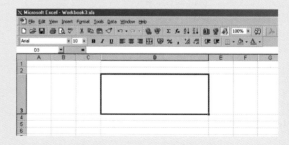

# Spreadsheet features

## Moving, cutting and pasting

Cells can be moved or copied to other areas of the worksheet. When this is done, any formulae held in the cells being moved or copied will also move. The way that the original formula was set up will affect the way it works when it is copied to a new place.

Care has to be taken to make sure that the formula is suitable for use in the new position. The cell references can be **absolute** cell references or **relative** cell references.

Some spreadsheets will default to relative values and some to absolute values.

## Sorting cells

Cells can be sorted into a chosen order depending upon the contents of the row or column. The most common sorts are carried out to produce data in alphabetical order, or ascending and descending numerical order.

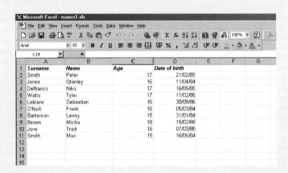

This sample below shows the same worksheet after an alphabetical sort was carried out, using the surname.

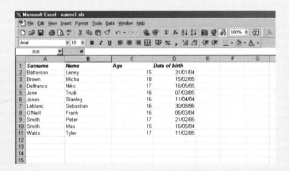

## Printing

Printing spreadsheets can be quite tricky. Spreadsheets are often very wide and deep, and would not fit upright (in the portrait orientation) on to a standard page however small the font size.

To get around this problem, printers can be set up in the landscape orientation, or sections of a spreadsheet can be printed along with a graph to make the copy easy to follow.

## Cell content

Cells can contain data in different formats, as described below.

## Numbers

Numbers may be set up in different formats such as:

| | |
|---|---|
| *money* | £32, £32.50 |
| *integers* | 2, 34, −5, 0 |
| *real numbers* | 2.00, −2.00, 7.777 |

Dates and times are also treated as numbers, but can be formatted to be displayed in a special way. For example, 25/12 could mean either 25 December or 25 divided by 12. To make it clear that this is a date, the cell has to be formatted as a date.

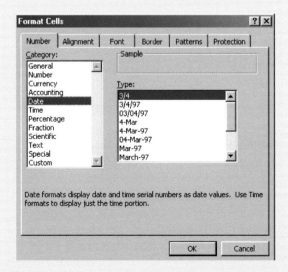

## Characters

Characters or text can be entered into a cell to create headings or to give a title to a row or column. The characters can be displayed in any font on the system, and in a range of styles, eg bold or italic.

## Formulae

Formulae can be used in a cell to allow the contents of a cell to be calculated by processing the contents of other cells in some way. If a formula is set up correctly, it can be used to carry out difficult calculations. The formula will not change unless a user changes it, so when in place it is a very reliable way of making calculations.

Formulae are made up of cell references, arithmetic operators and comparative operators. In most spreadsheets it is possible to use programming statements such as **if/then** as well as logical functions like **and**, **or** and **not**.

### Arithmetic operators

| | | |
|---|---|---|
| + | addition | C6+D6 |
| – | subtraction | C6–D6 |
| / | division | C6/D6 |
| * | multiplication | C6*D6 |
| * % | percentage | C6*25% |
| =sum( ) | sum or total | =sum(C6:D6) |

### Comparative operators

| | |
|---|---|
| = | equal to |
| < | less than |
| > | greater than |

When a formula is entered into a cell, the formula is not displayed, but rather the result of the formula. The value of a formula will be re-calculated automatically should the entry in one of the cells within the formula be changed. This is a very powerful tool in a spreadsheet as it saves the time that would be taken in going through all the entries and making changes.

As it takes a long time to enter the data initially, a careful operator will put a code on to a cell so that it is protected from accidental deletion or alteration. The protection has to be removed before the entry can be changed in any way.

## Functions

A function is a special pre-written formula that takes a value (or values), performs an operation, and returns a value. The functions are commonly used in formulae, but more complex ones can be written or adapted for special functions.

A common function used within a formula is =SUM. This is used to replace the formula of repeated addition, eg C1+C2+C3+C4+C5 could be replaced with =SUM(C1:C5).

## Absolute cell reference

If a formula is set up with absolute cell references, it will not alter when they are moved. For example, a formula E1*E4 moved from cell E6 to F17 will stay as E1*E4.

## Relative cell reference

If a formula is set up as a relative cell reference it will change as appropriate when moved. If the formula E1*E4 is copied across from cell E6 to F17, the formula will alter to become F1*F4.

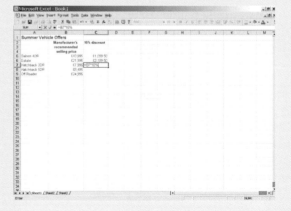

# System design

Designing a new system from scratch is a difficult task. The following items should all be worked out and checked to ensure that the system design and development will cover the required areas.

You could copy out these sections as a checklist.

---

**New system**

*Have you worked out:*

The use of the new system? ☐

What it will do? ☐

The effects of a new system on existing staff? ☐

---

**Data**

*Have you worked out:*

What data items are needed? ☐

What methods are to be used to acquire the data? ☐

The format the data will need to be in, eg numeric, characters, etc? ☐

The processes to be used on or with the data? ☐

---

**Methods**

*Have you worked out:*

The methods of input/output of data to be used? ☐

What the input/output screens or reports are going to look like? ☐

What methods or processes will be used to check for accuracy? ☐

How the data will be protected? ☐

What macros or programs could be written and used? ☐

The design of any documents generated by the system? ☐

---

**Support**

*Have you worked out:*

What hardware and software would be used? ☐

What documentation will be needed, eg system, technical and user guides? ☐

What arrangements would be needed to introduce the new system? ☐

What maintenance procedures need to be set up for the new system? ☐

---

# Graphs

Graphs can be used to display data. Most software applications allow for a range of different types of graphs to be used, as is shown below. It is important to choose a graph that will display the data in a meaningful way.

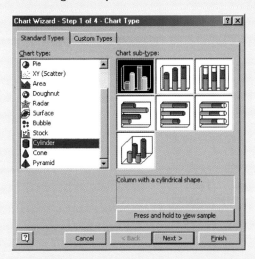

## Axes/legends

The bar chart shown below also has a **legend** placed alongside it to explain the information shown. Legends can be added to all graphs as well as labelling for the **axes**.

The fonts and colours used can all be set up to suit the type of graph. It is important to set the colours to contrast well, particularly if the graph will be printed in black and white.

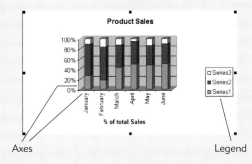

Axes                                          Legend

## 'What if?' analysis

Organisations often need to know what might happen in the future to their profits, sales or output levels if certain changes occur in the present situation.

For example, one type of question they could ask is: 'What happens if sales go up by 5%, or 10%?'

A spreadsheet can quickly calculate the effects of any changes. To carry out a re-calculation, a variable in a formula would need to be changed or added. The sample below shows how a basic sales record can quickly be altered to show a 5% and a 10% rise in sales, both by the month and as a total.

## Goal setting

In addition to the re-calculation feature, some spreadsheets allow a user to set up a desired outcome, known as 'goal setting'. An example might be: 'I am only looking to increase the food sales total. How much must I make from food sales if I am to make a 5% increase overall?'

The software can be set up to re-calculate in the spreadsheet to show the outcome (goal) that has been asked for, and the figures necessary to reach it.

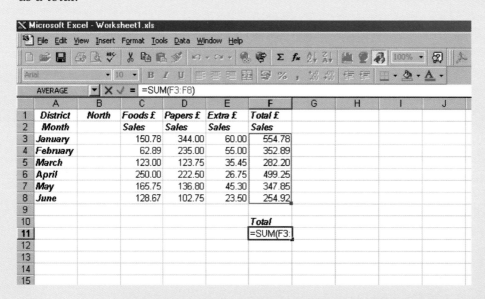

Increase of 10% and 5% in the spreadsheet

# Import/export

A range of software packages such as word processing, desktop publishing, multimedia and graphics applications have a feature to allow the import of files directly into documents.

This is a useful tool for the production of reports and presentations. The worksheet file or files from a spreadsheet can be imported directly into a document using a menu command such as 'place', 'insert' or 'import'.

The file can be imported in different formats. It can be imported as a copy. Sometimes this can be done through 'cut' and 'paste' commands. This will place a copy of a spreadsheet file into the other document. There is no link between the spreadsheet file and the document. It is just like sticking a photograph into the document with glue! The spreadsheet file cannot be changed without opening the spreadsheet application.

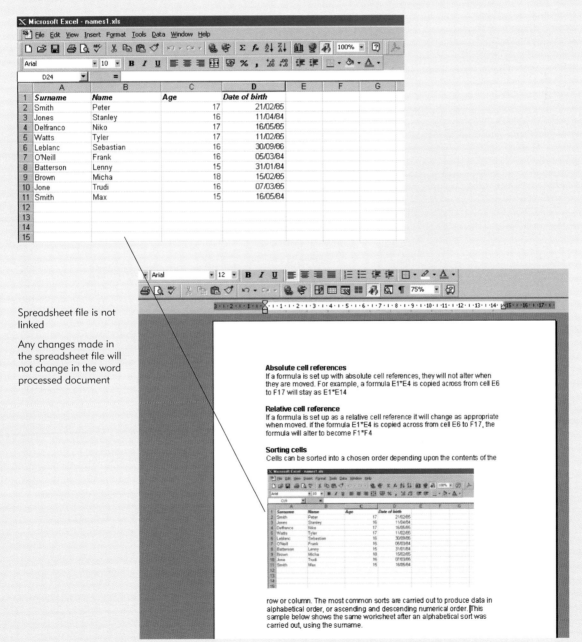

Spreadsheet file is not linked

Any changes made in the spreadsheet file will not change in the word processed document

**Absolute cell references**
If a formula is set up with absolute cell references, they will not alter when they are moved. For example, a formula E1*E4 is copied across from cell E6 to F17 will stay as E1*E14

**Relative cell reference**
If a formula is set up as a relative cell reference it will change as appropriate when moved. if the formula E1*E4 is copied across from cell E6 to F17, the formula will alter to become F1*F4

**Sorting cells**
Cells can be sorted into a chosen order depending upon the contents of the row or column. The most common sorts are carried out to produce data in alphabetical order, or ascending and descending numerical order. This sample below shows the same worksheet after an alphabetical sort was carried out, using the surname.

A second way is to keep an active link between the file and the document. A spreadsheet file can be imported through commands such as 'paste link', or 'paste special'. When the spreadsheet file is in place it can be altered at any time. If the spreadsheet file is changed, the linked file in the document will also change.

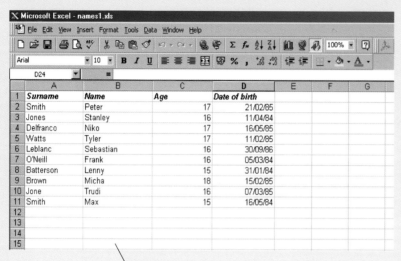

Spreadsheet file is permanently linked so that an alteration in the file will be included automatically in the document, even if it is not open at the time

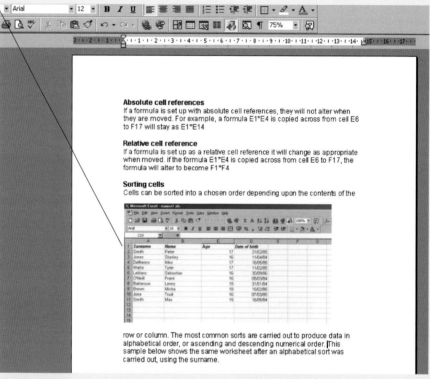

**Absolute cell references**
If a formula is set up with absolute cell references, they will not alter when they are moved. For example, a formula E1*E4 is copied across from cell E6 to F17 will stay as E1*E14

**Relative cell reference**
If a formula is set up as a relative cell reference it will change as appropriate when moved. if the formula E1*E4 is copied across from cell E6 to F17, the formula will alter to become F1*F4

**Sorting cells**
Cells can be sorted into a chosen order depending upon the contents of the row or column. The most common sorts are carried out to produce data in alphabetical order, or ascending and descending numerical order. This sample below shows the same worksheet after an alphabetical sort was carried out, using the surname.

# Macros

A macro is a series of commands that software can carry out automatically when the appropriate key is pressed.

Macros could be used to replace such tasks as:

➤ printing several ranges of cells

➤ formatting new worksheets into a set format

➤ saving, printing and closing a file.

Because they replace several actions with a single key stroke, macros can reduce the chance of errors being made when data is input. They also save time and make some of the more boring tasks easier to carry out. Where a number of users all have to perform a series of tasks, macros can be set up to standardise the way that the tasks are completed.

For example, in most spreadsheet applications, to set up a worksheet like the one illustrated below means going through all of the following stages of formatting.

- ■ Open a new worksheet
- ■ Select cell D4
- ■ Key in 'Bayrich Motor Company'
- ■ Select the Format Menu
- ■ Select the Fonts Format and select Geneva font, 14pt size, Bold style
- ■ Select the Border Format and select Outline border and a style, then click OK
- ■ Widen the cell width and height to make sure the title will fit.

All of this sequence could be replaced by a macro, saving the user from having to repeat the stages with each new sheet that is created.

Macros can be programmed into a computer system. The software usually already has standard macros. Today, it is easy to program a macro as required, using simple programming languages such as Visual Basic.

An alternative to programming macros is to use a macro record feature, available in some software applications.

## Recording macros

Spreadsheet software allows you to 'record' a macro. Just as you can record a sound and play it back, a macro can record the actions you do and, when saved, will repeat them whenever necessary.

To record the macro for formatting a new worksheet as shown above, you would:

➤ select the 'record a macro' menu

➤ choose a name for the macro

➤ carry out the sequence of actions that you want to replace with the macro – it is important to know the actions well before you start to record the macro

➤ stop the recording and save the macro (sometimes it is saved automatically).

Choose a name for the macro that describes the actions it performs. In the above example, it could be 'newsheet'. The name can have characters, numbers and understrokes, but it cannot have spaces or punctuation marks.

Macros can then be stored for future use. Screen displays list all the macros available for use within a system.

## Testing systems

### Test data

Systems always have to be tested to check that they work in the way expected.

The testing process should make sure that:

➤ every part of the system is executed at least once

> the effectiveness of every section is verified

> every route through the system is tried at least once

> the accuracy of the data after processing is verified

> the system operates according to the original design specification.

The system designer or developer tests the system by using test input data. The test data should be typical data similar to that likely to be used in the system under normal conditions. However, it should also contain data that the system should not be able to cope with.

The idea is to check that the system can handle any data in the correct format that is entered. The system should:

> store it

> process it

> report if data is incorrect in some way

> continue running.

If the test data causes the system to crash, the designer/developer must find the problem and alter the system so that it will not crash if the same type of data is entered or the same action happens again.

The whole process of design, testing and editing goes on until the users are happy that the system is working correctly.

## Dry run tests

Dry run tests are another way to test systems. Some flow charting and system design programs will run a dry run test automatically. The system is set up to run and will 'hang' at places where there is a problem, without crashing. Software applications are becoming sophisticated enough to work out whether there is a problem and whether to ignore it, and to continue with data it can handle.

## Evaluation form

When a system is being tested, it is important to focus clearly on the areas that are being checked. To try to cope with everything at once would not be sensible.

To work out how to evaluate a system:

> Think about the different processes or items that will be used, eg the screen displays, the loading of data, saving files, getting printouts.

> Work this list into a logical order according to the way different items are used in the system.

> Produce an evaluation form with the items listed, like the one shown below.

> Select items that are to be evaluated at each stage. Ask for or write down a full report of the system performance.

| Item being tested | Tester's comments | Nature of problems, if any | Refinement |
|---|---|---|---|
| Clarity of screen display | | | |
| Quality of colours on the screen | | | |
| Suitability of default font | | | |
| | | | |
| | | | |

## Detecting errors

If after a system is tried out a number of times there are still errors, the problem can be dealt with in a number of ways.

One approach is to discuss the way that the system works, stage by stage, with another developer. This focuses on the way in which the system works, and just talking it through will often allow a developer to see where the problem is.

Another approach is to use debugging routines that are held in the software. Most software applications now have simple debugging routines within the operating system software, which can use a program capable of handling most programming languages to detect problems within systems.

## Computer Control

## Bayrich Motor Company

**Bayrich Motor Company** has recently been developing new ICT systems in its factory, production lines and offices. The management group has asked for a full update on all of the systems that are now in use. The group plans to produce a video to encourage people to come and work for the company. The video will be shown in the education centre that will be opened soon.

**Control Systems Co**. is a company that specialises in control technology projects. A team of three consultants from Control Systems Co. work with the Bayrich Motor Company.

They help the company find out where systems are working correctly, and they advise the company on possible improvements.

As these consultants already know the Bayrich systems well, the management group has asked them to decide which systems should be shown on the video.

Luke, Ali and Mary – the three consultants – decide to split the analysis work up between them. Luke will start by looking at the computer aided design (CAD) systems that the design team uses. Ali will look at the production lines and Mary will look at the research and development plant.

### Learning objectives

➤ Identify the uses of CAD systems in a real context

➤ Identify the advantages and disadvantages of CAD systems

ℹ Read through **COMPUTER AIDED DESIGN (CAD) SYSTEMS AND MODELLING** in the **INFORMATION BANK** (pages 156–157).

➤ In the role of Luke, produce a report for the management group at Bayrich highlighting the main features of CAD systems and modelling, including simulation. You should discuss the advantages and disadvantages of such systems from all aspects in order to paint a true picture.

## Action Plus

The design team has been introduced to a virtual reality software application. This will allow them to experience how it feels to be inside any new model they design, before producing a prototype.

*i* Read through **VIRTUAL REALITY WORLDS** in the **INFORMATION BANK** (page 158) to find out about these systems.

➤ As a group, discuss the implications for using this type of system in the design process.

Ali is looking at the production lines. Bayrich has already introduced some computer aided manufacturing (CAM) and robotics automation into the factory. Ali decides that it would be a good idea to look not only at the systems being used now, but also at those that could be introduced to improve efficiency.

When Ali has gathered information about the systems, he intends to produce a Challenge IT brochure to go with the video. The brochure will include problems for readers to solve.

## Action Point      1  2  3  4  5  6  7  8  9

*i* Read through **COMPUTER AIDED MANUFACTURING (CAM) AND ROBOTS** in the **INFORMATION BANK** (pages 158–159).

➤ Explain how computer-controlled robots are used in car factories.

➤ Ensure that you explain how a robot might operate in terms of:

- input
- process
- output
- feedback.

➤ List other areas of life where CAM and robots could be used and explain why this would be useful.

Ali has been working on his Challenge IT brochure. He has developed an idea for a problem where readers have to write simple control programs.

A sample of two of the pages in Ali's brochure is shown on pages 131–132.

Using the following syntax, or code, write down the instructions which would move a robot from point X to point Y on the diagram below.

1 square = 1 metre

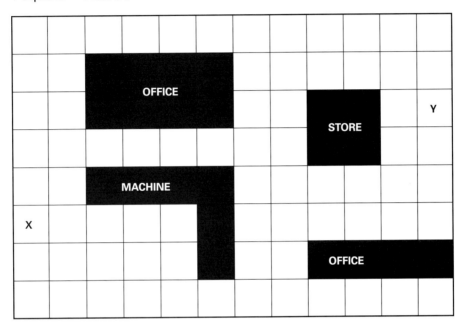

**Code:**

fd      forward
lt      left
rt      right

**Examples**

Instruction                 Code
Forward 6 metres            fd 6
Left 5 metres               lt 5

In which aspects of life might devices be controlled by programming them in ways similar to this?

## Sensors and feedback

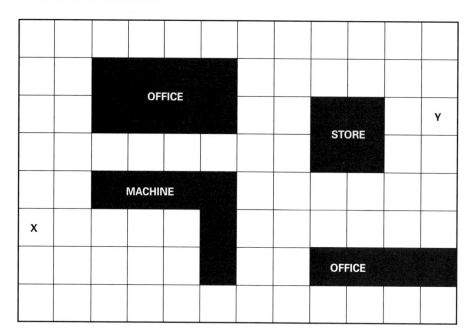

What would happen if, during the robot's journey from X to Y (on the diagram above), a large box was placed in its path? With the instructions that you have given it, could the robot avoid the box?

The answer is no, it couldn't. Unlike people, the robot has not been taught to think for itself. It would simply crash into the box and probably damage itself and the box.

To avoid this the robot could be fitted with sensors which detect any obstruction in its path. If a sensor on the front of the robot detected an obstruction, a signal would be sent to the controlling processor. This would then produce an output either stopping the robot or sounding an alarm. In a more sophisticated system the robot could be instructed to move around an obstruction.

List the types of sensors that would be needed to control the robot. In each case state why you have chosen that type of sensor.

## Learning objectives

➤ Identify the uses of computer programming

➤ Create a simple computer program to control devices

*i*   Read through **MOBILE ROBOTS** in the **INFORMATION BANK** (pages 159–160) to find out about programming robot systems. Make notes as you read.

*i*   Read about **EXPERT SYSTEMS** in the **INFORMATION BANK** (page 160) and how they can be used within industrial manufacturing. List the types of activities that could be replaced by Expert Systems.

*i*   Read through **SENSORS AND CONTROL** in the **INFORMATION BANK** (pages 160–162) to find out about the way that sensors are used in control systems.

➤ Complete the exercises that Ali has put in his brochure. If you have a LOGO program or similar control program and a turtle or buggy, you could carry out the exercise practically.

➤ Print your diagram and the sequence of commands that you used.

## Action Plus

### Learning objective

➤ Identify how programming is used in computer control

*i*   Read through **PROGRAMMING LANGUAGES** in the **INFORMATION BANK** (page 162–163).

➤ Make notes about the way programming is used in computer control.

While the others have been in the factory, Mary has been in the research and development plant (R&D). The work that goes on in R&D is very varied. Some sections look at the materials used in the production process and develop new ones. The materials that they have to think about are both the ones used in the cars and the ones used in the machinery that makes the cars.

To manage all of the different stages of the design and development stages, the R&D plant uses computer software for project management. All tasks in a project are displayed in sequence and the lengths of the tasks are shown. The following diagram shows a print-out for the first planning stages of the new car that Bayrich is manufacturing.

| Task | Jan | Feb | Mar | Apr | May | Jun | Jul | Aug | Sept |
|---|---|---|---|---|---|---|---|---|---|
| Market research | ▓ | ▓ | ▓ | | | | | | |
| Design | | ▓ | ▓ | ▓ | | | | | |
| Prototyping | | | | ▓ | ▓ | ▓ | | | |
| Testing | | | | | ▓ | ▓ | | | |
| Manufacturing | | | | | | | | ▓ | |
| Public trial | | | | | | | | | ▓ |
| Finance | ▓ | ▓ | ▓ | ▓ | ▓ | ▓ | | | |

The other issue that the R&D plant is concerned with is quality control.

*i.* Read through **PROJECT MANAGEMENT** software in the **INFORMATION BANK** (page 163) to find out how project management software can be used.

*i.* Read through **QUALITY CONTROL** in the **INFORMATION BANK** (page 164) and make notes about how quality control can affect production and development.

➤ Using project management software if it is available – or a different application if necessary – produce a management plan for a project that you are currently undertaking in school. Remember to take into account any quality control that you or others might think is necessary.

➤ Explain the advantages of project management software.

Mary also found that some of the developers use flow charts to work out the way that the processes will be carried out. Programmers use flow charts or system diagrams to help them with the logic of how a system will work before writing the program.

Ali has asked Mary to add some extra information about flow charts into his brochure. A sample of the information Mary has produced is shown here.

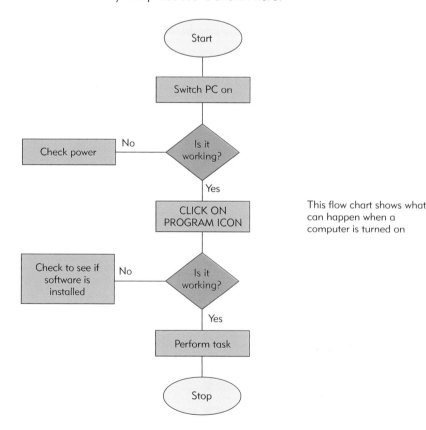

This flow chart shows what can happen when a computer is turned on

### Learning objective

➤ Examine and use flow charts

*i* Read through **FLOW CHARTS** in the **INFORMATION BANK** (page 164).

➤ Produce a flow chart for the program that you wrote in Action Point 3 (page 133). Remember that when the robot came across an obstruction it should have sounded an alarm until the obstruction was moved.

➤ Describe the role of people in this system. Give reasons why they would need to be involved.

## Action Plus

### Learning objective

➤ Describe the implications of using automated control systems

➤ Describe a method to overcome any need for human intervention into a control system like the one above.

➤ Explain what the implications would be for the workforce if this method were put in place.

## Knowledge Points

### Computer Aided Design (CAD) systems and modelling

➤ freehand sketching

➤ 3D modelling

➤ image manipulation

➤ modelling with computers

➤ testing with simulation

➤ how a simulation works

➤ why simulations are used

### Computer Aided Manufacturing (CAM) and robots

➤ controlling robots

➤ rapid prototyping

### Programming languages

➤ low level languages/assembly languages

➤ high level languages

### Sensors and control

➤ input sensors

➤ interface unit/ computer

➤ output devices

➤ feedback

### Project management software

### Quality control

## Knowledge Points (continued)

Mobile robots

Flow charts

Expert systems

Virtual reality worlds

## Skills Focus Point

➤ Discuss how to install software on a system

➤ Connect and install peripheral devices to a system, eg datalogging interface, sensors, input/output control boxes

➤ Open software application

➤ Save and name files

➤ Create and name folders

➤ Enter data

➤ Delete files

➤ Find location of files stored on a system

➤ Customise toolbars for specific documents

Mr and Mrs Sezer have had the opportunity to visit a major distribution warehouse. The warehouse is completely automated. Stock control robots are used to put stock on to the shelves and to collect the stock needed to complete orders as they come in.

As they went around the warehouses Mr Sezer noticed the differences in temperature between the different zones.

The Warehouse Manager, told them that the temperature zones had to be carefully controlled and frequently changed. The temperatures were set according to the types of goods that were being stored.

A feature that amazed both Mr and Mrs Sezer was that the warehouses were dark. The manager explained that although there was a full lighting system, it was used only for maintenance and when new installations were made.

Below is a plan of the warehouse areas, showing the amount of shelving in each area. Each full-length shelf holds a total of 150 pallets: 35 pallets in length and 4 in height.

| Frozen foods | Chilled foods | Loading bays |
| Perishables | | |
| Other goods | | |

Pallets are taken to the loading bay and split ready for distribution to the shops during the night. There is a temporary storage area in the loading bay where extra goods are kept when a shop does not require a whole pallet.

When pallets are removed from the warehouse this can affect the temperature in that section: it can become too hot or too cool for the safe storage of the goods.

## Action Point    [1]   2   3   4   5   6   7   8   9

### Learning objective

➤ Examine and report upon monitoring and control systems

ℹ Read through **MONITORING AND CONTROL SYSTEMS** in the **INFORMATION BANK** (pages 165–166) to find out how automated systems can be set up.

➤ Make notes about the system.

➤ In pairs, discuss the main aspects of a system.

➤ Use the plan of the warehouse and work out the temperature control zones that would be needed.

➤ Explain why you think the warehouse can be kept completely dark. State the implications for staffing in a situation like this one.

## Action Plus

### Learning objective

➤ Work out a monitoring program for set conditions

➤ Using the plan on page 137, construct a flow diagram that would take an automated stock robot the shortest distance around each aisle and through each temperature zone.

When Mr and Mrs Sezer return to their own Savastore, they find that the systems they use are quite similar. They have had problems in the past which have caused them to lose stock. The freezers have not been cold enough and the stock has been ruined.

They think that a similar monitoring system to the one that is used within the Automated Warehouse could be developed to run through their computer systems. They ask Luke from Control Systems Co. to come and look at their current system and see how they could improve its safety.

The information that the Sezers present to him is as follows:

- There are four fridges for the chilled goods that must be kept at 0–5°C.
- There are two large freezers, fitted with lids, that must be kept at –18°C.
- There are two small fridges that are used for drinks in the summer, but these are not close to the others.

In order to meet Health and Safety Hygiene Regulations, it is necessary to check the temperatures of the fridges and freezers at set intervals. It is also necessary to record the details in a log book, so that a Health Inspector can always see a detailed log.

## Action Point  1  **2**  3  4  5  6  7  8  9

### Learning objectives

➤ Analyse a data logging system

➤ Identify the hardware and software items required in a data logging system

*i* Read through **SENSORS AND CONTROL** and **MONITORING AND CONTROL SYSTEMS** in the **INFORMATION BANK** (pages 160–162 and 165–166).

➤ In the role of Luke from Control Systems Co., decide on and analyse the control system that would be the most effective for the Sezers to use.

➤ Describe what additional items of hardware and software the Sezer family would need if they chose to go ahead with the system.

To help the Sezers to see what the system would do and how the software would handle the data, Luke provides an outline structure diagram. He lists all of the different programs that would be used within the system and how they would work together.

They discuss the separate items.

- Fridges
- Freezers
- Drinks
- Perishables

## Action Point  1  2  **3**  4  5  6  7  8  9

### Learning objectives

➤ Read and report back about structure diagrams

➤ Construct simple monitoring programs

➤ Discuss the social and economic benefits of the use of a data logging system

*i* Read through **STRUCTURE DIAGRAMS** in the **INFORMATION BANK** (page 166) to find out what information should be given within a structure diagram.

➤ For each of the items, produce a simple control program that would keep the temperatures within the range that is needed.

➤ Create file names for your programs and produce a simple structure diagram to show the Sezers what the whole system could look like.

keep at 0–5°C

keep at –18°C

Read through **TO USE CONTROL OR NOT TO USE ...?** in the **INFORMATION BANK** (page 167).

➤ Describe the benefits of control systems for:
- the Savastore staff
- the Sezers.

## Knowledge Points

### Monitoring and control systems

➤ data parameters

➤ real-time monitoring

➤ analysing and predicting

➤ displays

### Structure diagrams

### To use control or not to use ...?

## Skills Focus Point

➤ Create and make use of sub-directories

➤ Demonstrate the ability to set the system settings for a specified user

➤ Customise toolbars for specific use

➤ Use different file formats for sending and receiving data from other sources

## The Small Theatre Company

Case study 3

The lighting engineers at the **Small Theatre Company** have put forward ideas for the improvement of the lighting systems within the theatre.

They want to introduce an automated lighting system and digital dimmers. They know that these systems can be used to control the lights which are difficult to reach manually.

The Small Theatre Company has decided that when further money becomes available they will develop the systems. In the meantime they want all of the staff to understand why it would be an advantage for the theatre to have these systems in place. They ask the consultants from **Control Systems Co**. to come in and discuss the possible systems with the lighting engineers.

### Learning objective

➤ Identify the components of an automated system in a given context

➤ Read through the information about automated spotlights that the Control Systems Co. consultants have brought to the meeting (see pages 142–144).

➤ In the role of Mary from Control Systems Co., produce a document explaining how one of the systems works.

There are two main types of lighting system to consider: these are automated spotlights and digital dimmers.

### Automated spotlights

Automated spotlights are fitted with electric motors so that the direction, focus and colour of the beam can be controlled from a remote location. They are installed in places which are dangerous or inaccessible for manual working. They could also be used to replace several conventional lights by being programmed to re-focus on different areas of the stage in each scene. They have to be accurately re-positioned for each performance and the movement during the performances must be very quiet.

The automated theatre spotlight has a special stirrup with two motors inside it. The motor at the top of the stirrup rotates the beam, and the other motor at the side changes the angle of tilt. Additional motors are sometimes added to adjust the focus, or to control the iris diaphragm. All of the motors and the colour changer can operate at the same time. The mechanism has to be very accurate because a 1° error over a distance of 40 m can mean that a spotlight misses an actor completely. The electronics needed to drive all of the motors and the optional scrolling colour changer are fitted on to the arm of the stirrup.

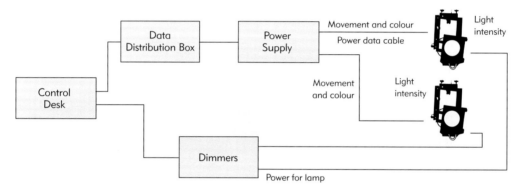

At the same time as the control desk sends the light intensity levels to a dimmer, an instruction goes out to all of the automated spotlights that are needed for the next scene. The command tells the microprocessor in the spotlight the location for the new position and the timing that is allowed to complete the move. The microprocessor then divides the distance of the move by the time needed for the move and adjusts its speed so it will reach the new position at exactly the right time.

Each motor is linked to a potentiometer which continually sends information about the current position of the spotlight back to the microprocessor. When the beam reaches the new position the potentiometer will tell the motor to stop.

There is always a manual default setting allowing people to override the system should it fail.

### Digital dimmers

Digital dimmers can be used to create different amounts of light levels very smoothly. It could be necessary to make a stage light go from bright to dark in a set time. Dimmers are used to do this.

Digital dimmers work in place of normal analogue voltage to control the brightness (intensity) of a lamp. The power is controlled by switching thyristors. The process of converting the instructions from the control desk to the dimmers is calculated by the microprocessor.

A digital dimmer recognises a number as a lighting level, eg 0 means no light, 255 means full light. The number is sent to the dimmer in binary code; this code is formed by eight pulses which are called bits. Each bit can be set as either ON or OFF.

In binary coding the first bit is 1 (ON) or 0 (OFF), the second bit is 2 (ON) or 0 (OFF), the third bit is 4 (ON) or 0 (OFF). This sequence continues up to a value of 128 (ON) and 0 (OFF). This means that if all of the bits are switched on at the same time the total is 255, ie full light:

1+2+4+8+16+32+64+128 = 255, full light.

The control lever is received by the microprocessor which calculates the exact moment that the power is turned on to give the needed intensity. The microprocessor supplies continuous information about the voltage, current and condition of the dimmer circuit to the control desk. This is a continuous feedback loop.

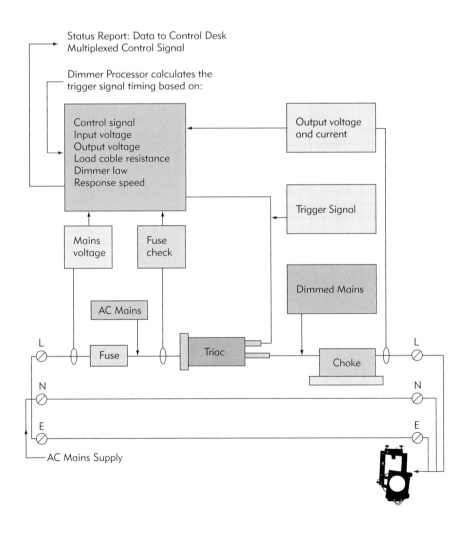

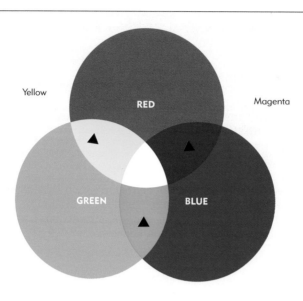

Yellow     RED     Magenta

GREEN     BLUE

Blue/Green

The three primary colours of light – red, blue and green – cannot be made by adding other coloured lights together. All of the other colours that are possible to see can be made by a mixture of these three colours.

When the three primary beams overlap each other, the middle of the overlap section combines to give white light.

Colour filters work by absorbing the light that passes through the filter, except the colour that is wanted, eg if you want the stage to look red, you would use a red filter. This effectively 'filters' all of the green and blue light only letting red light out.

The following is a list of some of the filters and special-effect filters that can be used.

| | | |
|---|---|---|
| Azure Blue | Light Rose | Light Salmon |
| Bright Rose | Middle Rose | Pink |
| Gold Tint | Follies Pink | Dark Pink |
| Pale Salmon | Slate Blue | No Colour Straw |
| Pale Chocolate | Bastard Amber | White Flame Green |
| Deep Orange | Steel Blue | Cyan (Blue/Green) |
| Magenta | Dark Blue Primary | Daylight Blue |
| Peacock Blue | Pea Green | Light Blue |
| Medium Red | Moss Green | Bright Purple |
| Pale Red | Dark Green (Primary) | Deep Lavender |
| Fluorescent Green | Dark Lavender | Dark Steel Blue |
| White Frost | Congo Blue | Light Salmon Pink |
| Blue Frost | Light Red | Chrome Orange |
| Mauve | Brushed Silk | Daylight Blue Frost |
| Smoky Pink | Cosmetic Burgundy | Neutral Density Frost |
| Bright Pink | Apricot | UV Filter |
| Moonlight Blue | Light Amber | Heavy Frost |
| Medium Blue | Medium Amber | Clear |
| Cosmetic Silver Rose | Lipstick Pink | Cosmetic Peach |
| Yellow | Pale Gold | Golden Amber |
| Straw | Red Primary | |
| Orange | Pale Rose | |

## Action Plus

### Learning objective

➤ Produce a sample program to meet a specified context

Programming languages are codes that programmers can use to give instructions to the computer to enable it to carry out a process.

➤ Read through the information about colour filters that the lighting engineers gave to Mary.

➤ Devise your own code for different colour combinations that can be created.

➤ Using your coding, write a program to turn on and off lights to create a colour sequence through the rainbow and back again.

➤ Write an explanation of what your program does or show a flow chart.

Before using the lighting systems within rehearsal and performances the lighting engineers need to carry out dry runs to test the system. The engineers have trouble in getting the time to try out the new systems as the stage is always busy with rehearsals or performances.

## Action Point        1  2  3  4  5  6  7  8  9

### Learning objectives

➤ Identify the use of dry run testing

➤ Identify the advantages and disadvantages of computer simulations

➤ Explain why a system must be tested to make sure that it is working in the way intended.

➤ The dry run test could be a computer simulation or it could be done in stages. Explain the advantages and disadvantages of each method.

The stage hands have seen the way that the automated lighting system has improved efficiency. There are now few problems with lights.

They have come up with the idea of automating some of the more difficult scene-changing processes that they have to do again and again. The main process that they would like to automate is the raising and changing of the large flats (pieces of scenery) in between scenes. Sometimes as many as 25 different flats have to be raised and changed during one performance.

On the next page is a sample of the scenery changes in Act 1 of a production of *Cinderella*. The items listed are the only items needed so the others have to be removed each time.

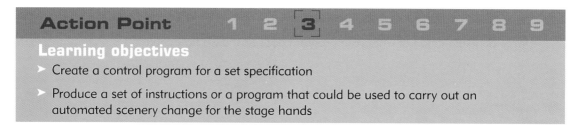

Flats are numbered F1–F8
Left stage side flats are numbered L1–L15
Right stage side flats are numbered R1–R10

**Act 1**   Scene 1   F1, F3, L2, L4, L5, L6, R3, R5
Scene 2   F2, F3, L3, L4, L9, L10, R5, R6, R10
Scene 3   F1, F2, F4, F8, L15, R10
Scene 4   F1, F3, L2, L4, L5, L6, R3, R5
Scene 5   F5, F8, L1, L2, L5, L8, R4, R9, R10
Scene 6   F1, F2, F4, F8, L15, R10
Scene 7   F1, F3, L2, L4, L5, L6, R3, R5

## Action Point   1   2   **3**   4   5   6   7   8   9

### Learning objectives

➤ Create a control program for a set specification

➤ Produce a set of instructions or a program that could be used to carry out an automated scenery change for the stage hands

To go ahead with any of the new systems would require a lot of careful planning.

The management group ask all the staff to produce a bullet point list of issues related to the way that the existing systems work and how the new systems would affect the way in which they will need to work in the future.

## Action Point   1   2   3   **4**   5   6   7   8   9

### Learning objective

➤ Identify the different methods used for implementing new systems

*i* Read through **IMPLEMENTATION** in the **INFORMATION BANK** (pages 167–168) and make notes about the different methods.

➤ Explain which method you think would be suitable for the introduction of a new lighting system in the theatre. State your reasons for choosing the method.

## Knowledge Points

### Implementation

➤ parallel running

➤ change over

➤ phased change over

➤ planning implementation

➤ Use embedding and linking facility with objects/files

➤ Incorporate two or more different formats of data into a single document

➤ Compress files to ensure maximum storage efficiency on a system

➤ Transfer files to external devices, eg writable CD, zip cartridges, for use on other systems

One of the main exhibits at the exhibition that the **Newschester Fire Service** is organising is to be about fire safety in the home. The service is keen to raise awareness of how smoke and fire can damage a home.

The early detection of fire in buildings is essential if lives are to be saved. This is no less important for homes than it is in public buildings of all types. Unfortunately, many of these systems are inadequate. People can become trapped in fires because they are unable to find their way out, or the fire is discovered too late for them to escape. People with disabilities are often at a disadvantage.

Steve Thomas, the Senior Fire Officer, has been in touch with a local college to find out how much the students know about fire protection. He would like some of the students to participate in the exhibition as he thinks this might help to put across the message.

One student, Gemma, has become increasingly interested in fire protection

both in the home and public buildings. She was pleased to discover that her parents had installed smoke detectors in their home. This made her look more closely at fire detection and safety in the college.

To Gemma's surprise, the fire detection and alarm activation system was purely manual and there was no system in place when the college was closed.

**Action Point**  **1**  2  3  4  5  6  7  8  9

**Learning objectives**

➤ Review sensors and control systems

➤ Review data logging systems

➤ Review the components of a system

➤ Read through the briefing document on page 149 which Steve Thomas has given to the students.

➤ In the role of Gemma, but using your school instead of the Newschester College (use one block if it is a large building), design a computer control system for fire detection 24 hours a day.

▸ Read through **SENSORS AND CONTROL** and **MONITORING AND CONTROL SYSTEMS** in the **INFORMATION BANK** (pages 160–162 and 165–166) again to help you with the system.

➤ Make notes on aids to help people escape from the building, eg lights to lead people along the safest route away from a fire. Remember that people who are blind or deaf will need to be considered.

# Fire detection

A lot of publicity has been given to the installation of fire detectors in homes. Fire regulations require the installation of fire detectors in public buildings, such as hotels and nursing homes.

The most common detectors in use are smoke and heat detectors.

**Heat detectors** are usually bi-metallic strips. As the heat increases the strips bend and make contact, completing the circuit. An alarm sounds as a result of the contact. This is a similar system to the one found in automatic kettles.

**Smoke sensors** are lights or laser beams directed on to a sensor. When smoke thickens at ceiling level, the lights are dimmed or the beam is broken, which activates the alarm. This system works in the same way as the infra-red beams used in automatic doors.

More sophisticated sensors are being produced all the time. One of the latest products detects the flame itself. It has been discovered that flames have their own frequency of flicker. The sensors can detect these and set off an alarm if the flicker remains at the same frequency. This sensor avoids the problem of the system being triggered by other heat sources. These sensors are placed on the ceiling and scan the room in separate quadrants (sections) in sequence. Quite often, in a large room, two sensors are used in conjunction. If one sensor detects a flame, the other sensor is contacted and then looks for the same signal. If both sensors agree on the source of the flame, the alarm is activated.

Automatic notification to the fire services is also an important feature of fire detection. The automatic notification can be made through the system sending a signal to the emergency room at the fire station. Any delay could cost lives. It is also important that this system is fail-safe: false alarms can cost lives too. It is sometimes useful for someone to check that the system is working correctly before the signal is sent through to the fire station.

### Evacuation
Getting out of a building quickly and safely when there is a fire is very important. Much research is being carried out into how buildings can be evacuated safely. Features being used to help safe evacuation include: sprinkler systems to help curb the spread of fire; automatic release of chemicals in areas of danger; and signs and indicators showing the nearest safe exit.

All of these factors have to be considered by architects, managers and the fire services when devising a system of fire detection and safety within public buildings.

Read through **MOBILE ROBOTS** in the **INFORMATION BANK** (pages 159–160) again to find out how robots could be used in this situation.

➤ Identify the input, process and output stages of the system and discuss the components for the fire detection system that would be needed at each stage.

## Action Plus

### Learning objective

➤ Use a flow chart to show processes involved in a control system

The computer control system needs to incorporate an automatic contact to the fire station.

➤ Draw a flow chart or flow diagram to show what would happen when a fire alarm went off.

Should the college choose to install the fire protection system that Gemma has developed, the system would have to undergo a 'dry run' period. This is a safety requirement for public buildings.

The dry run would be carried out when the equipment is installed. It could also be run as a computer simulation to prepare staff and students to react effectively should a fire occur somewhere in the college, eg in the kitchens. Using the computer simulation would be one of the first introductory activities that students and staff would carry out when they joined the college.

## Action Point 　　1 **2** 3 4 5 6 7 8 9

### Learning objectives

➤ Review the use of simulations to model real-life situations

➤ In a group, discuss points for and against using a computer simulation like this for the students, staff and the fire service

The siting of all the sensors is carried out as part of the contract work of Control Systems Co. They use a CAD system to draw out the shell of the building and then add the sensors and control centre in the best places.

## Action Point 　　1 2 **3** 4 5 6 7 8 9

### Learning objectives

➤ Review the use of CAD systems

➤ Describe how the features within a CAD system can make the planning of a control system more effective than producing it in other ways

# Action Plus

## Learning objective

➤ Review system documentation

The Control Systems Co. team have to draw up the implementation plan for the new system. They have the most knowledge about how the system works.

➤ Produce suitable documentation and support for the system that you have designed so that a new member of staff could see

- how the system works
- what they should do in case of a fire.

*i* Read through **SYSTEM SUPPORT** in Chapter 1's **INFORMATION BANK** (page 40) to remind you what type of documentation is needed.

## Review ICT

Throughout the case studies in this chapter, you have had the opportunity to explore a number of areas of knowledge. Make a copy of the following table and complete your table to show where you have used the Knowledge Points.

| Knowledge Points | Where Used |
|---|---|
| **Computer Aided Design (CAD) systems and modelling** | |
| ➤ freehand sketching | |
| ➤ 3D modelling | |
| ➤ image manipulation | |
| ➤ modelling with computers | |
| ➤ testing with simulation | |
| ➤ how a simulation works | |
| ➤ why simulations are used | |
| **Virtual reality worlds** | |
| **Computer Aided Manufacturing (CAM) and robots** | |
| ➤ controlling robots | |
| ➤ rapid prototyping | |
| **Mobile robots** | |
| **Sensors and control** | |
| ➤ input sensors | |
| ➤ interface unit/computer | |
| ➤ output devices | |
| ➤ feedback | |
| **Programming languages** | |
| ➤ low level languages/ assembly languages | |
| ➤ high level languages | |

| Knowledge Points | Where Used |
|---|---|
| Project management software | |
| Expert systems | |
| Quality control | |
| Flow charts | |
| Monitoring and control systems | |
| Structure diagrams | |
| To use control or not to use ...? | |
| Implementation | |

Implementation

- parallel running
- change over
- phased change over
- planning implementation

## Learning Objectives

The following Learning Objectives have been covered in Chapter 4.

Decide whether you have sufficient knowledge of each item to be able to use or write about them in the future. Leave blank the 'tick' column for any objective that you need to know more about.

| Learning Objectives | ✓ |
| --- | --- |
| Identify the use of CAD systems in a real context | |
| Identify the advantages and disadvantages of CAD systems | |
| Identify the use of virtual reality systems | |
| Identify the advantages and disadvantages of these systems | |
| Examine the way that CAM and robot systems are used | |
| Identify how programming is used in computer control | |
| Identify the uses of computer programming | |
| Create a simple computer program to control devices | |
| Use project management software, or techniques, to manage a project | |
| Identify the place of quality control within project development | |
| Examine and use flow charts | |
| Describe the implications of using automated control systems | |
| Examine and report upon monitoring and control systems | |
| Work out a monitoring program for set conditions | |
| Analyse a data logging system | |
| Identify the hardware and software items required in a data logging system | |
| Read and report back about structure diagrams | |
| Construct simple monitoring programs | |
| Discuss the social and economic benefits of the use of a data logging system | |
| Identify the components of an automated system in a given context | |
| Produce a sample program to meet a specified context | |
| Identify the use of dry run testing | |
| Identify the advantages and disadvantages of computer simulations | |
| Create a control program for a set specification | |
| Identify the different methods used for implementing new systems | |

You should have used the practical skills listed below in following the case studies in this chapter.

Decide whether you feel confident about using a skill again or are able to write about it. Leave blank the 'tick' column for any objective that you need to practise.

Record the filenames of the control programs or sequences you have created and copies of source materials.

Keep your own records of the control systems and the stages of development you used to get the results you needed.

Remember to record how you tested your system.

| Skills Objectives | ✓ |
|---|---|
| ➤ Discuss how to install software on a system | |
| ➤ Connect and install peripheral devices to a system, eg datalogging interface, sensors, input/output control boxes | |
| ➤ Open software application | |
| ➤ Save and name files | |
| ➤ Create and name folders | |
| ➤ Enter data | |
| ➤ Delete files | |
| ➤ Find location of files stored on a system | |
| ➤ Customise toolbars for specific documents | |
| ➤ Create and make use of sub-directories | |
| ➤ Demonstrate the ability to set the system settings for a specified user | |
| ➤ Use different file formats for sending and receiving data from other sources | |
| ➤ Use embedding and linking facility with objects/files | |
| ➤ Incorporate two or more different formats of data into a single document | |
| ➤ Compress files to ensure maximum storage efficiency on a system | |
| ➤ Transfer files to external devices, eg writable CD, zip cartridges, for use on other systems | |

Computer control

# Computer Aided Design (CAD) systems and modelling

## Computer Aided Design (CAD)

Computer Aided Design is a sophisticated system which enables designers to produce sketches and complete engineering drawings of any manufactured item.

Using CAD in car manufacturing requires very powerful computer equipment. The computer processing power/speed for CAD systems is generally greater than micro-computers such as the ones you probably use at school. The monitors which designers use need to be very large and have a high resolution.

CAD has a number of different features:

### Freehand sketching

This is performed with a 'pen' or 'brush' using a graphics tablet. These enable the designer to draw freehand with the image appearing on the monitor.

### 3D modelling

Once an image is created, a 3D effect can be created by plotting the co-ordinates of shapes. When all the co-ordinates are connected the designer can see a 'wireframe' image of the car or component.

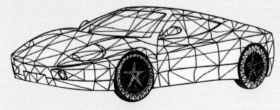

### Image manipulation

Once images are input into the computer, they can be manipulated or altered very easily. For example, a 3D design can be rotated or stretched to enable the designer to make changes.

CAD drawings are usually made up of objects. Objects are simple shapes (sometimes known as primitives) which, when combined together, make up the whole design.

A CAD system will operate as follows:

### Input

A 'pen' or stylus is used with a graphics tablet to sketch or manipulate shapes.

### Process

Procedures like rotation or re-sizing mean that the processor needs to perform complex mathematical operations.

### Storage

Modern CAD systems are large programs which require a large amount of storage and RAM. Many systems rely on 'object databases'. These databases store shapes and designs which the designer can select and use.

### Output

Most CAD systems require large monitors so that the designer can see the whole image or parts in great detail. Hard-copy output is usually obtained from a pen-plotter which is used to draw clear lines.

## Modelling with computers

One crucial aspect of car development is testing the behaviour of the car and its components whilst moving, braking or, most importantly, during an accident. You have probably seen physical crash testing on television where dummies are seated in the car and the car is driven into a stationary or moving object.

Crash testing is clearly a very expensive business as each prototype car is destroyed in the process. This must be done during development but car makers are able to program computers to simulate what happens to a car in different situations.

A computer simulation is one aspect of modelling. Computer modelling enables a situation to be reproduced in which simulated objects behave just like real ones.

### Testing with simulations

During computer simulations, many aspects of the car's performance can be tested. For example:

➤ how the car body deforms (gets pushed out of shape) during an impact

➤ how the occupants move in a crash

➤ how individual components, eg the suspension, behave whilst moving or in a crash.

### How a simulation works

In a simulation, a 'model' car is programmed to behave like a real car.

This means that engineers give the programmers details of how parts of the car will bend or how they will break during an impact. These 'rules' can be altered to make the simulated car behave differently. For example, if, during a simulated crash, the doors bend inwards towards the passenger, the programmer can strengthen or change the shape of the door before the car is 'crashed' again.

### Why simulations are used

Although computer simulation equipment is costly, it is cheaper than crashing real cars over and over again. However, there are other reasons for using simulation:

➤ Simulated crashes are safer – no one is likely to get hurt!

➤ Computer simulations save time as changes to designs can be made quickly before re-testing.

➤ Design improvements can be made on the basis of results from simulations.

Simulating a car crash for effects on humans

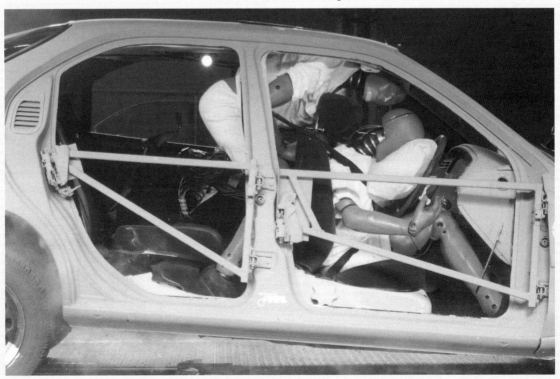

# Virtual reality worlds

One very new tool available to the designer is virtual reality (VR). A VR system is a complex computer simulation where the user can experience a situation in many dimensions. Environments are built up through very powerful modelling programs. At first the environments were of room or building interiors. Objects could then be placed in the environments. The modelling program would relate the position of an object to the interior, giving it a 'real' position in three-dimensional space.

Objects can be drawn, placed, moved and rotated to appear to act naturally within the environment. New developments in virtual reality have now linked the movement of the whole environment to a headset, gloves and shoes that a person wears. The equipment is connected to the computer through cabling or infra-red systems. The environment is then controlled by the way that the person moves, handles things or walks.

Car designers can now use VR to enable them to see what the interior of a car will look like before the car is even built. A 3D image of the car is created using a computer and this can be displayed on a monitor or more often on a headset which covers the user's eyes. All that the user can then see is the 'virtual' image of the car interior. Whichever direction the user looks, the interior can be viewed.

# Computer Aided Manufacturing (CAM) and robots

In car factories there are many repetitious tasks that can be uninteresting and where the worker can easily make mistakes.

Take a car worker who has the job of welding one particular part of the car. This might be repeated once a minute for seven hours. The job could be considered an inefficient use of resources. All that the welder is doing is lifting the welding gun into place and producing one small 'spot-weld'.

It was realised over 20 years ago that a robot could easily perform this task. A robot is a machine which can be instructed by a program to do work normally carried out by a person.

Robots can be either mobile or stationary (they either move or stand still). Because robots simulate the actions of a person, they are designed to have parts which move like human arms.

Some robots, however, are simpler and just move around a factory carrying parts from one area to another.

Computer-controlled robots in car factory

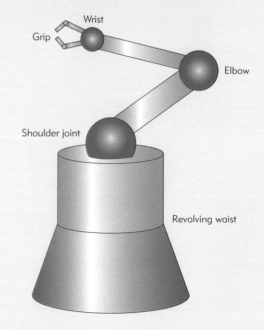

Wrist

Grip

Elbow

Shoulder joint

Revolving waist

# Controlling robots

To perform a task, robots must be programmed with instructions.

Robots are 'taught' tasks. Like a video-recorder, they can be set to 'record' mode. A human operator then moves the arm of the robot through the sequence of actions needed to perform the job. Once the sequence is complete, 'record' mode is stopped and the sequence is stored in the computer which controls the robot.

In some very modern systems, robots have tiny video cameras installed which enable them to 'see' what they are doing. The controlling computer can be programmed to recognise the shapes of different car components and then send instructions to the robot to perform the correct action.

## Rapid prototyping

A very recent development, which links CAD and CAM, is the ability to take a 3D design directly from the design engineer's computer and to produce a model (prototype) automatically.

The 3D design created using co-ordinates can be linked to a model-making machine. For example, this machine might cut paper using a laser which is programmed to cut the shape of the design. The model is built up by layering and gluing hundreds of sheets together. When this is complete, the engineers have a correctly shaped model which can be reviewed and then cast in metal or plastic.

Another method, known as 'stereo lithography', builds up a model by a laser 'curing' or hardening a special gel. After the laser has cured the gel in the correct shape of the design, the unused gel is removed and the engineers are left with a 3D model which can be cast as above.

The advantage in using these methods is the speed at which designs can be converted into models. Normally this would require skilled tool-makers and might take months. With rapid prototyping the process takes only a few weeks and so saves money.

# Mobile robots

Control systems have to follow a series of instructions to be able to work correctly. The instructions are written in a code that the computer can understand – a program. Programs are written in different languages, just as people speak different languages in different countries.

In many factories, robots are used to transport items. They can be controlled in a number of ways. The simplest method is to program the robot to follow a bright metallic strip on the floor. Sensors measure the light reading between the robot and the strip. If the robot moves off the strip the light reading will drop. The computer controlling the robot will alter the course of the robot until the sensor is in line with the metallic strip.

The robot could be programmed with instructions controlling distance and

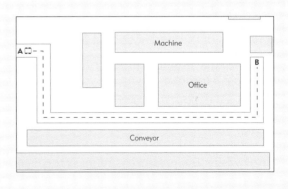

directions. In the diagram above, the robot has to move parts between point A and point B. The robot could be programmed as follows:

| Instructions | Program |
| --- | --- |
| 1 Move forward for 6 metres | fwd 6 |
| 2 Turn right 90 degrees | rt 90 |
| 3 Move forward for 10 metres | fwd 10 |
| 4 Turn left 90 degrees | lt 90 |
| 5 Move forward for 30 metres | fwd 30 |
| 6 Turn left 90 degrees | lt 90 |
| 7 Move forward for 8 metres | fwd 8 |

If a sensor is added to make a sound when the robot hits an object, then the program must include instructions for how the sensor is to operate.

An instruction written in this way is called an algorithm.

The sensor program might be written:
1 REPEAT
2 IF sensor OFF THEN move fwd ELSE
3 IF sensor ON THEN HALT AND SOUND ALARM UNTIL switch A is off
4 FOREVER5

In simple English this program means:

1 Keep doing this
2 If the sensor does not sense an obstruction keep moving normally, otherwise:
3 If the sensor senses an obstruction then stop the robot and sound an alarm until someone presses a switch to silence the alarm
4 Do this until the system is stopped.

## Expert systems

An expert system is software that can be programmed to mimic human expertise. If we are ill we consult a doctor. If the chain keeps coming off your bike you ask someone at the local bike shop about it. If we have problems with our tax assessments we consult an accountant. These people are experts in their own field.

If we can program an expert system with the knowledge of such people we no longer consult the expert – we consult the computer. Within expert systems, the user has to determine exactly what the goals and rules of the system should be.

A knowledge base consists of rules. Here is a simple example:

'It will be a sunny day *if* the pressure is high.'

'It will be a sunny day' is often called the **goal** while 'the pressure is high' is the **rule**. The goal is true if the rule is true.

We often talk about 'building' a knowledge base. This is because it is constructed in stages, making it more detailed all the time. You will see what this means when you look at the examples.

A knowledge base is made up of a set of rules. These rules are usually linked together with the word *'and'*. This is because all the statements must be true for the goal to be met. The word *'and'* is called an operator.

In the example above we might want to say:

'It will be a sunny day *if* the pressure is high *and* the sky is clear.'

Both rules must be true for the goal to be true. You might find the term *'succeed'* used to mean true. The goal succeeds if both rules are true.

## Sensors and control

Control systems usually have the following components:

➤ sensors (input devices)

➤ an interface unit linked to the central processing unit (CPU)

➤ computer

➤ actuators

➤ feedback loop.

### Input sensors

#### Touch

These sensors can be simple on/off devices that will stop a machine if it runs into a wall. The sensor touches something and the power is switched off. Other touch sensors sense the pressure between the machine and the object and can make a robot arm grip different objects with enough force to lift but not crush them.

### Light

These sensors sense the amount of light given off by objects. Many robots sense colour in this way as colours give off different light intensity and in this way they can select and sort by colour.

### Infra-red

These sensors respond on exposure to infra-red radiation. These are often used in modern security devices.

### Tilt

These sensors are used on lifting equipment to ensure large and heavy loads are lifted without the danger of falling over. They are rather like a tube with a chemical substance in it which triggers a response when it rolls to the end of the tube and comes in contact with it.

### Heat

These sense the temperature and can be used to control the heat in houses, thermal imaging cameras, the temperature of a greenhouse, etc.

### Video

These sensors film the object and the picture can be compared to ones in the memory to ensure the machine selects the right shape. They can also be used by robot arms to ensure the object is rotated into the right position for placement.

### Sound

These sensors detect sound of any type. They are commonly used in alarm systems and detect noise in buildings.

### Movement

These are also often used in alarm systems, security lighting, etc. They can sense movement within an area and are often infra-red sensors.

### Humidity

These sense the moisture in the area and can be used to control windows and fans in buildings such as swimming pools and greenhouses.

### Speed

These sensors can detect the speed of objects that are moving. They are used to sense wind speed (anemometers) for meteorologists and car speed for police.

### Smoke

These detect the presence of smoke and set off an alarm. They are commonly used in homes and public buildings to ensure safety from the threat of fires.

### Interface unit/computer

The interface unit provides a link between the computer and the input/output devices in the control system. The sensor will usually send an analogue signal. This is converted by the interface unit into a digital signal suitable for the computer. The interface unit will also enable output signals from the computer to control power to the actuators (see below).

### Output devices

These include bells, lights and sounds. Actuators are output devices that carry out an action under instruction from a computer, eg a motor.

### Feedback

Control systems use feedback loops involving a sensor, an interface and computer; controlled output devices; and the environment or situation being monitored.

### Example

Air temperature in a room could be controlled by simply switching a heater on at a certain time and off again some time later. The effectiveness of this system is limited by a lack of interaction between the air temperature and the heater. The room is likely to be too hot or too cold.

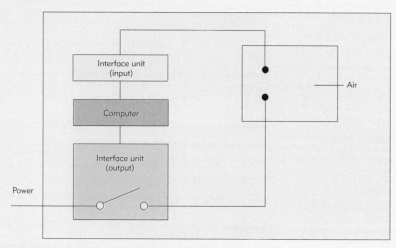

Interface unit (input)

Computer

Interface unit (output)

Power

Air

Interface unit

Matters would be improved if we could feed back information to the heater control about the effect the heater is having on the air temperature.

If a temperature sensor monitors the air temperature and sends signals to the input of a computer (via an interface) the computer can be used to switch on and off the power supply to the electric heater. If the signal shows the air temperature has fallen to a pre-set minimum temperature, the computer will output a signal to switch on the power supply to the heater. As the air temperature rises, a point will be reached where the signal from the sensor will show a pre-set maximum temperature has been reached, and the computer will switch off the power supply to the heater.

There is a loop between the components of this control system, with the final stage in the loop being the item controlled – the air. This loop is called the feedback loop.

## Programming languages

To execute an instruction a computer needs to be told what to do. It needs to be told in a code that it can understand. Programs are written in a special language and converted into machine code. Every computer has its own machine code. The languages used for programs are divided into low level languages and high level languages.

### Low level languages/assembly languages

Programmers have to know about how data is stored to be able to write a program in a low level language. The code contains details about what process is to be carried out as well as instructions to the computer about where to find the data in its memory.

The main terms to be aware of for low level programming are:

### Machine code

Program instructions in binary code, eg 0100.

### Assembler

A program that converts a program written in assembly language into machine code.

### Assembly language

A low level computer language that is close to machine code, where each instruction is a machine code instruction.

## High level languages

Programs written in high level languages are much easier to write and to understand. They still contain instructions in code, but the more advanced the language, the more structured the codes are and the easier they are to understand.

New versions of high level languages are being developed as new technologies are developed. The simplest versions of high level languages are LOGO and BASIC, but today languages like Visual Basic, C++, Java and DELPHI are more frequently used.

High level languages allow programmers to detect bugs within their programs much more easily than is possible in machine code or assembly languages. They make use of arithmetic and algebraic phrases that most people can understand, eg C=A+B or D=(4*B)/C, where the letters all represent variables.

A high level language still has to be translated into the machine code that the computer can work with. The conversion from high level to machine code is carried out by an interpreter program. Although this program checks to see that the program has been coded correctly – ie there are no syntax errors – it does not check to see that the program is logical. That is the task of the programmer.

## Project management software

The whole process of researching, designing, testing and building a car can take many years. The process also involves many people and other resources. It is vital that a project is organised in such a way that everything falls into place at the right time and in the right order.

Imagine cooking a meal. You are preparing a roast chicken, vegetables and a dessert. At 8 o'clock your chicken is cooked but you suddenly remember that you have not bought the ingredients for the dessert. You go out to the supermarket, having asked your friend to cook the vegetables. When you return, the vegetables are over-cooked and the chicken has now gone cold. By the time your guests arrive at 9 o'clock you have not made the dessert and you need some more vegetables. This project was a disaster!

If a car-designing project was organised as badly as the example above there would be delays, time-wasting and inefficient use of financial resources.

To overcome this problem, many organisations use project management software. This is modelling software which is similar to a spreadsheet program in that changes made in one section have an effect in another.

All the events associated with a project (designing, prototype building etc) are input into the system with an estimate of the time required. The software then sequences the events and displays the time required. In this way, anyone can see where they fit into the project and when. If, for example, the design of the engine takes three months longer than expected, everything moves back by three months.

# Quality control

Assembling a car is a very complex procedure and, because of the many stages, errors and faults can occur. The process of checking for mistakes and problems is known as quality control.

Car buyers want to be sure the cars they buy are built well. The last thing you want is for your new car to have a strange rattle or for the doors not to fit properly.

The planning, development and refinement stages of any project has to include quality control. If the outcome has to meet a set size, colour, weight or time, then procedures have to be set up to make sure that the quality will be maintained.

To make sure that the final product reaches the quality required, it is sometimes necessary to develop new equipment to carry out the checks.

Automated procedures are of benefit for a number of reasons. Tolerances can be set to be met which are far smaller than the human eye could detect – robots are often used to check for mistakes. Robot arms are fitted with sensors which measure the distance between the door and the body of the car. If it detects that the distance is too great, then the robot might sound an alarm to get the door removed. The checks can be done at any stage in any process, even where it could be dangerous for a human to carry out a check. The checks can be done in rapid succession, far more quickly than a human could carry out the repetitive actions.

# Flow charts

Flow charting is a way of explaining a system and the actions involved.

Flow charts use the symbols below.

The starting point or end of a system or procedure is a circle:

START/END

Any action or operation such as 'move forward' or 'turn right' is contained within a rectangular box:

OPERATION

A decision or question such as 'Is there an obstruction?' is contained within a diamond-shaped box:

DECISION

A wide range of symbols are used within systems diagrams to indicate printing/output processes and storage media.

The following flow chart shows how to make a cheese sandwich.

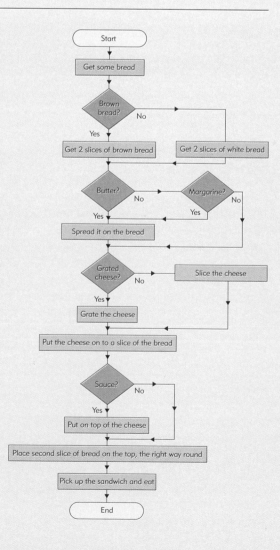

# Monitoring and control systems

The combination of sensors and computer data manipulation offers the potential for very powerful control systems such as data logging.

Data logging is the obtaining and storing of data about a physical system. You might data log the temperature of a room at one moment in time, but it would be far more sensible to use a conventional thermometer. The data logger is useful when, for example, you need to monitor the temperature of the room over a 24-hour period.

It is important to realise that in connecting any peripheral device, eg keyboard, monitor or printer to a computer, each device has to be connected via particular electronic circuits known as interfaces. Thus, when connecting sensors to a computer they are connected via either a digital sensor interface or an analogue sensor interface, according to the nature of the sensor/s being used.

A standard computer can be used as a data logger by running the appropriate data logging software. Sensors are connected via the appropriate interface.

However, more convenient – especially for longer-period monitoring and remote-site monitoring – is the battery-operated, data logging unit. This would be connected to a computer to be set up for the required task; disconnected and taken, with its sensors, to the site of the data logging; and switched on to log. At the end of the logging period it would be reconnected to the computer and the logged data would be down-loaded from the logger's memory to the computer's memory. It would then be stored on disk.

Data logging software will allow the displaying of the data in different forms such as tables, bar charts, pie charts and graphs. It is also possible to transfer the data into a database or spreadsheet for processing and analysis.

Sample data logging screen showing the recording of temperature over a period of time.

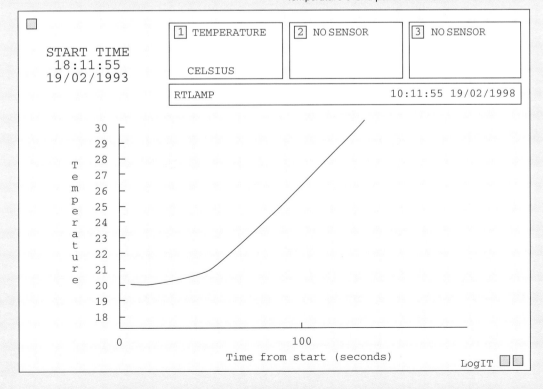

The same data recorded in a table, in numeric form, is as follows:

```
LogIT results:   RTLAMP
Sld'rttime: 18:11:55  (19/02/93)

No  Actual time     TIME
TEMPERATURE
    of reading      SECONDS  CELSIUS
1   18:11:55        0.0      20.4
2   18:12:11        16.0     20.4
3   18:12:27        32.0     21.1
4   18:12:43        48.0     22.2
5   18:12:59        64.0     23.7
6   18:13:15        80.0     25.3
7   18:13:31        96.0     27.1
8   18:13:47        112.0    28.5
9   18:14:03        128.0    30.0
10  18:14:19        144.0    31.7
11  18:14:35        160.0    33.2
12  18:14:51        176.0    34.7
13  18:15:07        192.0    36.0
14  18:15:23        208.0    37.2
15  18:15:39        224.0    38.3
16  18:15:55        240.0    39.4
17  18:16:11        256.0    40.2
18  18:16:27        272.0    41.0
19  18:16:43        288.0    41.6
20  18:16:59        304.0    42.3
```

An important use of data logging is remote use. This is when, because of the particular nature of the system to be monitored, only the sensor, suitably protected, can be situated at the monitoring site with the logger positioned at some distance from the sensor. This makes it possible to place sensors in extremely hot, cold or toxic conditions.

Another important advantage is that the user has control of the choice of time period over which the data logging is to take place.

The time intervals can be set to correspond with a working day, climatic changes or whatever periods are needed to log a situation accurately. This can range from 20 seconds to several months.

The stopping and starting of the logging can, itself, be controlled by sensors.

## Structure diagrams

Structure diagrams can make it clear how a system is set up and the links and relationships that exist between the different parts of a system.

The items shown on the diagram can be the files used to store data, the items of data stored, the macros used or even the menus themselves.

Below is a very simple diagram that shows the menus that are part of a stock control program.

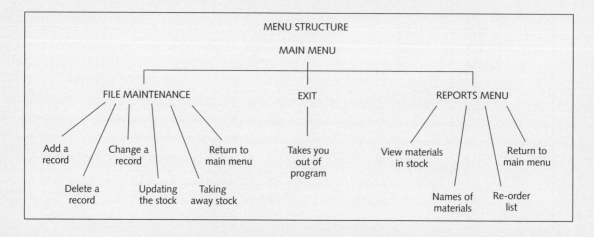

# To use control or not to use ...?

Rather as some commercial concerns have bought in computer systems only to leave them gathering dust in a corner, so robots sometimes gather dust in some factory corner. The reasons are basically the same – following fashion without due assessment of needs or due attention to specification of equipment.

It is essential, when considering a robotics system, to carry out a feasibility study. This should, ideally, involve all sections of the workforce and therefore create enthusiasm and commitment.

Technical factors which affect the decision will involve comparing robot performance with human performance, at one end of the scale, and with 'hard' automation at the other. Generally, once capable of carrying out a particular task, robots will outperform humans in speed, quality, reliability and endurance. Robots can be designed to work in conditions hazardous to humans. Hard automation will easily outperform robots if the cycle time is short and flexibility unimportant.

The potential for exceptionally high levels of quality control is a major advantage of robot technology. For example, a vision-based laser gauging system measures 148 critical dimensions of the complete body shell of the Rover 800 series, comparing them with a database-generated model to an accuracy of 0.1 mm – all within 43 seconds. Previously, the human-based system could check only two body shells per shift and then only on a limited number of dimensions!

Economic factors, of course, are the main factor in the decision. The introduction of a robotics system involves considerable financial investment that can be justified only by considerable financial gains. Cost benefits can be expected from improvements in productivity, product quality, maximisation of the use of the plant (robots can work 24-hour shifts, 7 days a week, in the dark), rapid response to changing market demands, no absenteeism and no sick-leave (if properly maintained).

Social factors are also important. Gaining the commitment of a workforce to the introduction of robots has to be achieved against the workforce's fear of losing their jobs. Even removing the need for people to do hazardous or boring jobs has to be balanced against the problem of long-term unemployment.

## Implementation

When new systems are being introduced into organisations, care has to be taken to choose the correct method of implementation.

There are a number of ways that the system could be implemented:

➤ parallel running

➤ change over

➤ phased change over

### Parallel running

To implement a system using parallel running will mean allowing the old system to run at the same time as the new system, until everyone understands the new system. The old system can then be stopped. This allows for problems to be sorted out, and gets the staff involved before the organisation becomes dependent solely upon the new system.

However this is an expensive way of implementing a new system. Extra staff and resources are needed and it may be difficult to know whether mistakes that are made are in the old or the new system.

The two systems can be very different: one with a lot of manual activity, using older equipment; the second with new unfamiliar equipment. Comparing the two systems is difficult.

## Change over

To implement a new system with a change over means to shut down the old system before starting the new system. If this method is used, the change over will usually happen when the old system is not very busy, for example in a shop it could happen in the middle of the night.

With computerised financial transactions and communications such as e-mail being sent after normal work hours, it is becoming more difficult to find a quiet time to allow a change over to happen.

Change-over implementation can create a number of problems for an organisation. The new system will not have been tried in full, and unforeseen problems could occur. This could be costly for a company if it means sales are lost or valuable data is corrupted. Another problem is that staff would not know the new system and could be slow or unhappy about its use.

The change-over implementation system is useful for a small company with limited resources available.

## Phased change over

This can be a way for a system to be introduced into large organisations that have a number of different sites or locations. The method could involve either a parallel or a change-over implementation system being used in each location.

The other common use for this method is in a large organisation, on one site, where a completely new system is to be implemented. The different stages of the system could be introduced as the staff and technical support teams are ready to implement the new system. If the old system and the new system are compatible, then the phased change over is a secure way of guaranteeing that the new system is working well.

## Planning implementation

When planning implementation, it can be useful to draw up a table like the one below, listing all the different tasks covered by the old system.

The tasks would either be replaced by new ones, with the actions for carrying out the tasks listed, or they would no longer exist. Completely new tasks would appear only in the new system column.

| Old system | Change needed | New system |
|------------|---------------|------------|
| Task 1 | | Task 1 |
| Task 2 | | Task 2 |

## Communications

### Sezer's Savastores

The Sezers have started to use their computer system for a wide range of different tasks. Although they want to expand their own network to all of their other stores, they want to know if they can communicate, without such expense.

Frederick Muzungu, from **IS..IT Ltd**, has begun to show them the benefits of simple computerised communication systems as this could be all they need.

Mrs Sezer likes the idea of the system and has asked for their own computer system to be set up so that they can start straight away. Frederick brings along a modem and some software to start with.

When their system is set up, Mrs Sezer is a bit disappointed to find that she cannot use it to communicate with as many people as she thought she would be able to.

**Action Point**   **1** 2 3 4 5 6 7 8 9

#### Learning objective
➤ Identify the main communication systems used

*i.* Read through **COMMUNICATION LINKS** in the **INFORMATION BANK** (pages 192–193) and make notes about how systems can be set up.

➤ In the role of Frederick, discuss with some members of your class (in the role of the Sezers) the best system for the Sezers to use.

### Action Plus

#### Learning objective
➤ Determine the nature of the transmission

The transmission could be set up as simplex, half duplex or duplex transmission.

*i.* Read through **DATA FLOW** in the **INFORMATION BANK** (page 193) to find out which system would be the most beneficial to the Sezers.

Mrs Sezer has a number of contacts, including some customers, that she could contact by e-mail. She has an idea to send information to them about some of the new products that they have in the shop.

## Action Point    1   **2**   3   4   5   6   7   8   9

### Learning objective

➤ Investigate the use of e-mail and send an e-mail message

ℹ Read through **ELECTRONIC MAIL** in the **INFORMATION BANK** (pages 194–195) to find out what type of communications Mrs Sezer could develop.

**Check for permission before completing the next point!**

➤ Prepare and send an e-mail to someone you know well that could be from Mrs Sezer to one of her contacts. (You should also tell the person that this is part of your GCSE work!)

Mrs Sezer has already been able to start sending e-mails to the suppliers for whom she has e-mail addresses. She is much happier with the system now, and can see that there are plenty of ways that it could help them in the stores.

Mrs Sezer has an idea that would enable any customers who have e-mail addresses to send in their orders and arrange for times to collect the goods. She hopes that this will encourage new customers to use the stores as well.

Mr Sezer likes the idea, but he cannot see how they could publicise this new service, therefore it would actually take time and money without any gains for the company. Frederick Muzungu suggests that they should consider having a bulletin board available for their customers, new customers and suppliers to use.

## Action Point    1   2   **3**   4   5   6   7   8   9

### Learning objectives

➤ Identify the ways that e-mail can be used

➤ Investigate the use of other information display systems

ℹ Read through the **INFORMATION DISPLAYS** in the **INFORMATION BANK** (page 195) to find out about other display systems.

➤ Produce a report that highlights the main factors of these systems.

## Action Plus

### Learning objective

➤ Create a suitable information display

➤ Use an appropriate software application to build up a screen image for a service similar to the Teletext service.

➤ Construct some information pages about your school or yourself.

The Sezers have decided to install e-mail on all of the computers in the Savastores. With all of the Savastores set up to receive and send messages, they decide to produce a weekly news-sheet to replace the weekly phone call they usually make to all of the stores.

**Learning objectives**

➤ Create a document suitable for electronic transmission

➤ Send an e-mail communication

➤ Receive and retrieve an e-mail communication

➤ Attach and send a document using e-mail

➤ Produce a sample news-sheet that could be from a Savastore. The contents can be invented: eg special offers, special opening hours for a bank holiday and details about new staff coming to join the company.

**Check for permission before completing this next stage!**

➤ Send an e-mail message to a number of people informing them of the news-sheet service.

➤ Ask for an acknowledgement or reply.

➤ Attach the news-sheet document to your e-mail as an attached file.

## Knowledge Points

### Communication links

➤ wired pairs/ coaxial cable
➤ fibre optics
➤ microwave transmission
➤ satellite transmission
➤ protocol
➤ baud rate
➤ ISDN

### Electronic mail (e-mail)

➤ e-mail addresses
➤ multiposting/mail lists
➤ attached files
➤ address book
➤ redirected or forwarded mail
➤ prints
➤ bulletin boards
➤ communication activities log

### Data flow

➤ simplex
➤ half duplex
➤ duplex

### Information displays

➤ Teletext
➤ Oracle

Communications

## Skills Focus Point

- ➤ Discuss how to install software on a system
- ➤ Open software application
- ➤ Alter format/layout of documents for specific reasons
- ➤ Save and name files
- ➤ Demonstrate the use of different file formats for sending and receiving data from other sources
- ➤ Create and name folders
- ➤ Enter data
- ➤ Delete files
- ➤ Find location of files stored on a system

The Publicity department at the **Small Theatre Company** thinks that the company would benefit from a more up-to-date approach to its marketing and publicity.

A number of the staff already use the Internet at home, and are starting to make use of it within the office as well. The company has an internal e-mail system and the staff think that this facility should be extended through an Internet provider.

The main items that they would like to promote are the productions that the company is putting on in the season and the sponsorship schemes that it has launched.

The publicity staff have asked for the **PR Inc Co**. consultant, Nick Hyde, to come back in and work with them to establish the best way for the Small Theatre Company to make use of the Internet.

When Nick arrives he suggests that they should spend some time looking at some of the items on the Internet to see which ones they think are the most effective.

**Action Point**   **1**  2  3  4  5  6  7  8  9

**Learning objectives**
- ➤ Investigate and make notes about the structure of the Internet
- ➤ Use the Internet to obtain specific information
- ➤ Report on useful sites on the Internet

*i* Read through **INTERNET** in the **INFORMATION BANK** (pages 195–196) to find out about the structure of the Internet.

*i* Read through **WORLD WIDE WEB** in the **INFORMATION BANK** (pages 196–197) to find out more about the World Wide Web.

**Check for permission before completing the next point!**

- ➤ Use a computer that is linked to the Internet to find a series of sites relating to actual theatres and their productions. Take care, you could end up with a lot of sites if you do not use the search engines correctly!

- ➤ If you are unsure where to start, contact somewhere big like:
  http://www.film.com   *(film/actor news & reviews)*
  http://www.bbc.co.uk/education   *(BBC site)*
  http://www.eb.com   *(Encyclopaedia Britannica site)*

- ➤ Create bookmarks of the sites that you have used.

- ➤ Report to other members of your class, in the roles of the staff at the Small Theatre Company, about the sites that you have found.

Having found out which sites the publicity staff at the Small Theatre Company liked, Nick Hyde is able to advise them on how to create a web page of their own.

The page is to be very simple with only a few hyperlinks at this stage. He suggests that they export it in HTML format (see below).

The Publicity department pull together the following information for Nick to work with. The first page will have:

An image of the Small Theatre Company building and their logo as shown below.

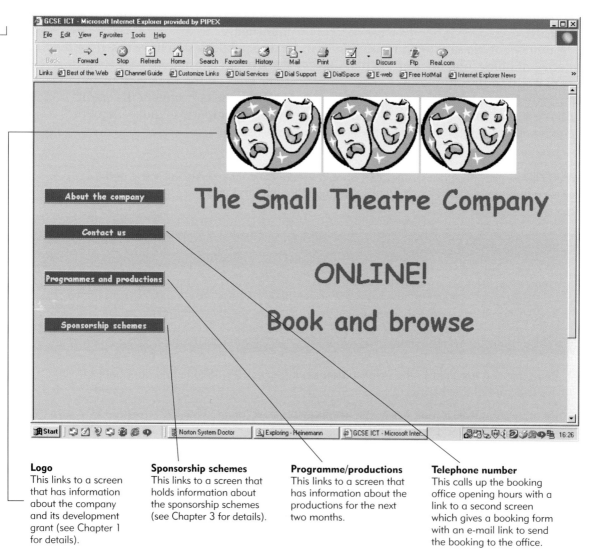

**Logo**
This links to a screen that has information about the company and its development grant (see Chapter 1 for details).

**Sponsorship schemes**
This links to a screen that holds information about the sponsorship schemes (see Chapter 3 for details).

**Programme/productions**
This links to a screen that has information about the productions for the next two months.

**Telephone number**
This calls up the booking office opening hours with a link to a second screen which gives a booking form with an e-mail link to send the booking to the office.

### Learning objectives

➤ Investigate and report on the creation of Internet web pages

➤ Create a series of web pages, with hyperlinks where appropriate

*i* Read through **PORTABLE DOCUMENT FORMAT (PDF) AND HYPERTEXT MARKUP LANGUAGE (HTML) WITH HYPERTEXT LINKS** in the **INFORMATION BANK** (page 197) to find out about designing Internet web pages.

➤ Use an appropriate software application to design these pages. If you cannot create the links, then design the pages separately, and indicate the links on printouts.

➤ You can get the information about the Small Theatre Company that you need from Chapters 1 and 3. If you are unsure about what productions to use, look in a newspaper for information about local theatres and picture houses and use seven of those titles.

## Action Plus

### Learning objective

➤ Investigate the use of video and sound within web pages

Video clips and sound can also be included with web pages.

*i* Read through **SOUND, GRAPHICS AND VIDEO** in the **INFORMATION BANK** (page 198) to find out about the type of file formats that have to be used to include video and sound in a web page.

The web pages have been put on to the computer system in the Small Theatre Company for all of the staff to give their opinions. The evaluation is to be done on-line.

## Action Point    1   2   **3**   4   5   6   7   8   9

### Learning objectives

➤ Create an evaluation form

➤ Carry out an evaluation of a system

➤ Analyse evaluation results

*i* Read through **EVALUATION TECHNIQUES** in the **INFORMATION BANK** (page 198)

➤ Create a screen that can be added to the others to evaluate the web page design

OR

➤ Create an evaluation form and print out a copy of your form. Consider the questions carefully. You should use closed questions to make sure that the system can be used effectively.

➤ Add the screen to your other screens or give out printed copies of the form.

➤ Ask several members of your class or other groups to try out your system and to carry out the evaluation as well.

➤ Analyse the results of the evaluation.

## Action Plus

### Learning objective

➤ Create a link to an evaluation analysis file

➤ Create a link to a file that can record the results of the evaluation. The system could be set up to produce a graph of the results.

## Knowledge Points

### Internet

➤ What is the Internet?

➤ FTP (File Transfer Protocol)

### World Wide Web

➤ WWW addresses

➤ search engines

➤ bookmarks

➤ Usenet

### Portable Document Format (PDF) and Hypertext Markup Language (HTML) with Hypertext links

➤ FAQ (frequently asked questions)

### Sound, graphics and video

### Evaluation techniques

## Skills Focus Point

➤ Obtain suitable hard copy by altering print quality and orientation

➤ Discuss how to connect peripheral devices to a computer, eg modem

➤ Demonstate the ability to set the system settings for a specified user

➤ Use linking facility to link objects/files

➤ Find location of files stored on a system

➤ Demonstrate the use of different file formats for sending and receiving data from other sources

The **Bayrich Motor Company** is carrying out development jointly with two other companies, one based in America and the other based in Germany. The work they are doing is taking longer than it should.

It is very difficult to get all of the people needed together at the same time. The time and costs of travelling are also beginning to cause problems.

The **IS..IT Ltd** consultant who has been working with the company suggests that they could look into the idea of teleconferencing. This would help development teams from all of the companies.

## Action Point  **1** 2 3 4 5 6 7 8 9

### Learning objective
➤ Investigate the use of tele/videoconferencing

ℹ Read through **TELECONFERENCING** in the **INFORMATION BANK** (page 199) to find out about this system.

➤ Describe the advantages and disadvantages that there would be for:
- the development team
- the Bayrich Motor Company itself.

The Bayrich Motor Company has quite a lot of sales and marketing staff based in the main office. Sometimes these staff are away from their desks for days on end. They have to visit dealers and agents all over the country.

The company has high running costs for the offices and is looking for ways to cut down on costs. The offices are all well lit and heated and feel very comfortable to work in. Each of the sales and marketing staff has his or her own desk, with a telephone/fax, and most have basic computer systems as well.

Some of the administration staff in the Finance department are already using a teleworking system, or telecommuting. This allows them to work at home most of the time and only come to the office for meetings or when they need access to restricted areas. The aim is to become a paperless office.

## Action Point    1 2 3 4 5 6 7 8 9

### Learning objective

➤ Investigate and report on teleworking and telecommuting

*i* Read through **TELEWORKING/TELECOMMUTING** in the **INFORMATION BANK** (page 199) to find out what the systems would mean for the sales and marketing staff.

➤ In the role of the Bayrich managers, prepare a case suggesting that the sales and marketing staff should move over to this way of working.

➤ Include the equipment that the staff would need to work in this way.

➤ Discuss your case with some members of your class, in the roles of sales and marketing staff.

## Action Plus

### Learning objective

➤ Identify the way on-line developments are affecting everyday life

New developments in technology are changing the way that people live their lives. Consider the users of the Internet.

*i* Read through **ON-LINE LIFE** in the **INFORMATION BANK** (page 200) for some ideas.

➤ Produce a short report about the way technology is changing the world we live in, using the following headings:
  • services, eg banking
  • shopping
  • leisure
  • health.

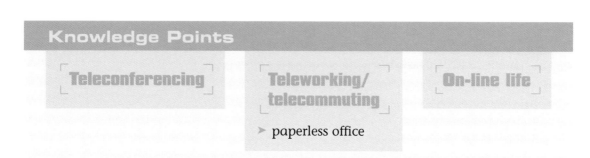

## Knowledge Points

| Teleconferencing | Teleworking/ telecommuting | On-line life |

➤ paperless office

➤ Incorporate two or more different formats of data into a single document

➤ Compress files to ensure maximum storage efficiency on a system

➤ Transfer files to external devices, eg writable CD, zip cartridges, for use on other systems

➤ Enable security procedures on a system, eg user defined passwords

## Newschester Fire Service

The exhibition that the **Newschester Fire Service** is to hold is now coming together well. There has been a good response to the plans and plenty of organisations and groups would like to take part.

The fire station office staff are worried that they cannot manage to keep up with all of the contacts and have asked for some temporary help.

Marion, from **TempIT**, has been brought in to keep in contact with all of the groups and organisations that are going to take part in the exhibition.

Her first task is to make sure exactly what type of exhibition stand or area each of the different people would like to have at the exhibition. Marion has been accustomed to using e-mail to contact people and thinks this would be a good start for her organisation of the exhibition.

She prepares the following booking form for the exhibition. She has created this file with a standard word processing application and has saved it as a normal word processing file, eg as form.doc.

| Name of organisation | Exhibition stand/area required |
|---|---|
| _____ | |
| **Contact name** | Area    10 m × 5 m ☐ <br>         5 m × 5 m  ☐ <br>         3 m × 2 m  ☐ |
| _____ | |
| **Nature of business/interest** | Stand   3 m × 1 m  ☐ <br>         2 m × 1 m  ☐ <br>         1 m × 1 m  ☐ |
| _____ | |
| Please complete and return to: <br> Marion Day <br> Newschester Fire HQ <br> Newschester <br> CH13 2BS | or e-mail directly to: <br> marion.exhib@newsfire.co.uk |

### Learning objectives

➤ Review the use of e-mail

➤ Review the method of attaching files in e-mail transmissions

➤ Prepare a similar form that could be used for booking a place at an exhibition.

**Check for permission before completing the next point!**

➤ Prepare an e-mail message that could be sent out to all interested parties, and include the booking form as an attached file.

➤ Send the e-mail to several people. Let them know this is part of your GCSE work.

## Action Plus

### Learning objective

➤ Review importing files and linking data

The way that the form has been created will not necessarily be the most effective way for Marion to be able to use the data returned.

➤ Set up a form that would allow the data to be imported directly into a spreadsheet or database, for future analysis.

Marion makes use of the Internet quite a lot at home. Her children are always asking questions for their school work and if she does not know the answer she uses the Internet to find the information. She is aware that the Internet can also be used to advertise or promote things. She suggests that the exhibition could be advertised through the county web page. Her contact at PR Inc Co., Nick Hyde, has agreed to help her with the idea.

## Action Point    1   **2**   3   4   5   6   7   8   9

### Learning objectives

➤ Review the use of the Internet for a specified reason

➤ Review the production of bookmarks

**Check for permission before completing this point!**

➤ Log on to the Internet and use an appropriate search engine to find out information about the Fire Service in the UK. Remember, the more accurately you phrase the search request, the more accurate the information you will find. Try something like 'Fire Service' AND 'United Kingdom', or 'Fire Stations' near 'United Kingdom'.

➤ Produce a bookmark list of the sites that provide interesting information.

Steve Thomas thinks this is a great idea and lets Marion go ahead and produce a draft of the layout for the page as long as it does not interfere with her other work.

The first idea she comes up with looks like this:

Click on the Events button to bring up details about the exhibition and other events being held around the county. This could then link to another screen that could have an on-line booking form, with a button that is linked to the e-mail address of the fire station.

Click to bring up details about the county fire service.

Click on the Services button to bring up details about the services that they offer.

Marion thinks that it would be a good idea to have more information about the Fire Brigade and the county provision as well as just the exhibition.

Steve has got the agreement of the County Council to have the page included on their server, but will have to get the layout and data agreed first.

**Action Point**    1    2    **3**    4    5    6    7    8    9

**Learning objectives**

➤ Review the production of web pages

➤ Review evaluation techniques

➤ Create the web pages that Marion and Nick have designed using an appropriate software application.

The following information, which is given out to the public when they ask for details about the fire service operations, might help you. Look back at the information about Newschester Fire Service in Chapter 1 for more details.

# GEC-Marconi Limited – Integrated Command and Control System

## Mobilisation equipment
In times of emergency, protection of lives, property and the environment requires a firm, fast response from professional fire fighters.

To give such dedicated people the best chance, they require correct, verified and reliable information as quickly as possible. Our mobilisation system guarantees that bridge between incident and response. Based on advanced computer hardware, tried and tested software and databases provide the necessary tools for secure mobilisation.

Once customised to take account of the local addresses, postcodes etc, the system can verify addresses instantly and accurately and assess their risk status from minimal information.

The system takes account of fire service operational procedures, location, resources and personnel data to give an instant suggestion for the number of fire fighters that should attend the scene of the fire.

Finally, the system must, upon command, mobilise the required resources. Throughout the process the system monitors all personnel and resources ensuring that status of all equipment, appliances and manpower is known and can be displayed.

The mobilisation system is further enhanced by total integration to the communication and management information systems.

The key, however, to operability is the man–machine interface. Marconi, through its work in a wide range of computer-based systems, is an acknowledged leader in this area, and through experience with many fire services has refined the interface to be practical, thorough and efficient.

Utilising a second computer in hot standby mode ensures that the system stands up against failure.

## Fire station equipment
The fire station end is rugged and flexible. Fully GD92 UK Home Office protocol approved, it is able to interface to any approved line, radio bearer system and local alerter system. It may also be configured to be the Management Information System interface at the fire station.

## Management information system
The continuous drive for improved performance and efficiency in the fire service means that large volumes of information regarding the operation of the fire service have to be collected, collated and analysed. In the past this has been a major manual task. With the new Marconi Management Information System the required information is gathered automatically by electronic means and then sorted and processed for presentation.

Much of the information is derived from the mobilisation system, and the Marconi system has all the required interfaces. However, the system can be interfaced by Marconi to any computer-controlled mobilising system.

Similarly, reports from fire services to the government or other authorities can, once authorised, be dispatched electronically and centrally processed.

The future of all electronic command and control systems rests on the free flow of information from one part of the system to another. Marconi is working to ensure that the latest advances are incorporated into its systems and that the various multimedia interfaces with the operators, users, management and policy makers are effective.

In addition to monitoring and improving performance, the system is able to help in the general management of the fire service, manpower rostering, fire safety records, breathing apparatus maintenance schedules, and many, many more can be included within the system for easy access and use.

To reduce personnel time, especially time in management, the ability to write reports electronically, both locally at control and remotely from a fire station, is a useful new facility in the gradual move towards a paperless system.

## Communications
The ability to integrate fully all manner of telecommunication systems into the mobilisation, control and management equipment is an essential part of any command and control system.

By utilising a modular approach Marconi is able to provide an initial operational solution for today which can be expanded and functionally adapted to meet evolving operational requirements.

Control of communications can be via keyboard and screen or, more commonly, via touch screen through a call concentrator suitable for any combination of operators, radio channels and digital or analogue telephone lines. The ability to record, archive and play back voice communications is provided by both instant replay and long-term recording systems.

## Resource allocation
To improve efficiency in the Fire Control Centre, continuously updated information on the status of all equipment and manpower resources needs to be available to all control staff. In the Marconi system this can be achieved either with a local monitor or large-screen resource display system which is fully integrated into the mobilisation and communications system.

Information from mobile data systems is also incorporated where available.

## Auxiliary systems
*Geographic Information System*
A high-speed electronic method of accessing maps, plans, data and photographs is becoming an essential part of any advanced command and control system. The Marconi system, based on flexible storage, allows almost instantaneous integration with icons representing all manner of risks to be immediately identified or linked to area-wide resources. Existing databases such as building plans can be accessed and integrated into the system.

- ➤ Create an evaluation form for users to complete about your web pages. Remember to phrase the questions very carefully to make sure that you get only the information that you need.

- ➤ Ask some other members of your class or other groups to access the pages, try them out and then complete the evaluation form.

- ➤ Refine the pages, if necessary, in response to their comments.

## Action Plus

### Learning objective

- ➤ Review importing files and linking data

The evaluation form could be an on-line form that is hyperlinked to the actual web pages.

- ➤ Create an on-line form, and set it up so that the data could be imported directly into a spreadsheet or database.

ℹ Read through **IMPORT/EXPORT** in Chapter 3's **INFORMATION BANK** (pages 125–126) if you need more help.

Marion had thought that the businesses that she is in contact with over the exhibition would be in office buildings somewhere in the county. She is surprised when talking to one of the contacts to find out that he is in his front room! Mike Taylor has been telecommuting for the last six months.

As a temp, Marion thinks this could be a good way for her to work in the future.

## Action Point 1 2 3 4 5 6 7 8 9

### Learning objective
➤ Review teleworking/telecommuting

➤ Explain what is meant by telecommuting.

➤ Describe all of the items that Marion will have to consider if she decides to try to work in this way in the future.

Nick Hyde has enjoyed the development of the web pages and puts another idea forward for the exhibition. He knows that there are to be seminars held during the day at the exhibition and suggests that one of these could be a tele/video conference for visitors to hear a discussion between some of the Newschester County Fire Officers and some from another area. The County Officers think this would be a good way of promoting the fire service as a forward-looking outfit. They ask Nick to arrange for a full videoconferencing link to be set up, and suggest that it could be with the fire service in the town that Newschester is twinned with in France.

## Action Point 1 2 3 4 5 6 7 8 9

### Learning objective
➤ Review methods of tele/videoconferencing

➤ Produce a briefing document for Nick to give to the officers about how the system would work and what they should be prepared for if they are to take part.

Whilst all of the preparations for the exhibition are going on the emergency room staff have had to deal with all of the on-going alarm calls and other support duties that the service offers.

They have a special communication system that makes use of high-speed transmission. The system is not connected to the normal phone lines in the station but is a separate system. It is a network system linked directly to the other emergency rooms in the county, as well as to the police and ambulance headquarters.

Calls are automatically logged and recorded as they come on-line. On the next page is a sample of a call log. It is recording the locating and controlled explosion of a suspect package. The timing of the calls is on the left, and the coded messages are in the main part of the display.

```
091629      WCI      MSG      Z34    INFORMED
091755      CJV      MSG      Z34    INFORMED
092543      BAH      1CM      INCOMING MESSAGE

INFM BOMB SQAD IN ATTENDANCE RELIEFS NOT REQUIRED AS WILL NOT BE ABLE TO REACH
INCIDENT DUE TO TRAFFIC

093B12      WBB      FCD      MOBILISING MESSAGE
            MSG NO   20433    WBB      0938      140896
            472      WrLI TO STANDBY AT 16
            TOO 0938

093907      IAICI MSG         FROM 317 BY LND LINE - 317
            417 STILL DET FURTHER 15 MINS
            - 472 TO STBY AT STN 16
0958008     CJU      MOB      CALLSIGN Z34 ATTENDING
095611      BAH      1CM      INCOMING MESSAGE
            317      StnO     X

INFM CONTROLLED EXPLOSION CARRIED OUT
EXAMINATION IN PROGRESS

0956        BAH
102321      BAN      1CM      INCOMING MESSAGE
            317      StnO     X

STOP        SSC ACB SUSPECT PACKAGE CONTROLLED EXPLOSION DEVICE FOUND TO BE SAFE
ALL APPLIANCES TO BE MADE AVAILABLE SHORTLY

102321      BAH      STP      FINAL CLASS SSC - AUTOCLOSE
103114      BAH      STA      AUTOMATICALLY CLOSED
110624      WBB      UNC      INCIDENT REOPENED
110648      WBB      LOC      F2A SUSPECT PACKAGE
110650      WBB      LOC      F2A SUSPECT PACKAGE
110709      WBB      CLO      INCIDENT CLOSED MANUALLY

- NUMBER OF APPLIANCES ATTENDING -
        I WrL1   2 WrL2   I TL
```

The emergency room has to be sure that they have a communication link that is secure, fast and reliable.

**Action Point**    1   2   3   4   5   **6**   7   8   9

**Learning objectives**
➤ Review different communication links
➤ Review network topologies

A number of types of communication links are available, and there are a number of methods of communicating.

➤ Produce a short report that describes the best system and hardware and software needed for:
  ● the emergency room (see earlier information)
  ● the rest of the fire service communications, eg telephone, e-mail and Internet communications.

*i* Look back through **COMMUNICATION LINKS** (pages 192–193) and **NETWORKS** in Chapter 2's **INFORMATION BANK** (pages 84–86) for help if needed.

## Review ICT

Throughout the case studies in this chapter, you have had the opportunity to explore a number of areas of knowledge. Make a copy of the following table and complete your table to show where you have used the Knowledge Points.

| Knowledge Points | Where Used |
| --- | --- |
| **Communication links** | |
| ➤ wired pairs/coaxial cable | |
| ➤ fibre optics | |
| ➤ microwave transmission | |
| ➤ satellite transmission | |
| ➤ protocol | |
| ➤ baud rate | |
| ➤ ISDN | |
| **Data flow** | |
| ➤ simplex | |
| ➤ half duplex | |
| ➤ duplex | |
| **Electronic mail (e-mail)** | |
| ➤ e-mail addresses | |
| ➤ multiposting/mail lists | |
| ➤ attached files | |
| ➤ address book | |
| ➤ redirected or forwarded mail | |
| ➤ prints | |
| ➤ bulletin boards | |
| ➤ communication activities log | |
| **Information displays** | |
| ➤ Teletext | |
| ➤ Oracle | |
| **Internet** | |
| ➤ What is the Internet? | |
| ➤ FTP (File Transfer Protocol) | |

| Knowledge Points | Where Used |
|---|---|
| **World Wide Web** | |
| ➤ WWW addresses | |
| ➤ search engines | |
| ➤ bookmarks | |
| ➤ Usenet | |
| **Portable Document Format (PDF) and Hypertext Markup Language (HTML) with Hypertext links** | |
| ➤ FAQ (frequently asked questions) | |
| **Sound, graphics & video** | |
| **Evaluation techniques** | |
| **Teleconferencing** | |
| **Teleworking/ telecommuting** | |
| ➤ paperless office | |
| **On-line life** | |

## Learning Objectives

The following Learning Objectives have been covered in Chapter 5.

Decide whether you have sufficient knowledge of each item to be able to use or write about them in the future. Leave blank the 'tick' column for any objective that you need to know more about.

| Learning Objectives | ✓ |
|---|---|
| Identify the main communication systems used | |
| Determine the nature of the transmission | |
| Investigate the use of e-mail and send an e-mail message | |
| Identify the ways that e-mail can be used | |
| Investigate the use of other information display systems | |
| Create a suitable information display | |
| Create a document suitable for electronic transmission | |
| Send an e-mail communication | |
| Receive and retrieve an e-mail communication | |
| Attach and send a document using e-mail | |
| Investigate and make notes about the structure of the Internet | |
| Use the Internet to obtain specific information | |
| Report on useful sites on the Internet | |
| Investigate and report on the creation of Internet web pages | |
| Create a series of web pages, with hyperlinks where appropriate | |
| Investigate the use of video and sound within web pages | |
| Create an evaluation form | |
| Carry out an evaluation of a system | |
| Analyse evaluation results | |
| Investigate the use of tele/videoconferencing | |
| Investigate and report on teleworking and telecommuting | |
| Identify the way on-line developments are affecting everyday life | |

You should have used the practical skills listed below in following the case studies in this chapter. Copy this table for your records.

Decide whether you feel confident about using the skill again or are able to write about it. Leave blank the 'tick' column for any objective that you need to practise.

Record the manner in which you have made use of electronic communications in carrying out the Action Points. State the way in which you communicated with others, eg through sending faxes, e-mail messages or on-line. Remember to record the file names of any documents that you sent as attached files.

| Skills Objectives | ✓ |
|---|---|
| ➤ Discuss how to install software on a system | |
| ➤ Open software application | |
| ➤ Alter format/layout of documents for specific reasons | |
| ➤ Save and name files | |
| ➤ Demonstate the use of different file formats for sending and receiving data from other sources | |
| ➤ Create and name folders | |
| ➤ Enter data | |
| ➤ Delete files | |
| ➤ Find location of files stored on a system | |
| ➤ Obtain suitable hard copy by altering print quality and orientation | |
| ➤ Discuss how to connect peripheral devices to a computer, eg modem | |
| ➤ Demonstate the ability to set the system settings for a specified user | |
| ➤ Use linking facility to link objects/files | |
| ➤ Incorporate two or more different formats of data into a single document | |
| ➤ Compress files to ensure maximum storage efficiency on a system | |
| ➤ Transfer files to external devices, eg writable CD, zip cartridges, for use on other systems | |
| ➤ Enable security procedures on a system, eg user defined passwords | |

## Communication links

The cost for connecting widely spread computers is very high. It is partly due to this cost that alternative methods of communicating have been developed.

Telephone lines are by far the easiest way to communicate because most places already have lines installed.

The main types of communication links (the physical joining of the sites) used today include:

➤ wire pairs/coaxial cable

➤ fibre optics

➤ microwave transmission

➤ satellite transmission.

### Wired pairs/coaxial cable

The most commonly used type are twisted wire connections. These are very cheap and used mainly because they are already in place in telephone systems. However, the standard of transmission can be spoilt by interference. The coaxial cable is a single conductor wire that is shielded by an outer sheath. Bundles of cables can be laid together underground or even under the sea.

### Fibre optics

Instead of using electricity to send data, fibre-optic systems use light. The cables are made of glass fibre that is thinner than human hair. The fibre is capable of carrying light beams for miles. The fibres can send and receive a wide range of data frequencies. The range of frequencies that a link can handle is known as the bandwidth. The broad bandwidth of a fibre-optic cable means it can be used to send and receive multimedia applications. It is a good link for transmission of voice, pictures, music and video.

### Microwave transmission

Microwave transmissions are quick and effective between sites with 'line-of-sight'. This means that the signals must go directly from relay station to relay station, with no obstructions in between. Microwave relay stations can be seen on the top of mountains or on high sites. The stations need to be within 30 miles to guarantee continuous transmission. Microwave links are not very useful in built-up areas, such as town centres, as tall buildings will break up the signals.

### Satellite transmission

Transmissions are sent from earth transmission stations to a satellite which is in orbit above the earth. The satellite receives the signal, changes the frequency of the signal and relays it back to a different station on earth. The signal has to be changed so that the incoming calls differ from the outgoing ones.

### Protocol

A protocol is a set of rules for the exchange of data between a terminal and a computer, or between two computers.

Before communications can be sent between systems, the systems need to be set up to work together. The systems have to tell each other that messages are being sent or received and to keep track of any problems that are occurring with the sending or receiving of data.

If the protocol is not accurate, the two systems could both be working well together, but the users might not be receiving the communications that they should. Standards for the speed and format of transmissions have had to be agreed amongst the range of computer manufacturers and software providers.

## Baud rate

The baud rate refers to the number of electronic signals that can be sent along a communications channel every second. Modern baud rate settings are measured in kilobytes per second (Kbps).

## ISDN

ISDN or Integrated Services Digital Network is a method of using standard telephone technology (although this is mainly fibre-optic today) to communicate digital signals. This is not as easy as it sounds as most of the telephone network was designed for analogue (voice) phones.

As computers can only 'understand' digital signals this has always meant the need for another piece of hardware to translate the digital to analogue and vice versa. You already know about this device, the modem (see page 86 in Chapter 2's **INFORMATION BANK**). Analogue signals are converted to digital and back again. This is what still happens whenever you use a telephone.

ISDN can deliver, at full capacity, 144 Kbps (kilobytes per second). This may sound very fast but it is only just capable of running a desktop conferencing system running at 128Kbps. It is, however, capable of faster delivery than a modem although it still requires a special box called a terminal adapter. New modems and upgraded ISDN lines are always coming on line and in the near future digital networks will also be in use.

---

## Data flow

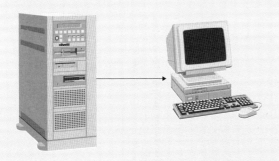

### Simplex

Data that flows in one direction only is called a simplex system.

### Half duplex

A half duplex system supports the transfer of data in both directions, but not at the same time. One channel can be transmitting data, the other one cannot, and this can then be reversed to send data the other way

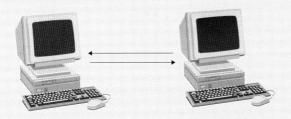

### Duplex

Duplex systems support the transfer of data in both directions, at the same time. There are two channels permanently open. There is an alternative duplex system – the asymmetric duplex – that allows the flow to be set at different speeds in the different directions.

# Electronic mail (e-mail)

Electronic mail is the process of sending messages directly from one computer to another. This could be between computers in the same room, building or to someone on the other side of the world. To run e-mail systems that go to external computers, the computers have to be connected to a modem. Most new systems today have an internal modem. For more information about modems, see **NETWORKS** in Chapter 2's **INFORMATION BANK** (pages 84–86). The computers or the network server must also have a communication software application installed.

E-mail will work only if the person to whom the mail is sent also has an e-mail facility on his or her computer. Since the introduction of the Internet, many more people can make use of e-mail, with a lot of service providers available and offering the facility at cheaper and cheaper prices.

A service provider will hold a message when sent until the receiver is ready for it.

Transfer is done very quickly, often taking only a few seconds. The mail is stored with the provider, in a mail box, until the other person 'logs on' and the program automatically collects the mail. Special software is required although most modern operating systems incorporate some support for e-mail.

# E-mail addresses

An e-mail address is made up of sections, that identify a 'unique' address, like an address of a house in a street. The e-mail address is easy to understand when you know what the different sections are, eg

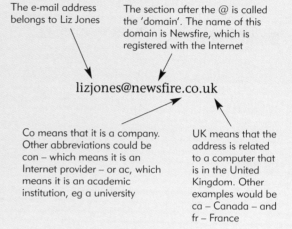

The e-mail address belongs to Liz Jones

The section after the @ is called the 'domain'. The name of this domain is Newsfire, which is registered with the Internet

lizjones@newsfire.co.uk

Co means that it is a company. Other abbreviations could be con – which means it is an Internet provider – or ac, which means it is an academic institution, eg a university

UK means that the address is related to a computer that is in the United Kingdom. Other examples would be ca – Canada – and fr – France

# Multiposting/Mail lists

A very useful feature of e-mail is the ability to multipost to a large number of users/locations at once. This is useful for sending one message or file to many users.

# Attached files

Another useful feature is the ability to attach a file to a message so that the recipient can extract the file and then use it on his or her own computer. This can be any file including graphic and picture files.

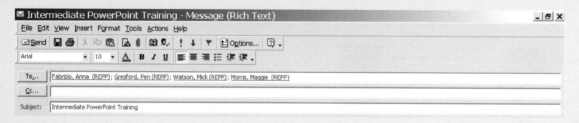

## Address book

A list of the most frequently used e-mail addresses can be stored on the computer system. If the user needs to contact someone in the address book, the software can be used to select the correct address from the list in the address book.

## Redirected or forwarded mail

When a message is received, the receiver can send on the message to other people directly. This saves keying in any documents or messages as the message will have a 'subject' section that will inform the recipient that it has been redirected or a copy sent from another source.

## Prints

If necessary, hard copy can be taken of any messages, although this does go against the principle of having e-mail in the first place!

## Bulletin boards

A bulletin board uses communication software to allow personal computers to act as public access systems. Most bulletin boards link people who have the same interests or jobs. People can have 'conversations' through a bulletin board.

To work, the computer must be switched on all the time as people can use a bulletin board at any time and it works only if messages are posted immediately – ie it is in real time.

## Communication activities log

When e-mail messages are sent, it is often important for the users to know how big each message was and how many transmissions there have been in a period of time. The software will automatically generate a report, known as an activity log, that shows where the transmissions went, and how long they took to send.

## Information displays

Teletext systems were developed before the Internet. They provide a free public information service, through television channels. The services that are common in the UK are Ceefax and Oracle systems. The data is stored on a huge database which is held centrally. Thousands of pages of information can be accessed through a keypad, usually the remote control for the television. The information is changed regularly throughout the day. People can find out information about the weather, travel conditions, news, TV programmes etc. The service is slow compared to other information systems and the user has only limited control. The system is not interactive, the user can only see the data and not add to it.

## Internet

### What is the Internet?

The Internet is essentially a worldwide connection of computers. These may be owned by businesses, governments, universities and other places of learning, and also by private individuals. Being 'on the Net' means you can access all of the information on these computers from your home computer. A computer joins the Net by installing the system and software set-ups necessary to allow the Internet to recognise it as a part of the Net.

To be connected to the Internet you need to have a modem connected to your computer. This piece of equipment translates the normal signal from the phone lines (analogue) into digital which is recognised by the computer. It also converts digital to analogue for you to send out messages, etc. via the Internet. Modern modems can transfer data at very high rates and some are approaching ISDN speeds.

To access the Internet you must subscribe to a server. You can choose, from the many available, the one that suits you.

You also need software that will enable you to access and view other Internet sites. This is usually done via the World Wide Web.

## FTP (File Transfer Protocol)

This is a way of getting files of information or programs from other computers. It can

be very useful as there are hundreds of freeware and public domain software programs that can be accessed from the Internet. There are also up-to-the-minute weather satellite photographs and current NASA projects that can be accessed via the Internet and downloaded on to your computer.

## World Wide Web (WWW)

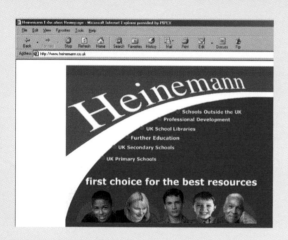

Users of the World Wide Web use a web browser, such as Internet Explorer or Netscape, and access a search engine such as Yahoo or Excite. The first site that appears is a home page. These pages are usually in HTML (HyperText Markup Language) format which allows links (hyperlinks) to be made to other pages across the world.

## WWW address

A WWW web site address is similar to an e-mail address except that it has even more information.

The web site addresses are known as URLs (**U**niform **R**esource **L**ocators) on the WWW.

The addresses all begin with

http:// this stands for **h**ypertext **t**ransfer **p**rotocol and tells the Web browser that a connection is being made.

www.bbc.co.uk/ is the server that is to be contacted in order to retrieve data.

## Search engines

In order to find a subject on the World Wide Web the search engine searches through thousands of web pages to locate areas of interest. There are web sites with web pages on every imaginable subject and they can include text, sound, movies and graphics. All of these can be accessed, read and – if you want – saved on to your computer.

When you have accessed a search engine you type in the word or phrase that you want to find out about. You can do this using capital or lower-case letters.

The way that the query is organised is very important. If you asked for 'small theatres', you would end up with thousands of sites to look at. To get around this problem search operators can be used. A search operator is similar to the query commands used in database and spreadsheet queries.

The most common search operators include:

**AND** searches for records that hold both of the words or phrases that it separates

**OR** searches for records holding either of the words or phrases that it separates

**NOT** searches for records that contain the first query word or phrase but do not have the second

**NEAR** searches records for details that are linked, eg 'dog near Labrador', would bring up only records about dogs that are Labradors.

There are other useful search engines which can be found on the Net itself.

The records displayed by a search appear in the 'best' order. The record at the top will be the one that fits closest to the search query. This does mean that when you get to record 155, you are probably not going to get much new information, and it will probably contain information about other things as well.

## Bookmarks

The Internet communication software allows users to save the addresses of the WWW sites that they like to use as bookmarks. Using a bookmark saves having to type in the long addresses each time you want to visit a site.

## Usenet

These are newsgroups formed on the Internet, where people 'talk' and send messages to each other about things that interest them. Whatever you are interested in there is probably a newsgroup for you. If not, you could set up your own!

## Portable Document Format (PDF) and Hypertext Markup Language (HTML) with Hypertext links

These are formatting tools that are needed to prepare documents for publication electronically, eg on the Internet. With modern software applications, documents are prepared and then they are 'exported' into PDF or HTML. When in HTML format the documents can be read by web browsers.

This is a method of presenting information that allows a user to jump between places in a document, usually by clicking on a word, an icon or a picture.

This allows a user to go anywhere he or she wants to throughout the document, rather than having to follow through in a set order (as with printed copy). Both help files and web pages make use of this facility.

Hyperlinks can also be linked to other web pages as well as other parts of the document.

## FAQ (frequently asked questions)

When using the Net, you will come across 'Help' buttons on different web sites. There is also often a FAQ button. This is set up with a list of the most frequently asked questions about the site. It is often a good place to look if you are having problems. The odds are that somebody else has already had the problem.

Bayrich Motors

Click Here

Bayrich Motors is a manufacturer of quality family and executive cars. The company is based at Landlow, near Newschester, where it was founded in 1924. The factory employs 3000 people, including designers, production workers and administration staff.

Source                              Destination

# Sound, graphics and video

Sound files, graphics files and video clips can all be linked into web pages. The files are created using the chosen software, eg Photoshop. When finished, the file has to be saved in a suitable format for electronic transmission. The file is accessed through hyperlinks and is 'played' whenever needed.

When creating multimedia displays for the Net, individual sound, graphics and 'movies' (video) are created first. These are then put together and saved in an authoring software application as a special type of file. To run on the Net, the file has to be lodged with a server that is set up to handle that type of file format, eg Director files are saved as .DIR files normally (which is recognised by HTML), but to be used on the Net, they are saved as .DCR files. DCR files combine compressed graphic, sound and video files together and then compress them again. The file formats are compressed so that they do not take up too much memory.

The most common file formats are:

- *Sound*   AIFF   audio interchange file format

            WAV   PC sound standard

            MIDI   musical instrument digital interface

- *Graphics*  GIF   a bitmapped colour graphics file format

            JPEG   joint photographic expert group

- *Video*   MPEG   motion picture expert group

            MPEGII   more common version that offers higher compression

            M-JPEG   uses high-quality compression from the JPEG group.

As yet not all sections and service providers fully support multimedia transmission, but in the very near future, all connections will support these systems.

# Evaluation techniques

A system is developed to meet specified needs. As a system develops, it is checked against the original specification and design criteria. Changes may be made which move the system away from the original specification.

An evaluation of a system, when it is up and running, is a good way to see how close it is to the original needs.

Sometimes the best evaluation is one by the people who are using it, watched by the developers.

An evaluation should be continuous as the system will need changing again in the future. Different aspects of a system should be looked at at different times.

Evaluation techniques can be built into the system, eg files which log errors and monitor the use of the Help file. Alternatively, a form could be developed that:

➤ has clear questions directed to the user of the system, eg can hard copy be obtained fast enough?

➤ is clear and easy to fill in.

The evaluation must be about the system and not the user ... although it could reflect problems that all users have with a system!

A simple table to record details to be imported into a database or spreadsheet is the most useful evaluation form.

| System feature | Good 1 | 2 | 3 | 4 | 5 | 6 | 7 | Poor 8 |
|---|---|---|---|---|---|---|---|---|
| Speed of printing | | | | | | | | |
| Saving files | | | | | | | | |

# Teleconferencing

Teleconferencing is the use of information technology and, in particular, satellite technology to enable face-to-face communication across great distances.

As businesses have become more international the need for better communication has become more important. International travel to business meetings is very expensive and very time-consuming. However, there is still a need for face-to-face communication.

This is the strength of teleconferencing (or videoconferencing). The virtually instant transmission available with satellite technology and the speed of modern computers have made it a viable alternative to actual face-to-face meetings.

The disadvantage is obviously the cost, but not when set against the cost of travel and the time wasted in travelling.

Great care must be taken to schedule meetings that are convenient to all parties

as time differences across continents can make it difficult for everyone to be available. Remember that when it is 9.00 am in the morning in the UK it is 5.00 pm in Singapore and 4.00 am in New York!

The equipment usually consists of a video camera, computer (to process or compress the signal) and a large screen to display the other party. The actual cost of the link via a satellite must also be borne in mind, but as it costs over £1000 to fly one person to New York on Concorde you are probably saving money!

# Teleworking/ telecommuting

Teleworking and telecommuting (the two terms mean the same) is the modern practice of using the advances in information technology to allow firms to change the way that their staff work. This often includes decentralisation from offices and making the workers' own homes their places of work.

This has many advantages for the firm and some for the worker. However, it is not always welcomed by everyone. There are disadvantages, including social isolation and greater stress for workers who have to use the home as an office.

The environmental advantage of less pollution from cars has to be set against more electricity consumption – and therefore generation – in the home.

Certainly with commuting becoming more difficult it has some advantages.

Any firm considering teleworking needs to weigh the advantages carefully against the disadvantages.

## Paperless office

When computers, and especially desktop computers, first started to become common in the 1980s, it was felt that their ability to store and process large amounts of work would lead to a 'paperless office'.

This was an ideal which has never been reached despite all the advances in information and communications technology since then. In fact, just the opposite seems to happen. Computers make us more productive and we therefore produce more paperwork. There is also the psychological problem that many people who use computers do not trust them. Many people feel happy only with hard copy – yet more paper!

# On-line life

As new technologies are developed, the future appears to be one where access to information and data communication will be made so easy that everyone will take advantage of it.

It is impossible to predict the future accurately. However, here are some thoughts on what could happen, and indeed has already started happening.

Computers and on-line services will be used as easily and frequently as people used to make phone calls. Everyone will know how to communicate through e-mail and Internet services.

Shopping will be done from the home. Electronic shopping malls will develop so that people will be able to 'walk around' their favourite stalls and major shops from their living rooms. Food orders and take-away meals will be ordered and delivery arranged through computers.

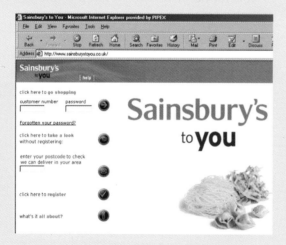

Telework will mean that working hours will not be restricted to 'office hours'. People will be able to work and communicate with others when they want to. This will help to overcome problems with time zones and travel problems.

There will be no need for the construction of huge office blocks or big business centres. However, alternative meeting places might be needed as people could become isolated if they had no contact with their colleagues at all.

Big companies will be replaced by smaller companies. New types of company will evolve where all of the workers are self-employed and work on set contracts with other people. Small companies will be able to use the Internet to reach markets all over the world, where before they would have been too small to consider international markets.

Personal services, such as banking, legal and health advice will be accessible via the communication networks, with visits being made only when necessary, eg for emergency health problems!

Interactive television, allowing the watchers to join in discussion programmes and decide on the outcome of drama programmes, will be possible. Video links will allow the system to switch from observing to one of being observed as the TV becomes a camera and transmits images of the watchers.

Electronic governments may be possible, where the borders of a country become irrelevant. People will be able to vote from home. The whole issue of where one country ends and another one begins will be open to question. With people from all over the world forming newsgroups, some of these could become the governments of the future.

## Case Study  [1] 2 3 4 5 6

## The exhibition

All the organisations are taking part in the exhibition that has been planned by the Newschester Fire Service. The exhibition is now going to be used to celebrate all walks of life, although the fire service is still to be the main focus.

- The **Small Theatre Company** is to hold a series of drama workshops at the exhibition, with the theme being 'Too hot to handle'. They will use a small work area and have a specially designed back drop.
- The **Bayrich Motor Company** is to have their new car, the Cryon, on their stand along with a simulation of a driving experience.
- The **Savastore** group are going to show a number of small demonstrations around their stand that will feature safety in the home (especially the kitchen area). They will also have display boards showing information for visitors.

- The **Newschester Fire Service** itself has decided to set up a stand with all of their publicity materials and information leaflets, but also to have a simulation of an emergency room where visitors can be involved in managing an emergency situation.

The first stages of organising the exhibition have gone well and the groups are all working to get their own areas in order.

**PR Inc Co**. has been given the task of coordinating the whole exhibition and is now ready to set up their work teams. The company has a wide range of staff who can be put into different project teams. There will be four teams, one to help each of the different organisations.

## Action Point  [1] 2 3 4 5 6 7 8 9

### Learning objective
➤ Investigate and describe the roles of different project team members

*i* Read through **PROJECT TEAMS** in the **INFORMATION BANK** (pages 217–218) to find out which types of staff should be on the teams.

➤ Select the team members with the right skills for each project. Each team might have the same types of staff, but PR Inc Co. would like to keep them as small as possible.

➤ Draw a spider diagram like the one on the next page to show what part of the project each member will be responsible for.

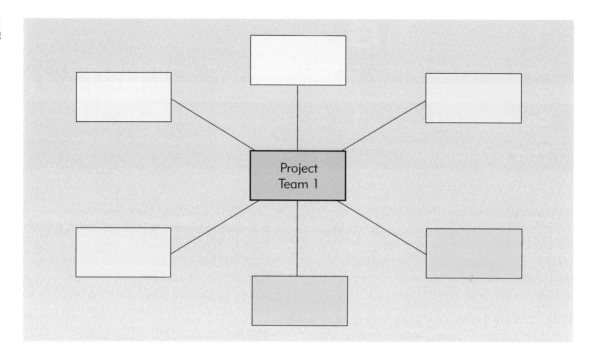

With the project teams sorted out, PR Inc Co. has called a meeting of the project team leaders. They need to work closely together to draw up an agenda for the first development meetings to be held with the organisations. They have to collect as much information as possible before they can start work with their teams.

Below are the main items that they have chosen for their meetings with the organisations.

They know that there may be items that they have forgotten about.

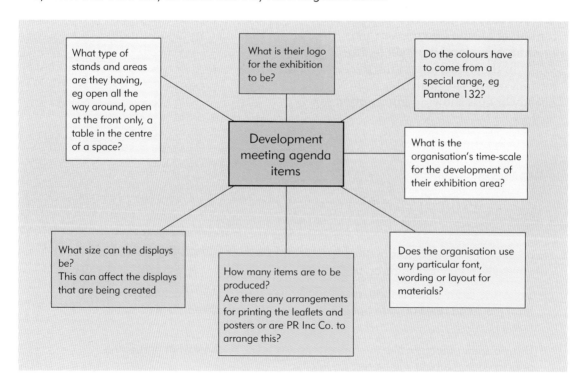

## Learning objective

➤ Carry out a basic analysis of the requirements of a project

➤ In the role of a project team leader, prepare a discussion document based on these agenda items.

➤ In the role of the project team leader, chair a development meeting with other members of your class in the roles of one of the organisations. You can choose any of the organisations at this stage.

## Knowledge Points

### Project teams

➤ managers

➤ graphic designers, animators, illustrators, image processing designers

➤ video engineers

➤ audio specialists

➤ technical engineers

## Skills Focus Point

➤ Open software application

➤ Save and name files

➤ Enter data

➤ Alter format/layout of documents for specific reasons

➤ Set up template files for pre-printed items, eg documents with letterheads, data entry into forms

*Presentations, graphics and multimedia*

The theme for the drama workshops that the **Small Theatre Company** are going to run at the exhibition is 'Too hot to handle'.

They intend to use a series of images projected on to the back of their work area to create the atmosphere.

James is the project team leader from **PR Inc Co**., and Rachel is the contact at the Small Theatre Company.

James suggests that they create a series of images in a presentation graphics application, and run as a 'slide show' by projecting them on to the back of the work area. The Small Theatre Company is going to use live music, so they do not need to have any produced for them by PR Inc. Co.

Four strong images based upon fire or heat

James has come up with the images above for use in the workshop.

The images are to be used over and over again with the resolutions and

colours being altered for different effects. He feels that the fewer images that are used, the stronger the effects will be.

## Learning objectives

➤ Investigate the use of presentation graphics applications

➤ Use a presentation graphics application to produce a slide show

*i* Read through **PRESENTATION GRAPHICS** in the **INFORMATION BANK** (pages 219–220) to find out how this software can be used.

➤ Use an appropriate software application to create a slide show of at least ten screens. Use images that you have created or scanned in to the computer.

➤ Manipulate the images so that they appear differently in the different screens.

➤ Allow other members of your group to view the presentation and refine your show, if necessary, in the light of their comments.

## Action Plus

### Learning objective

➤ Identify the methods that can be used to project images automatically

The slide show is to be projected on to the back of the work area.

*i* Read through **PROJECTION** in the **INFORMATION BANK** (page 221) to find out about methods that could be used.

➤ Prepare an information sheet that could be given to Rachel that explains how the system would work.

Rachel would like the following pieces of text to be added into the slide show. They should be placed evenly throughout the slides.

| HELP! | You scorcher | Don't touch! |

| What do you mean? | Well I'll be blowed! |

The actors will be performing to these and need each of them to be on-screen for 30 sec, 1 min, 30 sec, 45 sec and 1 min respectively.

## Action Point     1 **2** 3 4 5 6 7 8 9

### Learning objectives

➤ Add text to a presentation and graphics slide show

➤ Use automated procedures to improve an image

Read through **AUTOMATED DISPLAYS** in the **INFORMATION BANK** (pages 221–222)

➤ Add the timing sequences to your slide shows and alter the way the screen changes between the slides.

## Knowledge Points

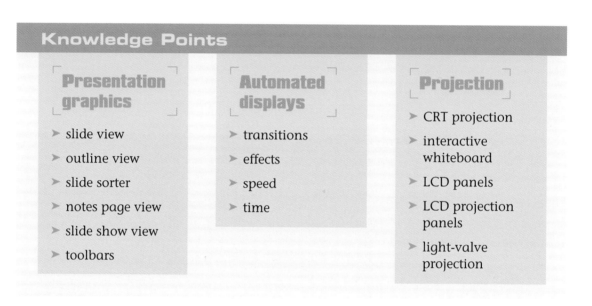

**Presentation graphics**

➤ slide view

➤ outline view

➤ slide sorter

➤ notes page view

➤ slide show view

➤ toolbars

**Automated displays**

➤ transitions

➤ effects

➤ speed

➤ time

**Projection**

➤ CRT projection

➤ interactive whiteboard

➤ LCD panels

➤ LCD projection panels

➤ light-valve projection

## Skills Focus Point

➤ Incorporate two or more different formats of data into a single document

➤ Use linking facility to link and embed objects/files

➤ Find location of files stored on a system

➤ Demonstrate the use of different file formats for sending and receiving data from other sources

➤ Demonstrate the ability to set the system settings for specified user, eg set to external projection unit display.

➤ Connect and install peripheral device to a system

## Bayrich Motor Company

The **Bayrich Motor Company** are quite happy to work on their own stand and area, but they would like to have some additional help from **PR Inc Co**. to advise them about their actual display boards.

They would like some high-quality, very large images of the new car on their stand. PR Inc Co. knows that it is an easy process to produce such images provided the pictures are created and saved in the correct format for printing.

The posters are to be full colour, which means that it could be expensive to print them using plates. Nick Hyde is leading the project team and has come up with some methods of printing and samples for the team to look at.

The images can be printed at any size, because of the way he has created and saved the image.

## Action Point 1 2 3 4 5 6 7 8 9

### Learning objectives

➤ Investigate the printing processes available for colour images

➤ Identify the file formats for graphic files

ℹ Read through **PRINTING IMAGES** in the **INFORMATION BANK** (pages 222–225) to find out how large prints can be obtained.

➤ Scan some images of cars into the computer. Make sure that you have permission to use them.

➤ Alter the size and resolution of each image and produce several images of differing size and resolution.

➤ If your printer supports 'tiling', produce large-scale images of your best image.

Read through **FILE FORMATS** in the **INFORMATION BANK** (page 225) to find out the different types of file formats for graphic images.

➤ State which file format you think would be most appropriate to use for sending the Bayrich Motor Company images to the printers.

With the poster agreed, the Bayrich Company needs to decide how it will run the simulation of the car ride.

They decide to work with an animation modelling package and to project four different animations on to the windows of a simulated car interior. The projection of the images will be synchronised so that the images appear to be moving past the windows.

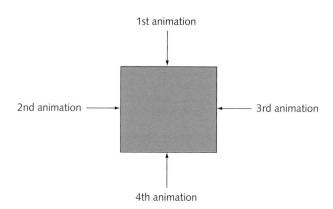

## Action Point   1  2  3  4  5  6  7  8  9

### Learning objective

➤ Create an animation sequence

 Read through **ANIMATION** in the **INFORMATION BANK** (page 226) to find out how they can be created.

➤ Use a software application to create an animation that could appear through one of the car windows.

## Action Plus

### Learning objective

➤ Create a second animation sequence linked to the first

➤ Work out how the images from one of the screens could then appear to travel back through the rest of the windows.

➤ Prepare a second screen that shows this effect.

Remember the objects in the animation will have to get larger and smaller with their position relative to the car.

## Knowledge Points

### Printing images

➤ modes

➤ process colour
spot colours and tints
on-screen images

➤ resolution
bitmap images
vector graphics
image size
monitor and printer resolutions

➤ printing methods
bubble jet
piezo ink cartridge
direct digital printing
➤ special effects

### File formats

### Animation

➤ frames
➤ 'between' tools

## Skills Focus Point

➤ Incorporate two or more different formats of data into a single document

➤ Use linking facility to link and embed objects/files

➤ Find location of files stored on a system

➤ Demonstrate the use of different file formats for sending and receiving data from other sources

➤ Demonstrate the ability to set the system settings for specified user, eg set to external projection unit display

➤ Connect and install peripheral device to a system

## Project Team  1  2  3  4  5  6

## Sezer's Savastores

The Savastore group is going to host a number of small demonstrations around its stand. The **PR Inc Co**. project team leader, Peter Jones, has suggested that they make a multimedia presentation that can be left running on the stand, whilst the staff talk to visitors about the displays.

The Sezers are keen to have some music with the displays, which pleases Peter as his idea for a multimedia display includes this. He also suggests that the display could be interactive with question-and-answer prize sessions for visitors.

Below are the notes taken by Peter Jones about the format for the display.

A small child is standing in front of a house with bags of shopping. The shopping will have come from a Savastore.

Child opens the door. Next scene is in the hallway.

From the hallway the child moves to the kitchen.

In the kitchen the child decides to put away the shopping and make a drink.

At this stage a number of different things could happen:

Mother in kitchen cooking, fire or safety hazards are pointed out, with suitable dramatic music, eg chip pan, overloaded plug socket

Child tries to light a fire and has problems with the matches, parents enter and there is trouble!

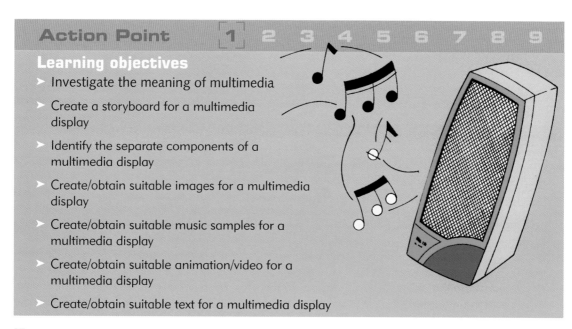

## Action Point   1 2 3 4 5 6 7 8 9

### Learning objectives

➤ Investigate the meaning of multimedia

➤ Create a storyboard for a multimedia display

➤ Identify the separate components of a multimedia display

➤ Create/obtain suitable images for a multimedia display

➤ Create/obtain suitable music samples for a multimedia display

➤ Create/obtain suitable animation/video for a multimedia display

➤ Create/obtain suitable text for a multimedia display

ℹ️ Read through **MULTIMEDIA** in the **INFORMATION BANK** (pages 226–228) to find out what is involved in a multimedia presentation.

ℹ️ Read through **STORYBOARDS** in the **INFORMATION BANK** (page 228) to see how to produce a storyboard.

➤ Produce a storyboard for one part of the Sezer's display.

➤ Work out:
- where the images are going to come from
- where the sound is going to come from
- what links and navigation route you are going to use.

➤ In the role of Peter Jones, have your ideas checked by some members of your class in the roles of the Sezer family.

➤ Make refinements to your ideas in the light of their comments.

➤ Create a short multimedia display for the Sezers based upon your storyboard.

## Action Plus

### Learning objective

> Use an authoring software application

Peter Jones suggested that the display could be interactive with a question-and-answer session.

> Contact the local fire service or look in libraries for information about fire safety and fire prevention in the kitchen.

> Create a series of questions that could be included in the display.

ℹ️ Read through **AUTHORING SOFTWARE** in the **INFORMATION BANK** (page 229) to find out about adding interactive links.

> Add additional screens to the multimedia display that you have already been working on to hold the questions.

> Make the display interactive by using an authoring application.

## Knowledge Points

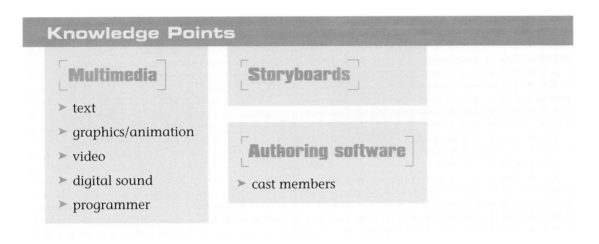

### Multimedia

> text
> graphics/animation
> video
> digital sound
> programmer

### Storyboards

### Authoring software

> cast members

## Skills Focus Point

> Open software application
> Save and name files
> Enter data
> Use linking facility to link and embed objects/files
> Alter the format/layout of documents for specific reasons
> Obtain suitable hard copy by altering print quality and orientation
> Incorporate two or more different formats of data into a single document

Steve Thomas, the Senior Fire Officer, is amazed how his little exhibition has now developed into a large-scale event.

The **PR Inc Co**. team working with the Newschester HQ staff has come up with the following ideas for the fire service stand. The layout of the area will look something like this:

Display with leaflets and booklets

Freebies to give out to the visitors

Multimedia display of the fire service in action

Series of computerised presentations that each show a different aspect of the fire service

## Action Plus

➤ Form a project team with other members of your class. Split up your project team into the following tasks:

- work out the display for the leaflets (CAD expert)
- work on a multimedia display (graphics, music and text personnel)
- work on a series of at least three short computerised presentations (text, graphics personnel)
- work out the overall effect for the stand (CAD, graphics, music personnel).

The jobs can be done by the same people, but they should not become too large for any one person.

➤ Use project management software, or work out a schedule manually, for the completion of the different stages of the project.

➤ Check with your teacher, in the role of Steve Thomas, to make sure that your plans are correct and that you have enough time. Review the points in your project plan.

➤ Start to create the Newschester Fire Service exhibition area.

➤ At an agreed time, invite a selected audience to come to the 'Newschester Fire Service exhibition area'.

➤ Set up all the displays to match the planned area.

Throughout the case studies in this chapter, you have had the opportunity to explore a number of areas of knowledge. Make a copy of the following table and complete your table to show where you have used the Knowledge Points.

| Knowledge Points | Where Used |
|---|---|
| **Project teams** | |
| ➤ managers | |
| ➤ graphic designers, animators, illustrators, image processing designers | |
| ➤ video engineers | |
| ➤ audio specialists | |
| ➤ technical engineers | |
| **Presentation graphics** | |
| ➤ slide view | |
| ➤ outline view | |
| ➤ slide sorter | |
| ➤ notes page view | |
| ➤ slide show view | |
| ➤ toolbars | |
| **Projection** | |
| ➤ CRT projection | |
| ➤ interactive whiteboard | |
| ➤ LCD panels | |
| ➤ LCD projection panels | |
| ➤ light-valve projection | |
| **Automated displays** | |
| ➤ transitions | |
| ➤ effects | |
| ➤ speed | |
| ➤ time | |

| Knowledge Points | Where Used |
|---|---|

**Printing images**

➤ modes
process colour
spot colours and tints
on-screen images

➤ resolution
bitmap images
vector graphics
image size
monitor and printer
  resolutions

➤ printing methods
bubble jet
piezo ink cartridge
direct digital printing

➤ special effects

**File formats**

**Animation**

➤ frames

➤ 'between' tool

**Multimedia**

➤ text

➤ graphics/animation

➤ video

➤ digital sound

➤ programmer

**Storyboards**

**Authoring software**

➤ cast members

The following Learning Objectives have been covered in Chapter 6.

Decide whether you have sufficient knowledge about each item to be able to use or write about them in the future. Leave blank the 'tick' column for any objective that you need to know more about.

| Learning Objectives | ✓ |
|---|---|
| Investigate and describe the roles of different project team members | |
| Carry out a basic analysis of the requirements of a project | |
| Investigate the use of presentation graphics applications | |
| Use a presentation graphics application to produce a slide show | |
| Identify the methods that can be used to project images automatically | |
| Add text to a presentation and graphics slide show | |
| Use automated procedures to improve an image | |
| Investigate the printing processes available for colour images | |
| Identify the file formats for graphics files | |
| Create an animation sequence | |
| Create a second animation sequence linked to the first | |
| Investigate the meaning of multimedia | |
| Create a storyboard for a multimedia display | |
| Identify the separate components of a multimedia display | |
| Create/obtain suitable images for a multimedia display | |
| Create/obtain suitable music samples for a multimedia display | |
| Create/obtain suitable animation/video for a multimedia display | |
| Create/obtain suitable text for a multimedia display | |
| Use an authoring software application | |

## Skills Objectives

You should have used the practical skills listed below in following the case studies in this chapter.

Decide whether you feel confident about using the skill again or are able to write about it. Leave blank the 'tick' column for any objective that you need to practise.

Record the file names and file formats for the variety of presentations and other files you have created. Make sure that you have sample files that include text, graphics and, if available, sound as well.

Remember to keep a copy of your analysis work and a record of the discussions that have taken place.

| Skills Objectives | ✓ |
|---|---|
| ➤ Open software application | |
| ➤ Save and name files | |
| ➤ Enter data | |
| ➤ Alter format/layout of documents for specific reasons | |
| ➤ Set up template files for pre-printed items, eg documents with letterheads, data entry into forms | |
| ➤ Incorporate two or more different formats of data into a single document | |
| ➤ Use linking facility to link and embed objects/files | |
| ➤ Find location of files stored on a system | |
| ➤ Demonstrate the use of different file formats for sending and receiving data from other sources | |
| ➤ Demonstrate the ability to set the system settings for a specified user, eg set to external projection unit display | |
| ➤ Connect and install peripheral device to a system, eg computer projection unit, interactive whiteboard | |
| ➤ Obtain suitable hard copy by altering print quality and orientation | |

# Project teams

To work together on graphics, presentation graphics or multimedia projects, teams of people with different skills need to be brought together.

The project team for the exhibition will have to demonstrate the following skills:

➤ produce a range of images from different sources

➤ produce work completed on time and within a tight, non-negotiable budget

➤ produce ideas in a range of formats, eg animation, screen- and paper-based images

➤ provide a system that works efficiently, is cost effective and is easy to handle

➤ provide text that is clear.

The following descriptions give an overview of the roles and nature of work that the staff for the project teams should be able to offer. It also itemises the types of hardware and software that the person should be able to use and have available for the work.

## Managers

They will administrate and manage all aspects of a project. A manager is always at the centre of the action with overall responsibility for the development and implementation of a project as well as the day-to-day operations.

Managers carry out work using spreadsheets, project management software, database queries, presentations and general text documents. The documents that they produce are automatically backed up each night by a tape streamer. They produce reports, analytical documents, budgets, financial projections, memos, slide shows for presentations and letters.

The systems that they use have integrated software packages (spreadsheet, database, word processing and presentation software) installed on them that allow easy transfer of files between the separate parts of the package.

Additionally, two lap-top machines are available with the presentation software installed. These are used when visiting clients. They use stand-alone 200 MHz machines with 2 GB hard drives. Because they do not carry out a lot of graphics work they have only 16 MB RAM. Some of the managers would like to have more RAM so that they could speed up the presentation software.

Most of their work is carried out by inputting the data via a keyboard, but all have a mouse and one system has a scanner with OCR software. The machines all have internal CD-ROM drives and internal modems. Some of the managers use the Internet and e-mail systems for keeping in contact with their clients.

## Graphic designers, animators, illustrators, image processing designers

The designers produce hard copy for advertisements, leaflets and other documents needed by clients. They also produce images that can be developed further or used by the clients themselves. Some clients bring in their own artwork and the designers set up and print the files for them. Other projects involve producing slide shows and presentation shows which have timed and phased changes between screens. They all use a combination of software programs for enhancing/altering scanned or digital images, creating computer-generated images, layouts and animated sequences. They all have QuickTime installed. Their work makes use of different colour systems and all of the software programs can handle both RGB and CMYK colour (see page 222).

Designers at work

They use the Pantone Colour system for setting the colours.

All designers have similar systems. The systems are all 275 MHz machines with 4 GB hard drives. Each machine has 128 MB RAM and a 12-speed CD-ROM drive. They have an internal 33k6 voice/fax/modem and are linked to shared scanners. Some of the designers choose to use graphics tablets whilst the others prefer to use a mouse. Some images are captured using digital cameras and are then worked on using the systems. In addition, all machines have external storage drives for back-up and file formatting for printing.

Each machine is linked to a large-format colour inkjet printer as well as the choice of a 600 dpi PostScript colour laser printer or a standard 600 dpi monochrome PostScript laser printer.

## Video engineers

The engineer produces files in the necessary format for the programmer to use with the authoring software.

The video engineers have similar machines to the graphic designers. In addition, their systems are connected to an editing desk. The analogue videos are played into the computers where the files are manipulated to change them from analogue to digital files.

The computer is linked to a broadcast standard VCR via a special cable. The computer contains a video capture card and video capture software.

The software allows the video engineer to alter the images and introduce special effects if needed. The video files are very large and although the software used compresses them as much as possible, the files are still very large. The best storage engineers have found for the files is CD-ROM, which is slow but accurate.

## Audio specialists

The audio specialists have computers that are connected to a mixing desk. The sound is recorded and the analogue signal from a microphone is manipulated to boost or dampen the different pitches. The audio specialist mixes different sounds and adds them to an animation or presentation.

The files are stored on CD-ROM where they are saved as digital sound files not as analogue audio tracks.

## Technical engineers

The programmers and software engineers have systems that are similar to the creative designers, but they have the full versions of the authoring software installed instead of the graphics/image manipulation software. The systems are not connected to the high-quality printers but use a 300 dpi laser. All of them have large monitors (20 in).

The engineers input most data via the keyboard, but use the mouse or keyboard short-cuts to navigate through the software.

One of their tasks is to plan the navigation route – how users will move around the system. They develop the 'run-time engines' of the systems. They develop software codes for different sections of the system and as the sections are finished they are plugged in directly to the run-time engines.

The programmers and software engineers work with the other team members to de-bug the system as it is being developed. If the program crashes or unexpected results are obtained, the programmers may need to search through vast amounts of coding to find the errors.

# Presentation graphics

Presentation graphics software applications have changed the way that displays and information can be presented.

With the common applications in use today items for a presentation can be created as:

➤ overheads

➤ paper printouts

➤ 35mm slides or

➤ on-screen presentations.

It is easy to provide speaker's notes, outlines of the presentation and handouts directly from the screen using the software.

One useful feature of this software is to create the handouts for discussion groups as the discussions are happening. A computer that holds the data is connected to a projection unit (see **PROJECTION** for details) and the software application is loaded. When a discussion is taking place, the notes or important points about the discussion can be displayed for all to see. This could mean that an existing screen is changed due to comments coming out of the discussion.

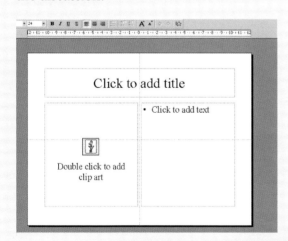

A presentation is prepared by creating a series of screens. The screens could be in a range of different views.

The common views that are available are as listed here:

## Slide view

In slide view one page is worked on at a time. It is possible to type, draw, add clip art, insert pictures and alter the look of text and objects, and to bring in files or graphics from other applications.

## Outline view

This enables you to work with the 'title' of each slide and the main text that is on the slide but no graphics. It is the easiest screen to use for editing the information in a presentation.

## Slide sorter

The separate images of the slides can be viewed as thumbnail images. You can see all of the images and text on the slides. In this view it is possible to set up timing and transitions between the slides. (See **AUTOMATED DISPLAYS**.) The order of the slides can be changed so that the flow of the presentation is improved.

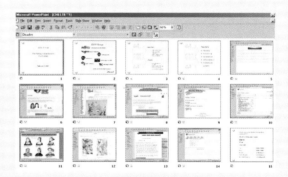

## Notes page view

To help to prepare the presentation an image of the slide to be displayed is shown along with a text area. Notes can be typed into the text area and printed so that when the presentation is given, the notes correspond to what is being displayed.

## Slide show view

The slides created are shown in the sequence that they are displayed. Each slide fills up the screen so that there are no toolbars or menus to be seen.

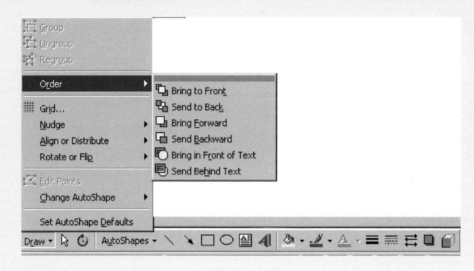

## Toolbars

As with a desktop publishing package, the toolbar contains a full range of tools to manipulate text and images.

Background and foreground colours can be altered to give desired effects.

The text is usually keyed in to text areas, and objects placed within frames. The text and objects can be altered and manipulated in the same way as any word processing or graphics applications.

Most applications will allow for the use of standard shapes, eg rectangles, circles. This speeds up the process and improves accuracy.

Shadows can be added to the shapes to emphasise them.

Overhead projector presentations like this one are being replaced more and more by computer projection presentations

# Projection

The multimedia programs are stored on a computer system which is then linked to a projection and sound system for use during the performance. The projection unit would be a traditional cathode ray tube (CRT) projector, liquid crystal display (LCD) panel attached to an overhead projector, stand-alone LCD projector or a light-valve projector. The unit is pointed at the place where the images are to appear.

## CRT projector

CRT projectors have been around for a long time. They use three separate projection tubes (red, green and blue). The three channels must join accurately on the screen. The set-up alignment and focusing is very important in order to get a clear image. CRT projectors can be used with most computers.

## Interactive whiteboards

Interactive whiteboards allow a user to project or link a computer directly onto a large surface that looks like a traditional whiteboard. The surface acts as a large monitor screen, but will allow touch screen facility. For example, a user who wishes to highlight a particular feature can write on the surface either by using a pen provided with the board or in some cases with any item (including a finger!).

The boards can also display software applications and can be used to run a presentation that includes an Internet link.

## LCD panels

An LCD panel is placed on the glass surface of the overhead projector. The panel is connected to a computer where the images are taken from stored files. The displays can be in thousands of colours with full video and animation display if required. Because the LCD displays are small and portable they are popular for business presentations and similar work.

## LCD projection panels

The display is as above, but the unit contains a projection lamp and lenses and therefore does not need a separate overhead projector. The units give out a brighter, clearer image, but as they are larger they are not very portable.

## Light-valve projection

This is at the top end of the range for projection. The unit can be compared to the very top end of CRT units. It uses LCD technology and produces a very bright, colour-saturated display that can be projected on to screens as wide as 10 m or more.

---

# Automated displays

As you know, with a slide show the slides are changed either manually or with a remote control device.

A slide show in a presentation graphics application can be set up to run on its own. To enable this to happen, the transitions between the slides need to be established.

The transitions can be set to change the screen by fading from one slide to another.

Effects can be chosen so the change comes about in different ways, for example:

➢ from top to bottom

➢ from left to right

➢ from bottom right diagonally to top left

➢ as small squares

➢ as shutters.

The speed of the change can be adjusted to happen at a slow, medium or fast speed.

The slide show can be set to change at timed intervals, and to do so automatically.

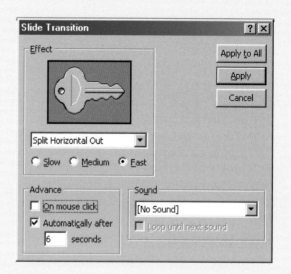

## Printing images

When creating a document to be printed in colour, it is important to think about the way the file is created before it goes to print.

### Modes

Files can be set up to print in RGB (red, green and blue) mode or in CMYK (cyan, magenta, yellow and black) mode. The true colour is only achieved through the use of CMYK mode when printing.

An image run purely on a system and not sent to print, should be set up in RGB mode, the mode of the screen image.

When CMYK files are printed, the printing is done through a subtractive method. Translucent (see-through) inks are printed on to pages, the inks absorb and reflect light. The colour we see is caused by the amount of absorption and reflection of the colour. Black is used to deepen shadows, type and lines.

### Process colour

Process colours are reproduced by printing overlapping dots of cyan, magenta and yellow. As these links are translucent, different mixes of the inks create the wide range of colours that we see every day.

If you want to produce a blue image using CMYK colour, then you add a little magenta to cyan and so on.

Care has to be taken when creating images: if cyan, magenta and yellow are added together, the result is a muddy colour, not black. If an image contains too much ink, the print becomes over-saturated and the quality is reduced.

### Spot colours and tints

Spot colours use pre-mixed inks on a printing press. There are hundreds of these colours to choose from and swatches of the colours are available for people to choose exactly which range they might want, eg Pantone colours.

Each spot colour is reproduced by using a single printing plate. The depth of colour is achieved by printing different levels of screened dots. 100% spot colour is solid, a tint is created by having 20% of the base colour in smaller dots.

### On-screen images

The image that appears on the monitor uses an additive method of colour. It transmits varying amounts of light. The light is red, green and blue. The monitor transmits different proportions of these and we see the colours on screen.

The combination of different intensities of the three wavelengths (red, green and blue light) can be used to give the same appearance as the range of colours that is found in nature. The screen image is made up of pixels of coloured light.

Where there is a combination of 100% red, green and blue light you see white as the 'colour', and where none of them is present you see black as a 'colour'.

## Resolution

Computer graphic images fall into two categories, bitmap images and vector graphics.

### Bitmap images

Bitmap images are made up of small squares known as pixels. Each pixel has a colour. Collections of pixels grouped together form shapes that are visible. When working with pixels, editing is carried out on groups of pixels rather than a single pixel. Bitmap images rely on the resolution setting. The lower the resolution the more jagged they appear and the higher the resolution the sharper they appear. If a bitmap image is scaled (stretched, rotated) on screen, the quality suffers.

### Vector graphics

Vector graphics consists of lines and curves that are defined by mathematical objects: vectors. Rectangles, circles and similar shapes drawn in vector graphics, can be stretched or rotated without losing any quality.

### Image size

The number of pixels used to display an image is called the image resolution. This is usually measured in pixels per inch (ppi). An image with a high resolution has more smaller pixels than an image of the same size with a lower resolution. If you had a square of 1 in × 1 in with a resolution of 72 ppi, it would contain 5184 pixels in total (72 × 72). If you had the same image and size but with an image resolution of 300 ppi, the total number of

pixels would be 90 000, but they would be much smaller, as they would be squashed into the same space.

### Monitor and printer resolutions

Resolution settings of a monitor and an image for printing have to be set up carefully. The screen dpi (dots per inch) and the print dpi is usually proportional but not the same.

Typically, a screen image on a monitor is in the range of 72–96 dpi. Image-setting printers and laser printers will print at output resolutions of between 300 and 2400 dpi.

When large prints are needed, the file size could be enormous if the dpi and ppi settings are not calculated carefully.

A low ppi setting of 72 ppi will still produce a high-quality print if the printer is set to print out at the correct high-quality setting, eg 1200 dpi. The pixel dimensions (how big each pixel is) is linked to the quality that is needed. The size of the image printed can change but there would still be the same number of pixels per inch, ie the pixels do not get bigger as the size of the print gets bigger.

Set at 72 ppi     Still set at 72 ppi, the print area is bigger but the quality has not changed

## Printing methods

Main types of printing computer files:

➤ bubble jet printing

➤ piezo ink cartridge

➤ direct digital.

### Bubble jet

A heater is built into the print head which receives a pulsed electrical current, causing many temperature rises a second.

**1** as the ink heats up a bubble is formed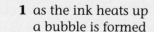

**2** the bubble expands

**3** the bubble forces out some ink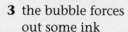

**4** the bubble cools and contracts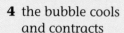

**5** a vacuum is formed which pulls more ink into the nozzle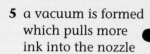

**6** the printer is ready to start again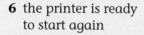

This type of printing is often used where large-format images are required. It is quite quick as the specialised software deals with the large files that are created in the printing process.

## Piezo ink cartridge

The piezo printing system has a permanent print head inside the printer. The print head contains a lot of tiny bumps which are powered by piezo crystals. These bumps act as small pistons and vibrate against the plate which is directly behind the ink layer. Ink droplets are pushed out of the nozzle by the vibrations. This system is useful for small amounts of accurate copies but is quite costly.

## Direct digital printing

Direct digital printing presses are connected to work stations that create postscript files from digital files and screen images, and send the files to the press. They do not require film or even, in some cases, any printing plates. One method transfers digital information on to electrographic cylinders instead of plates, and uses toner to print four-colour pages. Another method sends the digitised pages directly to plates mounted on the press.

This process produces fast turnaround times, low production costs and the ability to personalise publications. It is often used for on-demand or short-run colour printing where only a few copies are needed.

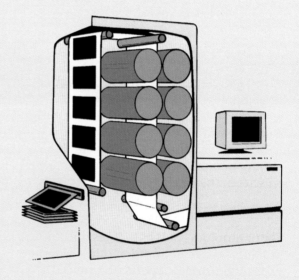

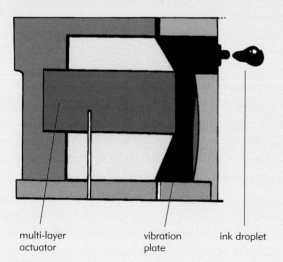

multi-layer actuator      vibration plate      ink droplet

## Special effects

Where images are to be used for display, specialist software, eg Photoshop or Kai's Power Tools, allows images to be manipulated to give special effects.

Many effects are available. A sample of these effects is shown below. This shows the same image altered by applying different special effects filters.

## File formats

Graphics files may be stored in a wide range of formats. The file format determines what can be done with the image. Some software applications will only support images in certain formats.

Below is a list of the most commonly used graphic file formats and where they can be used.

| | |
|---|---|
| **PICT** | Mac standard |
| **TIFF** | tagged image file format, used in most applications and computer platforms |
| **EPS** | encapsulated postscript |
| **PIC** | format accepted by Lotus 123, charts and graphs |
| **HPGL** | Hewlett Packard graphics language |
| **CGM** | computer graphics metafile |
| **Paint** | Mac |
| **Draw** | Mac |
| **RIFF** | raster image file format |
| **PNTG** | Mac 4 letter file type |
| **BMP** | bitmapped file (also as DIB, RLE) |
| **GIF** | graphic image file – a colour graphics file format for IBM-compatible systems. Often used in bulletin boards because of the high compression |
| **PCX** | PC paintbrush file |
| **JPEG** | joint photographic expert group |
| **Sprite** | |
| **Image** | BBC |
| **PCD** | photo CD, eg Kodak for photographs |

# Animation

All animation on computers is carried out using the same process. Step recording is the process of animating a moving object by taking 'snapshots' of its movement through a succession of frames.

**1** Create position 1

**2** Record position 1

**3** Step forward to position 2

**4** Record position 2

This sequence goes on until the animation is completed.

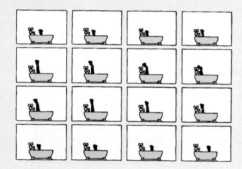

Animation can be created in a range of different applications. True animation software can be very complicated, allowing for timed movements and linking several different screens together to create whole environments.

One tool that is available in most animation packages is the 'Between tool' (called something different in each package!) The tool allows one shape to be altered between two points automatically, by the computer.

For example, two shapes are drawn. The software calculates the number of steps required to get from one image to the next. The software then automatically sets the changes so that one shape turns into the other one. These stages are then placed into frames and can be run as an animation.

In the same way that presentation graphics software can run through the slide display, animation sequences can be set to run through the frames.

# Multimedia

The different aspects of a multimedia system pull together teams with different skills and knowledge.

A multimedia presentation will have a combination of:

➤ text

➤ graphics (images)

➤ video/animation sequences

➤ sound.

A development team will work on the whole project with each person taking responsibility for a different section. The team will meet to discuss each person's progress and to see whether its plans need to change.

The members of the team will work on several different machines. These will not necessarily be the same type but will probably be connected on a LAN. However, all the computers will be multimedia systems, ie they will able to run CD-ROMs, have a sound card and be linked to speakers (either external or internal).

Each team member would create his or her own files which would be stored in a format compatible with the main multimedia authoring software. This would mean that the separate files could be compiled into one full multimedia system.

## Text

The whole team will decide upon the nature of the text to be used in the system. The text will be written (but not formatted) by a member of the team who is good with language, ie the author.

## Graphics/animation

Images for the system would be created by a graphic artist. Some multimedia artists draw and paint with a mouse, others use a graphics tablet connected to the computer. The tablets are pressure sensitive. This means that when the artist draws on the tablet the image appears on the screen, with the same degree of pressure as the artist used. If a heavy line is needed, the pen is pressed quite hard on the tablet. Images can be created not only from hand-drawn images, but also from scanned images or using a digital camera.

## Video

A video engineer produces clips of video to be included in the system. These could be from archived footage or from videos made especially for the system. The video must be of a high quality, which is expensive. This is why storyboard is used first to work out the minimum use of video. A normal video camera can be used but a camera stand and a method of easy movement is needed to ensure clear, crisp video images. When the filming is complete, rough edits can be made. This uses an analogue editing desk and it is then that editing decisions have to be taken, ie what has to go! The analogue video will be played into the computer while it is running software that creates a digital file of each frame. The video engineer will use a keyboard and mouse to input the data. When created, these digital images can be manipulated on the computer like any other. The same software will be used for the final editing of the video. Special backgrounds or touch-up techniques will be used to complete the clips. To make them manageable, the video clips need to be compressed to fit storage media such as CD-ROM.

## Music and sound

### Digital audio

A studio engineer can use a computer to record the sound picked up by a microphone. It stores numbers that precisely measure the height of the sound wave at regular time intervals. To reproduce the sound the numbers are converted back into a sound wave, as with a music CD. The software the engineer uses allows different recordings to be kept on separate tracks and then mixed together using a 'virtual mixing desk'. On screen this looks just like the real thing, but with controls that can be moved with the mouse. Digital audio can be accurate and predictable but needs large amounts of memory, a fast system and does not offer precise control over each individual note.

### MIDI

MIDI stands for Musical Instrument Digital Interface. It is an agreed language of codes for the remote control of equipment capable of synthesising sound electronically, including the soundchip inside most multimedia computers. MIDI codes can switch notes on and off, set loudness and control different effects (slides, vibrato, etc.) just like a real musician. There are special keyboards, drum pads, violins and brass and wind instruments that produce MIDI codes when played. These codes are recorded into a computer using sequencing software. Composers can then see and alter information in a number of ways, including traditional score notation, graphics on a grid and a list of events. A sequencer can also play back music by sending MIDI data on to the synthesiser, sampler or drum machine that will make the sounds. MIDI needs much less memory and processing speed than digital audio, and allows precise control over individual notes, but the quality of the sound produced is less predictable as it depends on the synthesiser.

## Programmer

When the rest of the team has finished work, the text, graphics, animation and sound files are handed over to the programmer to put together using authoring software.

## Storyboards

A storyboard should be used by each member of the multimedia team. A storyboard is a series of frames each representing a different action or screen image. They are also used in working out which sounds should accompany which frame of text or image.

Storyboards are often drawn on paper in the meetings so that edits and additions can be made easily and quickly.

To the right is a sample of a storyboard that can be used to record the MIDI track that will be on each channel.

## TRACK SHEET                    MT8X

TITLE _____  DATE _____
ARTIST _____  COMPOSER _____
ENGINEER _____  ENGINEER _____

| 1 | 2 | 3 | 4 | 5 | 6 | 7 | 8 |
|---|---|---|---|---|---|---|---|
| Drum | Bass | Piano | Vocals | Samples | | | |

| 1 | 2 | 3 | 4 | 5 | 6 | 7 | 8 |
|---|---|---|---|---|---|---|---|
| | | | | | | | |

| 1 | 2 | 3 | 4 | 5 | 6 | 7 | 8 |
|---|---|---|---|---|---|---|---|
| | | | | | | | |

## Authoring software

Authoring software is used to create multimedia systems. The software allows a programmer to bring together the separate components of the system – ie text, graphics, animation, videos and sound – into one whole.

The main authoring software applications treat the creation of a system like a stage production.

The different items, eg sound files and video clips, all become known as cast members.

As in a real production, each cast member will appear at a set time, in a set place, for a set length of time. The same cast member might come back again several times.

The software is a huge database of files – the cast members. The programmer will call together the different files that are needed to make up the screen images. Complex problems can occur when eight, nine, ten or more files are needed at once. The programmer has to set up links to all of these files on a master cast sheet. This allows the cast members to be kept in place or allowed to disappear off the screen.

The programmer has to work out the navigation of the system. People do not want to see things in a linear way, ie as in printed books. By using hyperlinks in the same way as in web page design, links between the cast members can be created to allow a user to go to many points in the system.

Multimedia systems can be made interactive by deciding that a 'movie' in the system will not start until there is a click on the mouse button, or a key is pressed. In this way, screens can be created with 'hot spots' that hold a code to allow the program to go on only if the correct input is given – ie the correct key is pressed or the mouse is clicked in the correct place.

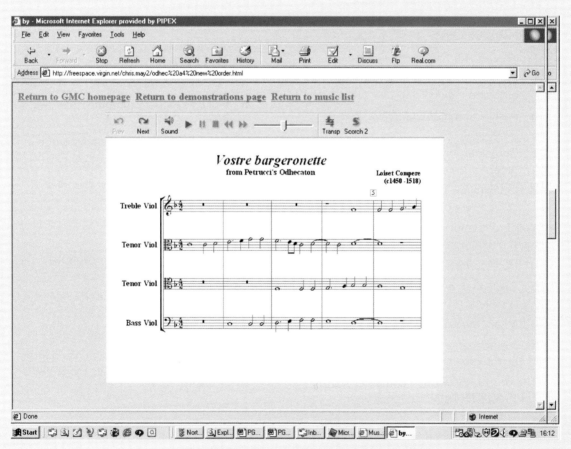

# So now you know?

## Multiple-choice questions

This set of multiple-choice questions has been included to test your knowledge and understanding of information technology systems and computers in general.

1  Which one of the following is **true**?
   a  A computer is a machine which processes data and supplies results.
   b  There is no difference between a mini and a microcomputer.
   c  All computers are dedicated computers.
   d  The three main types of computer are mainframe, medium and microcomputer.

2  Which one of the following is **false**?
   a  Computers find the results to any problems very quickly.
   b  Results from computers are always consistent.
   c  Computers can electronically store data.
   d  Calculations performed by computer can be very accurate.

3  Which of the following lists the three main types of computer?
   a  PC, Acorn and Mac
   b  Dedicated, general-purpose and personal
   c  Micro, macro and mini
   d  Mainframe computer, mini computer and micro computer

4  The process by which a computer makes itself ready for use once it has been switched on is called
   a  Starting up
   b  Booting up
   c  Shooting up
   d  Waking up

5  An inherent flaw in programming logic which may cause a computer program to crash is called a
   a  Byte
   b  Bit
   c  Bug
   d  Backup

6  Which of the following **best** describes a 'dedicated' computer?
   a  A computer designed specifically for one task
   b  A mainframe computer with a large number of terminals
   c  A home computer for simple accounts
   d  A mini computer with a printer

7  What are the four main components of a computer system?
   a  VDU, keyboard, computer and printer
   b  VDU, keyboard, computer and disk drive
   c  Input, output, process and storage
   d  Input, output, VDU and mouse

8  Which of the following **best** describes a computer peripheral device?
   a  A unit which enables a computer to manipulate data
   b  A unit which includes a control processor
   c  A device connected to and under the control of a computer
   d  A device for storing data

9  A small piece of silicon which has a large number of electronic circuits fabricated on to it is known as a
   a  Byte
   b  Bit
   c  Chip
   d  Port

**10** Which of the following **best** describes the term 'on-line'?

**a** The use of a computer to control a telecommunications network

**b** The procedure for powering up a computer

**c** The procedure for powering down a computer

**d** The connection of a peripheral device to, and control by, a computer

**11** A port is the

**a** External point on a computer where a peripheral may be attached

**b** Internal point on a computer where a peripheral may be attached

**c** Cable connecting a computer to a peripheral

**d** Point where a disk is inserted into a disk drive

**12** A keyboard is used to

**a** Input data

**b** Output data

**c** Control input devices

**d** Control output devices

**13** An inkjet printer prints characters on paper by

**a** Spraying a fine controlled jet of ink on to paper

**b** Depositing toner on to paper from an electrostatically charged drum

**c** Impressing a heated print head on to aluminium-coated paper

**d** Impacting pins on to a ribbon

**14** A VDU or monitor is an

**a** Input device

**b** Input device which provides storage

**c** Output device which provides high-quality print

**d** Output device similar to a television screen

**15** Which one of the following is **false**?

**a** A new disk must be formatted before use

**b** A corrupted disk has had its data changed in an undesirable manner

**c** Each time it is used a disk must first be formatted

**d** Corrupted disks may contain data which cannot be recovered

**16** The programs that run on a computer are known as

**a** Hardware

**b** Software

**c** Wetware

**d** Vapourware

**17** A set of instructions designed to enable the computer to perform a defined function is known as a

**a** Driver

**b** Program

**c** Specification

**d** Menu

**18** Which one of the following is required to make hardware usable?

**a** A program

**b** A disk drive

**c** A keyboard

**d** A VDU

**19** Computer memory is defined in terms of

**a** Pixels

**b** Baud rate

**c** Kilobytes, megabytes and gigabytes

**d** Millibytes and nanobytes

**20** Which one of the following would be described as 'a hand-held device with one ball used for controlling the movement of a screen cursor'?

**a** Joystick

**b** Bar code reader

**c** Mouse

**d** Trackerball

**21** For which one of the following is a monochrome monitor likely to be unacceptable?

a Data processing

b Word processing

c Textile design

d Spreadsheets

**22** RAM can **best** be described as

a Permanent, programmable memory, retained when the machine is switched off

b Temporary, programmable memory, retained when the machine is switched off

c Permanent, volatile memory, lost when the machine is switched off

d Temporary, volatile memory, lost when the machine is switched off

**23** Which of the following **best** describes a 'stand-alone' computer system?

a One connected to a network

b One connected to the Internet

c One not connected to a network

d A LAN connected to a WAN

**24** A multimedia computer is capable of

a Sound and moving pictures only

b Reading a CD-ROM

c Sound, high-quality graphics, moving pictures and reading a CD-ROM

d Sound only

**25** Which one of the following would best be used for output from a CAD system?

a A laser printer

b A plotter

c An inkjet printer

d A dot matrix printer

**26** Which one of the following would **not** be a suitable application for a computer network?

a The transfer of data between a head office and its branch offices

b The classroom use of a number of terminals sharing expensive peripherals

c The provision of internal e-mail within a large company building

d The distribution of electronic components from a factory to customers

**27** Which one of the following would **best** enable the urgent transfer of a page of text including a colour illustration?

a Telex

b E-mail

c Fax

d Postal system

**28** A digital signal is **best** described as one that

a Varies continuously

b Is continuous

c Is either a 1 or a −1

d Is either on or off

**29** Methods of capturing data that can be automatically entered into a computer include

a MICR

b OCR

c OMR

d All of the above

**30** Data capture is **best** described as a means of

a Obtaining data for a computer

b Processing data on a computer

c Outputting data from a computer

d Using data from a computer

**31** WIMP stands for

 **a** Windows, interface, mouse and pointer

 **b** Windows, icons, menus and plotter

 **c** Windows, icons, mouse and pointer

 **d** Windows, icons, mouse and printer

**32** The main advantages of bar codes include

 **a** Cheap to produce

 **b** Human-readable

 **c** Easy to spot if damaged

 **d** All of the above except b

**33** Passwords are a good method of protecting a computer against

 **a** Acts of God, ie flood, fire, earthquakes etc.

 **b** Viruses and theft of the system

 **c** Viruses and hacking

 **d** Theft and Acts of God

**34** Compression is

 **a** The production of smaller computers

 **b** The production of smaller computer chips

 **c** The production of smaller computer users

 **d** The production of a file of smaller size than the original to aid storage and possibly transfer

**35** An integrated package contains at least

 **a** Word processing software

 **b** Word processing and spreadsheet software

 **c** Spreadsheet, word processing, graphics and communications software

 **d** Spreadsheet, database and word processing software

**36** The computer programming language associated with 'turtle' graphics is called

 **a** BASIC

 **b** COBOL

 **c** LOGO

 **d** FORTRAN

**37** The hardware and software required to enable two devices to communicate is called

 **a** A port

 **b** A buffer

 **c** An interface

 **d** A bus

**38** Which one of the following is **true**?

 **a** MICR is used to read some details on cheques.

 **b** OCR is used to mark students' multiple-choice examination scripts.

 **c** OMR is used to code groceries for EFTPOS systems.

 **d** Bar codes are used by exam boards to mark students' exam scripts.

**39** What is the name given to the smallest addressable display space on a VDU?

 **a** A bit

 **b** A byte

 **c** A pixel

 **d** A character

**40** Which one of the following is the name for a computer network of limited geographical extent?

 **a** BAN

 **b** LAN

 **c** WAN

 **d** MAN

## Short-answer questions

**1**

Enter the items in the list on the left under the correct heading in the table

| Spreadsheet | Input | Output | Software |
|---|---|---|---|
| Barcode reader | | | |
| Monitor | | | |
| Database | | | |
| Desktop publisher | | | |
| Graphics tablet | | | |
| Keyboard | | | |
| Mouse | | | |

**2**

A local retail group has decided to buy a computer system to help them in the storage of their product details and to assist in re-ordering stock.

At the moment all these records are kept on individual sheets and will need to be transferred to the database.

They have decided to use an EPOS system with a barcode reader for this task.

What does EPOS mean?

_____

What advantage will an EPOS system have for the shopkeeper and his staff?

_____
_____
_____

**3**

The shop hopes to upgrade its system in the future to an EFTPOS system.
What is EFTPOS?

_____

What advantages will EFTPOS have for the shopkeeper and his customers?

_____
_____
_____

**4**

All the details of the products will have to be put on to a stock datafile.

List four fields that will be needed in order for the details to be stored.

**a** _____

**b** _____

**c** _____

**d** _____

These details will be stored in different field types. State one field type that is:

Alphabetic _____

Numeric _____

Alphanumeric _____

**5**

Data accuracy is important. Explain how the following methods help to ensure accuracy.

Validation

_____

_____

_____

Verification

_____

_____

_____

**6**

Quite often coding data is used when inputting details on to a datafile. Give an example of one field that could be coded in this datafile.

_____

**7**

The introduction of a new computer system to replace a manual one can have many effects on the staff in an organisation. Thinking in terms of job changes, training implications, staffing levels, etc discuss what these might be if the shop was computerised in this way.

_____

_____

_____

_____

_____

**8**

More and more people are 'hooking up' to the Internet every day. You cannot read magazines or watch television without seeing World Wide Web page addresses.

Many businesses now take advantage of this and will spend much time and effort placing information on the Net.

Many people now buy goods and book tickets etc. via the Web.

What advantages does this have for businesses that have web pages?

_____

_____

_____

_____

**9**

What equipment do you have to have to 'hook up' to the WWW?

_____

_____

**10**

Being able to access all this data is interesting but what implications does this have for data security?

_____

_____

_____

_____

**Page numbers in bold typeface refer to Information Bank sections.**